THE INNER EXPERIENCE
OF LAW

DAVID GRANFIELD

THE INNER EXPERIENCE OF LAW

A JURISPRUDENCE OF SUBJECTIVITY

THE CATHOLIC UNIVERSITY OF AMERICA PRESS
WASHINGTON, D.C.

LIBRARY OF CONGRESS CATALOGING-IN-PUBLICATION DATA

Granfield, David
  The inner experience of law.

  Bibliography: p.
  Includes index.
  1. Law and ethics. 2. Subjectivity. 1. Title.
BJ55.G65 1988   340'.1   87-38221
ISBN 0-8132-0657-X

CONTENTS

PREFACE

Law enjoys an anomalous position; it is on the growing edge of society, but it is always out of date; it is something everyone needs, but most people resist. It touches every aspect of life, operating analogously as a norm of action, but it remains, like life, puzzling in its complex profundity.

As a law professor, teaching both criminal law and the philosophy of law, I am inevitably aware of these juridic extremes. Moreover, my studies in philosophy and theology have prompted me to look beyond the positive law in order to understand the positive law. But above all, there is the hunger for a vision that, harmoniously blending meaning and value, can unify this multifaceted arena of human destiny.

In helping me in this task of synthesis, I owe much to many persons, some footnoted, all remembered. But I want to thank by name Professor Mary Ann Glendon, of Harvard Law School, and John T. Noonan, Jr., formerly Professor of law at Berkeley and now judge of the Ninth Circuit Court of Appeals, for their words of encouragement after they carefully read the manuscript. I am very grateful to Dr. Cathleen Going, O.P., of the Farmington Hills Monastery, whose perceptive and nuanced mind has deepened my grasp of cognitional theory and whose skillful editing has done so much to let the ideas in this book shine through. Finally, I thank my brother Patrick; his wisdom and scholarly expertise, his friendship and practical concern, have helped bring this project pleasantly to term. For me, the grand opportunity to attempt a jurisprudence of subjectivity and to share whatever light I may have discovered has been indeed a treasured gift.

In memory of
John Julian Ryan (1898–1983)
a great teacher, a revered friend

INTRODUCTION

Law is a familiar and inescapable presence. The *purpose* of this book is to examine the possibility of an inner experience of law. We begin with questions: How do we participate mentally in a legal event? What are the major spheres of our participation? How do we appropriate legal meaning and value in each sphere? What ultimate meaning or value is there to appropriate? And how can we experience legal meaning and value, both practical and transcendent, in a unified vision? Our questions respond in part to the frustration and the sense of absurdity that many feel in their quest for an intellectual and ethical ground for law.

The *means* used in answering these questions will be a jurisprudence of subjectivity, that is, a study of law and ethics from the perspective of the mental operations at work as we consciously participate in legal events. The focus is the inner experience of law. So we are interested, for example, in what goes on in our minds when we act with integrity; when we do justice or claim a right; when we wield authority or submit to its decrees; or when, admitting guilt, we accept punishment as just.

The *context* is important. In the seventeenth century, there began a shift from classicist to modern thought, from the philosophical and abstract to the scientific and historical. This change was characterized by "a turn to the subject." We follow that same turn here, but add a new level of experiencing it. We are not reapplying the old insights of Descartes and Locke; modern philosophy and jurisprudence have already done that. What we are doing is examining the legal subject from a subjective perspective, not treating the legal subject exclusively as an object to be held at arms length but trying to understand the legal subject from within as self-conscious. We do not want merely to learn about legal subjects; we want the inner experience of being legal subjects.

[handwritten margin notes: "what are the mental opers at work?" and "self-consc of legal subject"]

I

The *approach* of this book is not to mount an attack on other schools of jurisprudence; it complements rather than confronts them, for it involves law primarily on the level of interiority rather than of theory. Nevertheless, a jurisprudence of subjectivity is not just a methodology, free of content. By focusing on the mental operations that go into ethical and legal thought, one is able to ground content on a foundation more solid than theory alone. Moreover, because these mental operations are common to all thinkers—for example, Positivists, Pragmatists, Naturalists, Idealists, Utilitarians, Existentialists—the possibility emerges of a common basis for legal dialogue. Theories separate; subjectivities unite. To hope for a consensus may be over-ambitious, but to work towards a dialogue, even between opposing theories, is a responsible and necessary task. A jurisprudence of subjectivity is an ideal vehicle for just such a dialogue.

The *basis* of this approach stems from a personal search. When I first began thinking about a jurisprudence of subjectivity, the existentialist current was strong among contemporary Europeans such as Marcel, Jaspers, Heidegger, Camus, and Sartre, as well as among Neo-Thomists such as Gilson and Maritain. For many of us, Kierkegaard, in his reaction against essentialism and his focus on the subject, was a seminal influence. But for what I was trying to achieve, none of these thinkers, despite their valuable insights, sufficed. Although I had developed my jurisprudential ideas in some detail—even writing a first draft with the working title *Law and Subjectivity*—I was not fully satisfied with its philosophical component. German and French existentialists had not produced either a theory of law or a sound basis for such a theory; positivists and analytic philosophers had theories of law in abundance, but no place for subjectivity; and naturalists had an abstractly classicist jurisprudence, not adequately attuned to modern culture and legal developments.

Certain thinkers, sometimes called "transcendental Thomists," had begun to make profound philosophic advances in cognitional theory. Joseph Maréchal prompted this new approach through his study of Kant, which brought additional light to the philosophy of Aquinas. Going beyond Kant, others such as Karl Rahner, André Marc, and Emerich Coreth have continued this development, which reached its most systematic, methodological presentation in the work of Bernard Lonergan. Writing as a critical realist, in contrast to Kant's critical idealism, Lonergan critiqued and radically transformed his Kantian influences. He remained, however a Thomist, although admittedly a "transcendental" one.

Scientists, too, such as W.I.B. Beveridge, Gyorgy Polya, Michael Polyani, and Thomas Kuhn have written extensively on how knowledge is increased, decisions formed, and discoveries made. More recently, "cognitive psychology" has emerged with such contemporary thinkers as Jerome Bruner, Howard Gardner, J. P. Guilford, George A. Miller, and Ulric Neisser. Incidentally, Thomas Verner Moore, who was a psychiatrist and a professor at The Catholic University of America, wrote in 1939 the first book entitled *Cognitive Psychology*, a pioneering study of "the ways in which the human mind receives impressions from the external world and interprets the impressions thus received." In the last few decades, there has been a rash of books on various psychological aspects of the legal process, such as jury selection, competency proceedings, psycholinguistic analysis of confessions, and the insanity defense. Nevertheless, there has not as yet been any full-scale attempt by lawyers, scientists, or philosophers themselves to work out an integral explanation and evaluation of law from the viewpoint of subjectivity. That is the task of this book.

A *distinction* is in order. The very name "a jurisprudence of subjectivity" conjures up the ghost of subjectivism, with its capricious, idiosyncratic, and anarchic sequelae. We must therefore clearly distinguish subjectivity from subjectivism; otherwise, we have an open-ended jurisprudence with a problematic foundation. In a jurisprudence of subjectivity, we value reality so highly that we do not limit ourselves to a detached objectivity; we are convinced that subjectivity, properly understood and responsibly used, is a necessary component and safeguard of objectivity. Only if we are conscious of our experiencing, understanding, judging, and deciding can we guarantee the objectivity of the results. A jurisprudence of subjectivity rests on the twin supports of subjectivity and objectivity, but objectivity always depends on subjectivity.

The *subject* is the person as conscious. The turn to the legal subject and his subjectivity, if it is to be a fruitful component of jurisprudence, must be a turn to an integral subject, a subject free for the conscious realization of his full dignity and destiny. A diminished subject, politically or ideologically, has become the stock in trade of much juridic thought, almost as readily accepted as the abstract, "reasonable man." By scrutinizing how our minds operate when we participate in legal activity, we may learn to restore the subject to full human stature. This is a necessary task, for neither the law nor its subjects can reach perfection in a realm of diminished human beings. Noting the gradual rehabilitation of the legal subject as we move through the major spheres of legal activity, we may begin to appreciate the illumination and the strength that comes from authentic subjectivity.

The *legal spheres* emerge as we follow the road to meaning and value, which winds through a broad and diversified terrain. I direct my analysis of legal experience to four spheres of activity, progressively more and more complex, human, and conscious. The totality, I call the Nomosphere (from the Greek *nomos,* meaning law); it comprises the Monosphere (from *monos,* alone), which considers the legal awareness of the individual all by himself; the Isosphere (from *isos,* equal or fair), which considers the awareness of personal equality; the Koinosphere (from *koinos,* common or public), which considers the awareness of fellowship in a community; and finally the Theosphere (from *theos,* God), which considers the awareness of a relationship with the divine. The inner experience of law is then individual, bilateral, communal, and sacral. To phrase it more personally, we work through four dimensions of consciousness involving the I, the I-Thou, the We, and the We-THOU.

The *progression* is not purely rectilinear; nor are the spheres simply concentric or overlapping circles like Venn diagrams, with the greater including the lesser in whole or in part or not at all, although that image is more accurate than the linear one. To represent most faithfully what happens, we should combine line and circle to show the spiral ascendancy of the expanding development. If each sphere could be made fully conscious, it could be lifted up or sublated once and for all into a higher synthesis.

In practice, however, we must begin again and again; in a self-correcting process, we are ever trying to heighten, through our illumination from a higher sphere, the lower spheres of awareness; they then ground more firmly our ascent to the higher spheres. Nabokov's remark about the spiral as spiritual catches something of this movement. A familiar instance of this repeating spiral is seen in the fact that we know ourselves best when we know others, and we love ourselves best when we love others, but we cannot really know and love others unless we begin in some way to know and love ourselves. So, too, the ever-deepening circuit through the spheres of a jurisprudence of subjectivity becomes not only an adventure in self-discovery, but also an indispensable vehicle for the fullest experience of meaning and value in the law.

The *structure of the book* comprises a self-conscious focus, four spheres of activity, and an integral or unifying experience. First of all I discuss the overall subjective viewpoint in "The Eyewitness Perspective" (Chapter One). Sparked by the challenge of absurdity as exemplified in Justice Holmes and Franz Kafka, I search for a remedy for the pervading despair of ever making full contact with reality. Since the problem has surfaced in modern thought with its conspicuous "turn to the subject," I trace this turn from the Renaissance to the present time. Finally, to get an inner sense of what an adequate subjective perspective entails, I focus on key insights of Kierkegaard, Newman, and Ortega y Gasset. Then I am ready to attempt through this new viewpoint a fresh understanding of the various spheres of legal activity.

The *Monosphere* (Part 1) investigates the individual experience of law at its ethical source, as if there were only one person in the world. Here I discover the taproot of law, and I examine it positively and negatively, using the symbols of Greek mythology: "Eros: the Juridic Daimon" (Chapter Two) reveals the drive toward meaning and value, the positive dynamics of knowing and doing; "Nemesis: the Avenging Goddess" (Chapter Three) provides for the negative consequences of flawed actions and also, though less dramatically, for the positive consequences of proper actions. Through experiencing inclinations and limitations, the individual becomes intimately aware of law as a rule and measure of acts and as the inescapable condition of human destiny.

The *Isosphere* (Part 2) adds a new component, another subject. Here I discuss "Justice: the Bond of Intersubjectivity" (Chapter Four), which is grasped through self-consciousness and manifested as proportionate reciprocity, and "Rights: the Claims of Intersubjectivity" (Chapter Five), which are demands for justice based on equality and grasped fundamentally as participated values. This jural relationship uses the principles of the earlier sphere as applied to bilateral interactions. Ethics, thus, assumes also the dimensions of justice.

The *Koinosphere* (Part 3) has an additional component, a political construct made up of people civilly united. There are two major aspects. I first consider the structure itself, "The Dimensions of Community" (Chapter Six), justified by the need to protect and foster human interests, shaped as a system by constitutional and legal norms, and unified subjectively by communion in a political idea and by political friendship. Then, I discuss power in "The Dynamics of Governance" (Chapter Seven): its major forms, its relation to punishment, and, lastly, its highest manifestation as authority (power grounded in reason and conformed to community expectations). By internalizing justice, we are able to ensure the ethical character of the Koinosphere as the just bonding together of conscious subjects for a public order of self-protection and self-fulfillment.

The *Theosphere* (Part 4) introduces the sacral character of law, which has traditionally played a large role in jurisprudence. In "The Natural Law in Transition" (Chapter Eight), I compare a classicist and modern formulation of natural law, to judge how they comport with the insights of subjectivity, to determine whether human reason can discover general norms of conduct, and to discern the role of the divine in this overall normative process. In "The Divine Ground" (Chapter Nine) I look at some classical affirmations and then squarely raise the "God question," which is so crucial to the validation of ultimate meaning and value in law.

The *culmination* of this multileveled search is "The Vision of Law" (Chapter Ten). It suggests a way to experience the emerging unity of legal meaning and legal value. This achievement, which brings theory and praxis into consistent harmony with ultimate reality, is the ripening fruit of a lifetime of thought and moral integrity. To be human is to be conscious of law; to have an inner experience of the law permeated with wisdom and love is part of being fully human. A jurisprudence of subjectivity thematizes this inner experience.

Someone might well ask: what, very briefly, does this subjectivity do for jurisprudence, the science and philosophy of law? And what does it do for the persons involved in law? The answer is much in every way. First of all, by becoming conscious of the mental operations used in legal activity and really making them our own, we more easily return to the realm of theory with a clearer and more searching grasp of objectivity. Second, by grounding jurisprudence, not on divergent abstract propositions, but on mental operations commonly acknowledged to be shared by all, we can lay the foundations for an emerging legal dialogue.

Third, and more personally, by a jurisprudence of subjectivity, we are able to know ourselves profoundly as conscious participants in legal events. Members of the legal profession, since they expend so much of their time and energies directly on law, have to ask themselves whether they can afford to practice law as a fascinating technique for earning a living, if it remains separate from what they believe are the most vital and fundamental concerns of life. Inevitably they will develop a "legal mind." But will that mentality, as generally understood, contribute to their personal wisdom, goodness, and happiness?

Conscious participation in law is a concern not merely for judges and lawyers, but for everyone, whether a legal professional or not, for everyone is necessarily involved with the many spheres of law: its ethical base, its intersubjective relations, its political structure, its immanent and transcendent juridically sacred ambiance. We are all continually exposed to the law. It would, therefore, be tragic to conclude at the end of an exciting but all too short life that, in T. S. Eliot's words, "We had the experience but missed the meaning."

Let us see, then, as we move through the four parts of the Nomosphere, consciously participating in legal events, how normative interiority can give us an inner experience of law that, when objectified as theory, will form a jurisprudence of subjectivity that can be shared by all those who have appropriated their own conscious intentionality and, finally, how it can make of our lives a unified and luminous experience of profound legal meaning and transforming legal value.

CHAPTER 1

THE EYEWITNESS PERSPECTIVE

*All that I can say of my book is that it is a copy of my own
mind in its several ways of operation.—John Locke**

A fundamental question in jurisprudence is whether the law is ultimately meaningful or absurd. How we resolve this critical issue determines the quality and the magnitude of the role that the law will play
in our lives. Is it to be exclusively a matter of practical results? Is it at
best that systematic conceptualization called legal theory? Or can it
also be an enlightening and transforming experience of authentic legal
subjectivity?

[handwritten marginalia: INNER EXPERIENCE OF LAW]

[handwritten marginalia: three levels]

I. THE CHALLENGE OF ABSURDITY

To sharpen our focus on the question of the meaningfulness of law,
we will consider two radically different but consonant views of the
legal process, that of Justice Oliver Wendell Holmes, Jr., and that of
Franz Kafka. Both have concluded that the law is absurd. An understanding of their charges will help us determine the steps to take in
discovering the answer for ourselves.

[handwritten marginalia: Absurdity = chaos]

Absurdity, of course, need not appear clownish, stupid, or anti-
intellectual. Albert Camus best expressed the current connotation of
the term: "The world is not reasonable, that is all that can be said. But
what is absurd is the confrontation of the irrational and the wild longing
for clarity whose call echoes in the human heart."[1] It is this inner
frustration—quietly recognized by Holmes and dramatically portrayed

---

* John Locke, Letter to Edward Stillingfleet, Bishop of Worcester, *Works of John
Locke,* 12th ed., 9 vols. (London: C. and J. Rivington, 1824), 3:139.

1. Albert Camus, *The Myth of Sisyphus,* trans. J. O'Brien (New York: Vantage
Books, 1955), p. 16.

by Kafka—which centers the mind on its own subjectivity as it attempts to ground the legal process.

Early in life, Oliver Wendell Holmes, Jr. (1841–1935), concluded that the law was "a ragbag of details."[2] Undaunted, however, this "Yankee from Olympus" spent a long and successful life trying to bring order out of that chaos. In doing so, he followed his own advice: that one who would become a master of the law must "in the first place follow the existing body of dogma into its highest generalizations by means of jurisprudence."[3] He defined the latter as follows:

Jurisprudence, as I look at it, is simply the law in its most generalized part. Every effort to reduce a case to a rule is an effort of jurisprudence, although the name as used in English is confined to the broadest rules and the most fundamental conceptions. One mark of a great lawyer is that he sees the application of the broadest rules.[4]

In a letter to the Chinese jurist John Wu, Justice Holmes spoke of their common commitment to philosophy, "the greatest interest there is." What he meant by philosophy underlies his jurisprudence.[5]

My notion of the philosophic movement is simply to see the universal in the particular, which perhaps is a commonplace, but it is the best of commonplaces, if you realize that every particular is as good as any other to illustrate it, subject only to the qualification that some can see it in one, some in another matter more readily, according to faculties.[6]

This twofold task—generalization and application—operated most effectively in Justice Holmes: it brought him lasting international fame and the satisfaction of knowing that he did a job worth doing and did it superbly. But did it fulfil the longings of his mind? A remark he confided to his friend Sir Frederick Pollock, when he was seventy-eight and again a year later, seems to indicate that a sense of absurdity rather than a grasp of truth actually characterized his intellectual life. He wrote: "I always say that the chief end of man is to frame general

---

2. Oliver Wendell Holmes, Jr., *Collected Legal Papers* (New York: Harcourt, Brace, & Co., 1920), p. 299: "When I began, the law presented itself as a ragbag of details—the only philosophy within reach was Austin's *Jurisprudence*."

3. Idem, "The Path of the Law," *Harvard Law Review*, 10 (1897): 476.

4. Ibid., p. 474.

5. Idem, from a letter in *The Mind and Faith of Justice Holmes*, ed. Max Lerner (New York: The Modern Library, 1943), p. 421.

6. Ibid., pp. 421–22.

propositions but that no proposition is worth a damn."[7] Although said lightly and without self-pity, the statement is a sad summing up for one who many years earlier wrote so buoyantly: "It is through them [generalizations] that you not only become a great master in your calling but connect your subject with the universe and catch an echo of the infinite, a glimpse of its unfathomable process, a hint of the universal law."[8]

Something had to balance this cruel sense of absurdity, so that life could be still worth living, for "we are all very near to despair." That something was "faith in the unexplainable worth and sure issue of effort."[9] It was a "fighting faith," a faith not in passivity but in a romantic battle against all-conquering fate.

I do not know what is true. I do not know the meaning of the universe. But in the midst of doubt, in the collapse of creeds, there is one thing I do not doubt, that no man who lives in the same world with most of us can doubt, and that is that the faith is true and adorable which leads a soldier to throw away his life in obedience to a blindly accepted duty, in a cause which he little understands, in a plan of campaign of which he has no notion, under tactics of which he does not see the use.[10]

In commenting on this passage, Max Lerner noted perceptively, long before absurdity became a philosophic catchword: "Here is a sense of blind obedience which approaches the religious *credo quia absurdum*."[11] Holmes, of course, was speaking of more than military struggle. For him, war was the paradigm of life itself, meaningful only in fighting the good fight.

To the end, Holmes remained cynical, skeptical, absurd. With courage and clarity, he formulated the philosophic significance of his legal career: law was "a ragbag of details" to be given order and meaning through "the highest generalizations," none of which was "worth a damn," but faith in the "worth and sure issue of effort" alone gave that sense of the superlative that transmutes absurdity into joy. Because Holmes, like Camus, was so immensely gifted, highly productive, and

7. *Holmes-Pollock Letters*, ed. M. Howe, 2 vols. (Cambridge: Harvard University Press, 1961), 2:59. See also 2:13.

8. Holmes, "Path of the Law," p. 478.

9. Idem, speech given to the Bar Association of Boston, March 7, 1900, *Mind and Faith*, p. 43.

10. Ibid., a Memorial Day address, May 30, 1895, p. 20.

11. Max Lerner, ibid., p. 6.

widely acclaimed, he was personally able to carry off this paradoxical combination of absurdity and accomplishment. Equipped naturally and environmentally to function well, and given abundant positive reinforcement, he could be content with the principle—a bit thin for lesser men—that "To live is to function. That is all there is in living."[12]

The allegation that the law is painfully absurd becomes more credible in the works of Franz Kafka (1883–1924). For if Holmes stands for the successful judge, Kafka stands for the innocent and unfortunate accused. He was a lawyer, though hardly a legal scholar, but his book *The Trial*—finished in 1918, posthumously published in 1925, and translated into English in 1937, two years after Holmes's death—has been more widely read throughout the world than anything ever written by Holmes. Different as these two men were, however, their insights into the absurdity of the law complement one another.

A convenient way to manifest this complementarity is to apply to them a general distinction made by Edmond Cahn in another context to describe two ways of looking at the legal process.[13] Accordingly, Holmes, primarily but by no means exclusively, thought and wrote from "the imperial perspective," the point of view of the establishment, the authorities, the courts. So he could blend law and absurdity and still find the results personally satisfying and publicly rewarding. Kafka, on the other hand, took up wholeheartedly "the consumer perspective," looking at law as its subject and even as its victim. Predictably, the legal process is not as fulfilling to one caught up in the gears as it is to the one who runs the machinery.

Kafka, it should be remembered, was not a naive outsider, but one whose fate, even from his university days, was to be an absurd consumer. He never fell in love with the law as did men such as Pound and Brandeis and Llewellyn; his was not a practical, efficient, and confident mind. He initially chose law as a sensible though unattractive way of preserving his options, convinced that the law by itself would never be his ultimate choice. Even as a law student, he felt his situation to be absurd: "So I read law. That meant that in the few months before examinations, while wearing out my nerves at a great rate, intellectually

12. Holmes, ibid., a radio talk, March 1931, on the occasion of his ninetieth birthday, p. 451.

13. Edmond Cahn, "The Consumers of Injustice," *New York University Law Review* 34 (1959): 1166.

I fed myself exclusively on sawdust—sawdust, too, which had already been chewed by thousands of jaws before me."[14] Nevertheless, Kafka went on to receive his degree of Doctor of Laws in 1906, completed his year of clerkship, practicing in the criminal and later in the civil courts of Prague, and then went to work for an Italian insurance company: "It had never been my intention to remain in the legal profession."[15]

Kafka's jurisprudential questions could not be cast away that easily: he never lost his preoccupation with law and authority, with justice and guilt. In fact, he was to find in the legal process the perfect symbol for his own all-pervading sense of absurdity. His legal experience, filtering through his "dreamlike inner life,"[16] crystallized in *The Trial* to reveal the anguish that comes to a mind imprisoned in a juridic universe of shifting, impenetrable surfaces, ever frustrated in its passionate search for order, coherence, truth.

In his book Kafka portrayed the fate of an apparently innocent citizen, arrested and accused, who never learns what his offense is, never gets a trial, but after a nightmare of procedural complexities is led off to execution—by that time, half convinced of the justice of his official condemnation. Camus rightly said of *The Trial:* "It states the problem of the absurd in its entirety."[17] Here the absurdity of the civilization is reflected in the absurdity of the judicial process, for in it we confront what Kafka calls "the senselessness of the whole."[18] Note, as a summary statement bearing on legal and, by implication, social reform, how sharply Kafka distinguished between the imperial and the consumer perspective:

Although the pettiest lawyer might to some extent be capable of analyzing the state of things in the Court, it never occurred to the lawyers that they should suggest or insist on any improvement in the system, while—and this was very characteristic—almost every accused man, even quite simple people among them, discovered from the earliest stages a passion for suggesting reforms which often wasted time and energy that could have been better employed in other directions. The only sensible thing was to adapt oneself to existing conditions.[19]

14. Max Brod, *Franz Kafka,* 2d ed. (New York: Schocken Books, 1960), p. 41.
15. Ibid., p. 249.
16. From Kafka's diary, selections of which are appended to *The Trial* (New York: Schocken Books, 1968), p. 275.
17. Albert Camus, ibid., quoted on back cover without citation.
18. Kafka, *The Trial,* p. 46.
19. Ibid., p. 121.

To return to the comparison between Holmes and Kafka, we find two disparate personalities with different cultures and different perspectives, both experiencing the law as absurd: Holmes by reducing law to broad generalizations, which he eventually found inadequate; Kafka by particularizing concrete frustrations. Holmes faced this absurdity bravely and romantically—a mighty hero battling to the death in a lost cause. But Kafka was quickly defeated, vulnerable in the tender sensitivities of youth and in the acuteness of artistic experience.

Both men were sustained in part by their *Funktionslust*, to use Konrad Lorenz's term: the compulsion to exercise their powers, thereby redeeming the time because their days were absurd. For these jurists in transition lived during the heyday of positivism, nihilism, and "the death of God." Holmes apparently adjusted easily, internalizing much of contemporary thought—but not without his occasional black moods. Kafka, neurotically on edge, revealed the agony of a deeply religious temperament threatened by the humanistic *reductio* of nihilism. Holmes, in freeing himself from the rationalism of his predecessors, insisted that the life of law was not logic but experience. Kafka contended that law was certainly not logical and that the experience of the law was absurd. Where the reasonable man moved step by step, the artist plunged headlong. The judge defined law as a prediction of what the courts will do; the prophet revealed in a monstrous parable what the courts were actually doing—not the whole truth about them, but a horrible facet in all its starkness. Both men prompt us to confront the law at the core of our own creative subjectivity. For it is in the realm of subjectivity that the battle over the fountainhead of the legal process will ultimately be fought.

II. THE TURN TO THE SUBJECT

To respond adequately to that intellectual frustration which is absurdity, it is helpful to note the radical change in direction that modern thinkers have effected. Holmes, speaking of the power of ideas, noted "how a hundred years after his death Descartes had become a practical force in controlling the conduct of men," and he added: "Read the works of the great German jurists and see how much more the world is governed by Kant than by Bonaparte."[20] His point was well taken;

---

20. Holmes, "Path of the Law," p. 663.

but since the Renaissance a cultural change was occurring more pervasive than the ideas of the individual philosophers such as Descartes and Kant who contributed to it, a change that was to have a lasting effect on legal theory and on the institution of law. The great transition from medieval to modern thought consisted principally in a turn to the subject. Even a brief survey of this directional change as it has progressed to the present suggests the developmental ripeness of a jurisprudence of subjectivity and with it the possibility of a reaffirmation of legal meaning.

Rooted in its classical past, the intellectual synthesis of the Middle Ages focused on objects—material and formal objects. By the fourteenth century, however, Scholasticism had begun to deteriorate, falling into Conceptualism and, through the writings of Scotus and Ockham, into Nominalism as well. Certitude, of course, remained a goal of philosophers, but it had become largely an affair of logic and propositional truth. Reacting against the skepticism of his times as reflected, for example, in Montaigne, Descartes argued that true philosophy might be reborn if its focus changed from things to ideas, from objects to subjects.

At about the same time in England, thinkers such as Bacon and Locke were also turning to the subject in a more factual but still complementary way. The overall result was that the Continental rationalists and the British empiricists projected a *Weltanschauung* that would radically transform legal theory and, as an unfortunate byproduct, diminish the legal person. Modern thinkers had become preoccupied with the subject and his specializations, thus fragmenting the former cultural unity: natural science separated itself from philosophy, and philosophy from theology; an emerging historical scholarship questioned the traditional accounts of human development and human activities; the law, too, quickly staked out its claims to autonomy, legal history from the seventeenth to the twentieth century clearly revealing the various permutations of this turn to the subject as well as the declining status of the legal subject.

A. Break with Tradition

René Descartes (1596–1650), "the father of modern philosophy," tried to arrive at clear and distinct ideas through a process of methodic doubt; he grounded his thinking subjectively on what he considered an indubitable truth: *Cogito ergo sum*. Here was a memorable formulation of the turn to the subject, which was to characterize the modern era. Descartes' theory of innate ideas, however, boded ill for the law, for it resulted in an unworkable dichotomy between *res cogitans* and *res extensa,* between mind and matter, reason and experience.

This splitting of reality, which gave rationalism its narrow focus and consequent drive, Jacques Maritain called, "the sin of angelism," whereby man, an embodied spirit, presumed to act as if he were a pure spirit, an angel. To reject experience and rely on deductions from innate ideas seems today to have been a doctrinaire exercise in logic, neither truly philosophical nor scientific; it was to have deleterious effects on legal thinking, ever susceptible to formalism. The subsequent history of jurisprudence will be a chronicle of the attempts to cope with this imbalance. Nevertheless, the insight that repositioned the subject in the heart of philosophy had within it the seeds of wisdom as well; they would not mature, however, for many years.

Rationalism made its impact on law through the writings of Hugo Grotius (1583–1645), a contemporary of Descartes, who was caught up in the struggle for disciplinary autonomy for jurisprudence. The thinking subject was the justification for his so-called "impious hypothesis"—an affirmation of the validity of the natural law "even if we concede that which cannot be conceded without the utmost wickedness, that there is no God or that the affairs of men are no concern to him."[21] Grotius was a convinced Calvinist, even a theologian of sorts; God was essential to his religion and to his overall thinking. His formulation, however, took on a life of its own, so perfectly did it capture for law the spirit of rationalism. Eventually, it led to the "death" of the divine lawgiver in much of Western jurisprudence.

Actually Grotius said nothing new; Stoics and Scholastics had suggested as much. Even his contemporary, Robert Bellarmine (1542–1621), Saint and Doctor of the Church, had written: "If (*per impossible*) law did not come from God, it would still bind under pain of fault; just as if (*per impossible*) there existed a man not created by God, he would still be rational."[22] But the hypothesis coming from Grotius

21. Hugo Grotius, *De jure belli ac pacis. Prolegomena* (1646), trans. F. W. Kelsey et al., Classics of International Law 3 (Oxford: Oxford University Press, 1925), p. 9. The Latin reads ". . . etiam daremus, quod sine summo scelere dari nequit, non esse Deum aut non curari ab eo negotia humana."

22. Robert Bellarmine, *Opera Omnia. De controversiis christianae fide. De membris Ecclesiae militantis,* ed. J. Fèvre (Paris: L. Vivès, 1870), Lib. III, cap. 11.

in that particular cultural climate was widely taken as the basis for legal rationalism. Part of its appeal was its liberating power as an intellectualist weapon against the voluntaristic antagonists of natural law. The attack was not against God, but against canonists, theologians, and the entrenched authorities of church and state. Grotius was fighting philosophic voluntarism, theological dogmatism, and state absolutism. Rationalism, however, subjected legal theory to radical surgery: it cut off both its empirical and divine components. The legal subject, thus mutilated by the Cartesian dichotomy and the Grotian hypothesis, was institutionalized in a conceptualistic and God-free system, condemned to the frustrating task of trying to fashion by reason alone a meaningful and workable jurisprudence.

B. Emerging Empiricism

The turn to the subject elaborated by the rationalists was employed in a very different way by the British empiricists, especially Thomas Hobbes and John Locke.[23] During their lifetimes, modern science had become firmly entrenched and highly respected. Both philosophers incorporated scientific method into their own thinking on jurisprudence. Together, they shifted the basis of their ethics and politics from the law of nature to the rights of nature. Not divine law or even natural law but natural rights provided the foundation upon which they erected their social structures—Hobbes, on sovereign power; Locke, on shared power. This change of direction was to characterize the politics of modernity. Let us consider each briefly.

Thomas Hobbes (1588–1679) was inspired, by his reading of Euclid and by conversations with Galileo, to apply the scientific method to his political concerns. His empirical basis was natural appetite and natural reason. From observing man's appetites at work, he discerned the fundamental one: the passion for self-preservation. From this, he tried to arrive at natural right and natural law; the former was simply a descriptive fact: "Natural right is the liberty each has to use his power as he will himself, for the preservation of his own nature, that is to say for his own life; and consequently of doing anything which in his own judgment and reason he shall conceive to be the aptest means there-

23. The distinction between a rationalist and an empiricist is not a mutually exclusive one. Both Hobbes and Locke were men of their age. Hobbes, though materialistic and scientific, reflects a strong rationalistic tendency in his own system of natural law.

unto."[24] Obviously, in a world populated by naturally selfish beings, there would be conflicts resulting in a "war of all against all," and life would be "solitary, poor, nasty, brutish, and short."[25]

The subject, however, has been only partly described; in addition to natural appetite, the subject has natural reason. This power enables him to make prudential judgments based on a kind of rational self-interest. Indeed, man's passions prompt him to use his reason for peace, since he fears death, desires things needed for commodious living, and hopes by his industry to obtain them.[26] So he fashions laws of nature, deductions from the passion for self-preservation or, more accurately, from the right of nature. The classical tradition derived rights from the law of nature; Hobbes reversed the process. Laws have a very practical basis, not reason, nor faith, but utility—since men wish to live, this is what they must do. These "laws of nature" or commonsense judgments are three: (1) "that every man ought to endeavor peace so far as he has hope of obtaining it; and when he cannot obtain it, that he may seek and use, all helps and advantages of war"; (2) "that a man be willing when others are so too; . . . to lay down this right to all things; and be contented with so much liberty against other men as he would allow other men against himself"; and (3) "that men perform their covenants made."[27]

The social contract, in accordance with the laws of nature, is made by the citizens, who give all their power to the sovereign, though he is not a party to the contract. The sovereign is then absolute and unlimited, the authority for everything—truth and error, good and evil, justice and injustice. As for the liberties of the citizen, "they all depend on the silence of the law."[28] This statement of Hobbes reveals the sequence: first, the right of nature attests to total liberty; then, the laws of nature leading to the covenant give the sovereign the power to restrict as much of that liberty as he chooses; finally, the positive law by imposing duties also indicates the residual freedom.

In the process, however, the legal person has undergone a radical role reversal: once having been a subject able to act with full freedom, he has, for the sake of security, virtually become an object, one under

24. Thomas Hobbes, *Leviathan,* ed. C. B. Macpherson (Baltimore: Penguin Books, 1968), part I, ch. 14.
25. Ibid., I, ch. 13.   26. See ibid.
27. Ibid., I, ch. 14 for laws (1) and (2) and ch. 15 for law (3).
28. Ibid., II, ch. 21.

total subjection to an absolute sovereign. Indeed, the sovereign remains, in the fullest sense of the term, the only true subject, "for it is the unity of the representer, not the unity of the represented that maketh the person one."[29] So great is the authority of this "feigned or artificial person," however, that Hobbes called it "that mortal god, to which we owe under the immortal God, our peace and defence."[30]

Hobbes—although he has been said to be the founder of modern political philosophy, primarily because of his subordination of law to right and his enlargement of the idea of sovereignty—did not have an immediate and direct impact on law. By the nineteenth century, however, his empiricism, his scientific approach, his rejection of metaphysics and natural law, his assertion of the absolute power of the state, and his emphasis on law as a command, would strongly influence both analytical jurists as well as other legal positivists, giving great longevity to the reductively diminished Hobbesian subject.

In philosophical and legal matters, John Locke (1632–1704) made a more valuable contribution than did Hobbes. They had much in common—both made the subject central; both followed a scientific method; both subordinated law to right; both had a contractarian conception of the state. But where Hobbes held an absolutist position, Locke had a libertarian one, which recognized in the people a residual power limiting governmental authority.

Although both Hobbes and Locke were empiricists, Locke's greater importance in this area rested on his elaborate analysis in the *Essay Concerning Human Understanding* (1690), which was to influence Hume and Kant. Locke, a physician and student of science, had already incorporated the empirical approach in his thinking long before writing that book. Indeed, he was already using an empirical perspective with the subject as his point of departure when he wrote, sometime in the years between 1660 and 1664, a series of *Essays on the Law of Nature;* they were discovered almost three hundred years later and first published in 1954.[31] In the third essay, Locke denied that the natural law is inscribed in the mind of man; in the fourth, he argued that reason can attain to knowledge of the natural law through sense experience. The mind begins as a *tabula rasa*, but using the body as its instrument,

29. Ibid., I, ch. 16.
30. Ibid., II, ch. 17.
31. John Locke, *Essays on the Law of Nature*, trans. W. von Leyden (Oxford: Clarendon Press, 1954).

it can through sensation and reflection arrive at ideas, including the idea of the natural law. Having made his own the earlier scholastic maxim—"Nothing is in the intellect which was not somehow first in the senses"—Locke was convinced that if the natural law is to be known at all it will be through reason, the discursive faculty, working on sense data.

Locke opposed Thomas Hobbes on many points. For him, the state of nature was not a state of war. Although men were free, they were naturally equal and had from the law of nature duties to one another. Moreover, even after the social contract, the natural law with its rights and duties continued independently of the state. Rights were not irrevocably handed over as in Hobbes's commonwealth. This more reasonable approach, or at least one more consonant with traditional political and ethical philosophy, helps explain why Locke rather than Hobbes was the inspiration for American colonists. Nevertheless, Locke was clearly a modern thinker; no resemblances to the past or continuity with it should be allowed to conceal that fact.

Locke's avowed "historical, plaine method" contrasted with Descartes's contrived "methodic doubt." Although both methods dealt with the subject, Locke sought data outside himself and reflected on his perceptions; he relied on experience instead of on innate ideas, on induction more than on deduction. Clearly, Locke's most memorable impact on the law was in the area of civil rights and political theory; nevertheless, his recognition of the key role of empirical data would indirectly, but perhaps as significantly, influence Anglo-American legal thinking. Together, rationalism and empiricism would effect major changes in jurisprudence, as Kant's critical philosophy, the next step in this complex and erratic process, clearly shows.

C. Metaphysics Rejected

Immanuel Kant (1724–1804) brought the turn to the subject to a dramatic stage of development that would greatly influence legal thinking. Yet his own jurisprudence was largely a summation of the tradition of classical Protestant natural law; he brought this era to a close with a finely articulated theory of law and morals, conspicuous for its rigid deontological core. What inspired later legal thinkers, however, was not his natural law perspective, but what he called his "Copernican revolution."

Kant's revolutionary insight resulted from the convergence of two currents of thought: rationalism (Descartes, Leibnitz, and Wolff) first structured his thinking; then empiricism (Locke and Hume) provided the decisive spark. A question common to both positions involved the notion of substance, but it was David Hume's challenge to Locke's definition of substance that, as Kant admits in his *Prolegomena,* awakened him from his "dogmatic slumber." Hume's radical empiricism convinced Kant that although we can know the *phenomena* (sense impressions), we cannot know the *noumena* (substances, essences). Of course, Kant acknowledged the general acceptance of the reality of space, time, casuality, necessity, substance, and so forth, but he called such convictions a transcendental illusion. He had concluded that these areas of knowledge must be the result of *a priori* forms already in the mind; they are not innate ideas, but rather innate forms that are given to sensible data.

This "Copernican revolution" consisted in a complete turn-about: categories are not, as they were for Aristotle, derived from reality as modes of being that the mind discovers and conforms to; rather, they are patterns of understanding that the mind imposes on phenomena, the only reality that the mind can know, for it can never know the *Ding an sich,* the thing-in-itself. The result of his "Copernican revolution" was the assertion of the clear centrality of the subject.

Central or not, the subject was precariously poised on the brink of skepticism. Speculative reason, for Kant, could never attain certain knowledge; at best it could reveal antinomies, which dialectically contradicted one another, or regulative ideas, which enabled the subject to act "as if" they were true. Kant avoided absurdity by insisting on the primacy of practical reason. He based his solution on inner experience, on the subjective consciousness of duty or obligation. This is the *factum* of morality from which the Categorical Imperative with its universalizing function is articulated: "Act as if the maxim of your action were to become through your will a universal law of nature."[32] Then, in accord with the principle that if you ought to do something you can do it, he postulated three necessary truths—previously established by a then discredited metaphysics—human freedom, the immortality of the soul, and the existence of God.

However crucial they may be, these three postulates are personal and

---

32. Immanuel Kant, *The Moral Law: Kant's Groundwork of the Metaphysic of Morals,* trans. and ed. H. J. Paton (New York: Barnes and Noble, 1963), p. 89.

incommunicable; for example, "I must not say *it is* morally certain that there is a God . . . but *I am* morally certain."[33] The subject's competence to understand has been drastically limited; in its place is an intuition of an *a priori* form implemented by three postulates. Kant had devised a means of avoiding skepticism, at least temporarily; he did so by basing ethics and law on a kind of moralism or subjectivism. It did not prove difficult for later Neo-Kantians, like Kelsen, to reject the moralistic postulates and assert a pure theory of law grounded on power and its valid use. Indeed, positivism was a logical, though not inevitable, derivative of Kant's critical philosophy.

In assessing Kant's influence on the turn to the subject that has characterized the modern era, we note that he remained on a conceptualistic, even rationalistic, level. Moreover, his anti-metaphysical conclusions narrowed the scope of human reason, even more than did the earlier rationalism, so much so that many who did not experience an *a priori* call to duty nor accept as necessary his three postulates found a return to empiricism or a move to its cognate, positivism, logically appealing. In short, though Kant contributed many valuable insights, his legacy was a drastically limited legal subject, as if the more he scrutinized it, the more it shrank.

D. Idealist Conceptualism

The German Idealists—Fichte, Schelling, and Hegel—moved beyond Kant's critical philosophy and back into metaphysics, which had been thought to be totally discredited by Kant. Georg Hegel (1770–1831) brought this idealism to its culmination: the absolute spirit knowing itself. The absolute was the whole of reality, the universe. Hegel, however, defined it differently than did Spinoza or the Stoics: "Everything depends on grasping the true not merely as *Substance,* but as *Subject* as well."[34] This absolute spirit, through a necessary dialectical process, is ever unfolding to produce the world.

The absolute becomes self-conscious through the human spirit, specifically through philosophy, for "philosophy is concerned with the

33. Idem, *Critique of Pure Reason,* trans. Norman Kemp Smith (London: Macmillan, 1950), A 829/B 857, p. 650. For Kant's argument for the existence of God as a postulate of pure practical reason see *Fundamental Principles,* pp. 220–29.

34. Georg Hegel, *Werke,* ed. H. G. Glockner, 22 vols. (Stuttgart: Frommen, 1927–1939), 2:22.

true and the true is the whole."[35] Philosophy, thus, achieves reflective self-consciousness according to the principle: "The rational is the real and the real is the rational,"[36] whereby both the process and the product of the unfolding of the absolute are revealed by an ever-deepening conceptualization. Incidentally, Kierkegaard's criticism of this conceptualistic objectification would much later inspire the Existentialists of the twentieth century.

It is relevant to the purposes of this book that Hegel had worked out, as part of his larger schema on the philosophy of the spirit, a version of what I have called a jurisprudence of subjectivity. His is an insightful construct, unfortunately characterized by idealism and conceptualism and grounded on an inadequate cognitional theory. Nevertheless, it is enlightening to examine briefly the framework of his development of the relationship between law and the subject.

Hegel establishes three stages of his philosophy of the Spirit. *The first state,* the subjective spirit, involves three aspects: the finite spirit united to the body as its soul and existing in an undifferentiated state; the finite spirit as it becomes self-conscious on its various levels of differentiation; and the finite spirit as it becomes universal through the consciousness of intersubjectivity. *The second stage* is that of the objective spirit. The finite spirit, like the absolute spirit, objectifies itself, thus revealing ethical and legal components: right looks to the use of freedom in the external world and encompasses property, contract, and liability; poised against this external aspect is morality, which concerns itself with inwardness, purpose, intention, and, above all, conscience; social ethics is the dialectical synthesis of the external and the interior and examines concrete duties and objective values, as found in family, community, and state. *The third stage,* the absolute spirit, resolves the opposing forces of the subjective spirit and the objective spirit, whereby the absolute spirit knows itself reflectively. The finite spirit has been transcended; subjectivity and objectivity are reconciled in a higher level of self-consciousness and apprehended conceptually through art, religion, and philosophy. This brief sketch barely suggests the richness of Hegel's thought. It does, however, present a challenge to contemporary jurisprudence: to attempt once again the synthesis of law and subjectivity.

35. Ibid., 2:24.   36. Ibid.

E. Juridic Reactions

Although Kant and Hegel would decisively influence juridical thought, their impact was not immediately apparent in a culture still characterized by rationalism. The German thinkers had taken great strides in the development of modern philosophy; ethical, legal, and political thought would never again be the same. But law is conservative and rooted in common sense; it does not react readily to new philosophic insights.

Nevertheless, after almost two centuries, a reaction against rationalism on the part of legal thinkers became inevitable. They could not remain content forever with the great divorce between reason and experience and the splitting of the legal subject initiated by Descartes. Rationalism was a disappointing *tour de force;* it was not a philosophy of living law but an abstract imposition detached from concrete facts. Of course, an occasional interlude with formalism—with its logical coherence—may have a beneficial effect on the law, if clearly a temporary liaison, but it is disastrous if protracted.

Rationalism had indeed long outlived its usefulness. The growth of modern science and the increasing support for empiricism were steadily undercutting its intellectual foundations. The precipitating factor, however, was the legislative excesses following the French Revolution (1789) and the crowning of the goddess Reason on the high altar of the Cathedral of Notre Dame, a symbol of a spirit that felt no need of tradition or experience or facts.

The jurisprudential break with rationalism consisted in turning away, not from the subject, but from an exclusive reliance on abstractions and generalities. This reaction, sketched out here very boldly, took two major forms. Since rationalism, relying on reason, focused on *what the law ought to be,* the Historical School in Germany, studying customs, focused on *what the law was* and the Analytic School in England, using logic, focused on *what the law is.*

The Historical School of jurisprudence was a reaction against what was seen as the unfettered legislative license of the French rationalists. Its leading figure was Friederich Carl von Savigny (1779–1861), who wrote a small book, *Of the Vocation of Our Age for Legislation and Jurisprudence* (1814), in opposition to proposals to codify German law in the manner of the *Code Napoléon.* He was profoundly influenced by Edmund Burke's *Reflections on the French Revolution* (1790);

Burke very tellingly called *la liberté*, as understood by the victors, an object "stripped of every relation, in all the nakedness and solitude of a metaphysical abstraction."[37]

Hegel, too, influenced Savigny with his notion of the "popular juridic consciousness" and the historical unfolding of the absolute idea. But Hegel criticized Savigny's anti-legislative stand; this criticism is understandable, for in his thinking, Hegel, unlike Burke and Savigny, remained on the conceptual level, and, like Descartes, Hegel had an exaggerated confidence in the powers of human reason. Nevertheless, the Hegelian *Volksgeist*, narrowly construed, became an essential component of the Historical School, but one implying that only tradition and custom—not principles, deductions, and statutes—can produce sound law. Law, Savigny believed, is a social phenomenon that develops gradually; the jurist's task is to recognize and apply these maturing directives which come from the national spirit, the only authentic source of law. In Savigny, then, the legal subject had in part returned to his roots.

The Analytic School in England, founded by John Austin (1790–1859), manifested its opposition to the law-of-nature approach in another way; it preserved the logic of rationalism without its ideals and studied legal enactments themselves, not their underlying rationale. It asserted its autonomy from philosophy by keeping law for the lawyers, but its escape from the endless dialectics and sterile formalism of the rationalists led to a denial of the legal competence of philosophic reason. The law, which was once proudly called "an ordinance of reason" by Aquinas, was re-defined by Austin as "a command of the sovereign." The result was a further truncation of the existential subject, whose political fate was now to be decided in terms of power. The challenges of philosophy and the lessons of history became irrelevant; authoritative enactment was all that mattered.

John Austin's *The Province of Jurisprudence Determined* (1832) was committed to the construction of a juridical system based solely on the analysis of positive law. In some respects, however, Austin's writings seemed to offer a sequel to Hobbes's *Leviathan* by way of Bentham's

---

37. Edmund Burke, *Reflections on the French Revolution*, ed. T. H. D. Mahoney (Indianapolis: Bobbs Merrill, 1955), p. 8.

insights.[38] After almost two hundred years, the Hobbesian principles were precisely reformulated and applied to an ongoing system; the logical preoccupation of the Analytic School gave scientific shape to this positivist and absolutist core; justice was separated from positive law, and positive law was reduced to the four elements—sovereignty, command, duty, sanction—of an imperative theory of jurisprudence.

return to Hobbes

These two schools effectively bypassed rationalism: the Historical School moved in the direction of experience, although it tied itself to the dead hand of the past; the Analytic School concentrated on the present, but limited itself to the logical implications of power. As a result, the legal subject as such could no longer appeal beyond the positive law to God or to reason; he was at the mercy of the *Volksgeist* or the "mortal god." Of course, history and analysis are beneficial for the law, but they do not join together what Descartes and Grotius had rent asunder. Modernity's turn to the subject still continued, but it was a turn to a subject all too narrowly construed.

F. Positivist Reductionism

Auguste Comte (1798–1857), a contemporary of Savigny and Austin, was a philosopher, not a jurist, yet his positivism was to have a lasting effect on legal thinking. Not one prone to acknowledge the influence of others, he did admit, however, "Hume is my principal precursor in philosophy."[39] British empiricism reached him, not in its purest form through Bacon or Locke, but in its most radical form in Hume, and it did so directly, not shunted through the critical philosophy of Kant, who, as we have seen, was also inspired by Hume.

"The law of the three states"—first formulated by Comte, when he was twenty-four, in an article published in a book by Saint-Simon and later elaborated in his six-volume *Cours de philosophie positive* (1830–1842)—described the progression of *l'esprit positif* from the theological or fictitious state dealing with God, through the metaphysical or abstract state dealing with Nature, to the positive or scientific state

38. Although Hobbes spoke of law as a command in *Leviathan* (1651), e.g., Part II, ch. 26, his kinship with the Analytic School is more obvious in a work published posthumously in 1681, *Dialogue between a Philosopher and a Student of the Common Law* in *The English Works of Thomas Hobbes*, ed. W. Molesworth, 11 vols. (London: J. Bohn, 1839–1845), 6:3–160.

39. Auguste Comte, *The Catechism of Positive Religion*, trans. R. Congreve. 3rd ed. (Clifton, N.J.: A. M. Kelley, 1973), p. 7.

dealing with Fact. Comte had already experienced these states personally, having long been atheistic, anti-metaphysical, and positivist. He rejoiced perversely in the French Revolution for destroying religion and at the same time for exposing the emptiness of its own Enlightenment philosophy, thereby paving the way for the emergence of the fully realized positive spirit.

Comte considered himself the prophet of "the fundamental law of intellectual evolution" as it reached its final state. Sociology, a term he coined, described, not the area of specialization that we are familiar with today, but a universal science of man, a synthesis of all human knowledge. So far as law is concerned, Comte's specific contribution was to apply to social and political facts the methods of empirical science; this would be the core of legal positivism, enabling the social scientist to discover social facts and social laws for the purposes of social control. As for legal ideals, one should note, Comte believed that the Enlightenment notions of right and liberty were "metaphysical fallacies."

Legal positivism owes much to Comte, but not everything. It is also the result of the reductionist tendency of modern thought, whereby the subject remains central but becomes more and more limited. As we have seen, the influence of Hobbes, Hume, Bentham, and Austin, as well as the less direct influence of Kant, had given to the law an empirical, anti-metaphysical, and analytic character, well before Comte named it *l'esprit positif.* Moreover, the nation states that sprung up after the defeat of Napoleon in 1815 proved highly susceptible to a positivist approach.

Liberalism considered the law to be a product of individual wills implemented by sanctions; but where classical liberalism grounded law on human reason and human goodness, positivistic liberalism grounded it on power and legality. The tension between the individual and authority was resolved for liberalism by Voltaire's principle, "Freedom consists in being independent of everything but law,"[40] Yet positivism equated law solely with the directives of valid power. Where, then, does positivism leave the legal subject? In a drastically reduced state. Kelsen logically and matter-of-factly defined this ultimate dehumani-

40. Voltaire, *Pensées sur l'administration publique,* quoted by J. H. Hallowell in *Main Currents in Modern Political Thought* (New York: Henry Holt, 1950), p. 89. Hallowell's analysis of liberalism affords an excellent context for an understanding of the changes in legal thought.

zation: "The concept of physical (natural) person means nothing but the personification of a complex of legal norms."[41]

Legal positivists necessarily exclude God or justice from their personal lives, but they do conceive of the legal system as an analytically self-contained or a logically closed system, at least to the extent that it does not depend on ethical, metaphysical, or theological foundations. Law was to be a true science, empirically not trans-empirically grounded. But positivists differed widely in their emphasis: European positivists (Hobbes, Austin, Kelsen, Hart) were more analytic; American positivists (Gray, Holmes, Pound, Llewellyn) were more pragmatic.

It was John Chipman Gray (1839–1915) who helped give American positivism its distinctive direction by breaking with Austin, to focus not on the sovereign but on the judiciary: "The Law of the State or of any organized body of men is composed of the rules which the courts, that is, the judicial organs of that body, lay down for the determination of legal rights and duties."[42] So essential was this principle for Gray that he put it in a purposely shocking phrase: "The Law, except for a few crude notions of the equity involved in some of its general principles, is all *ex post facto*."[43] A strong emphasis on social facts and judicial behavior was to characterize American jurisprudence in the decades to follow; it was captured in the famous sentence of Holmes—written some years before Gray's book—"The life of the law has not been logic: it has been experience."[44] This new legal positivism blended well with the pragmatism of William James, and later of John Dewey, to structure the dominant American jurisprudence.

Despite its being in the ascendancy for some hundred years, positivism began to decline after World War II, primarily because of the increasing concerns and controversies over values and over the responsibility of the state to protect and foster them. Some of these issues were occasioned by the war itself, with its crimes against humanity: genocide, slavery, torture, and unjust war. Other issues have subsequently emerged: poverty, racism, women's rights, abortion, capital punishment, voting rights, immigration, self-determination, terrorism,

41. Hans Kelsen, *General Theory of the Law and the State,* trans. A. Wedberg (New York: Russell and Russell, 1971), part I, ch. ix, "The Legal Person," p. 95.
42. John Chipman Gray, *The Nature and Sources of the Law,* 2d and revised edition by R. Gray (New York: Columbia University Press, 1921), ch. iv, p. 84.
43. Ibid., p. 100.
44. Holmes, *The Common Law* (Boston: Little, Brown, 1881), p. 1.

and nuclear arms. Appeals were made beyond the law of the state or the international community to a higher law, that of reason, of justice, or of God. The heart of the appeal has been the pressing need, in the absence of adequate political power, to limit or change positive law.

Underlying these controversies over values has been a change in the relationship of the state to its citizens. With the rise of positivism, the state had intruded more and more into areas hitherto considered private, such as economics, education, and the family. Then, too, political unrest and revolutions have disrupted previously stable regimes. The net result has been a reluctant recognition that legal theory must take values into account.

Positivism—for all its resistance to the fully dimensioned existential subject—has begun to loosen its grasp on jurisprudence; it grows weak precisely in confronting the evils and sufferings of the times, the conflicts between justice and injustice, the competing value judgments, all of which it had previously scorned as fundamentally irrelevant to legal theory. Indeed, the main reason for the current struggle against positivism is that legal subjects, recognizing and resenting their diminished status under positivism, have begun to insist with more and more power on a fuller realization of their human values and civil rights.

G. Piecemeal Recovery

To resume our chronicling of the turn to the subject, we must note that Comte did much more than facilitate the growth of legal positivism. His emphasis on the need for a broad database with a "sociological" component suggested to many that such an addition be made to the earlier rationalistic, analytic, and historical approaches to jurisprudence. The result was the formation of three socio-philosophic schools: the Social Utilitarian, the Neo-Kantian, and the Neo-Hegelian. Each one of these took a step forward in the restoration of the integrity of the legal subject, but they did not achieve the goal either separately or corporately. Let us look at the contribution they did make.

The Social Utilitarians, under the leadership of Rudolf von Jhering (1818–1892), brought a social dimension to analytic theory. Looking beyond "the jurisprudence of conceptions" of rationalism and Roman law, he considered the claims and demands that the law secured. His basic insight was that a right was an interest secured by law, and he tested each law to determine what that interest was, whether it was worth while, and whether it was effectively secured. Jhering's utilitarianism moved from individual to communal concerns, paralleling the developments from Bentham to Mill, but he remained primarily analytic, producing a methodology but not a complete jurisprudence. Under his imperative theory of law taken from John Austin, the status of the subject was not appreciably changed, despite the introduction into juridic calculations of a communal component.

The Neo-Kantians, under Rudolf Stammler (1856–1938), brought a social dimension to Kant's critical philosophy. Stammler tried to achieve "justice through rules" by bringing back juridical idealism to legal theory. He went beyond Social Utilitarianism, with its simple complexus of individual laws, to a higher synthesis of law as unified by the ideals of reason and justice. Philosophy returned to jurisprudence under the guise of "a natural law with a changing content."[45] Gone was the immutability and deductive certainty of rationalism; in its place was a flexible although conceptual core as a standard for value judgments.

Stammler, however, proposed a pure theory of law involving form rather than content. Later, Kelsen, another Neo-Kantian, would reject his approach as neither pure enough nor formal enough. But at this point in time, Stammler's contribution was that he faced up to the philosophic problems implicit in the social dimension of law. He tried to resolve the tension between the individual and the community through the idea of cooperation between "men willing freely"[46] as well as the tension between egoism and altruism through the ideas of respect and participation with each person acting as "his own neighbor."[47] In doing so, he distinguished ethics (regulating the subjective intention in the internal forum) from law (regulating objective conduct in the external forum). The most important result of Stammler's social idealism was that it brought back as a legitimate topic of jurisprudential debate the philosophic component, which the rationalists has discredited and the analytic and historical schools had bypassed.

The Neo-Hegelians, especially Josef Kohler (1849–1919), added a sociological dimension to the methodology of the historical school.

45. Rudolf Stammler, *Wirtschaft und Recht nach der Materialistischen Geschichtsaffassung,* 2d ed. (Leipzig, 1906), p. 165.

46. Idem, *The Theory of Justice,* trans. I. Husik (New York: Macmillan, 1925), p. 153. This formula of "a community of men willing freely," he calls his social ideal.

47. *Ibid.,* pp. 161 and 163, the second and fourth of his four "Principles of Just Law." He deals with the question: "Who is my neighbor?" on pp. 217–23.

Kohler's goal was to be able to preserve the best of the past without being constrained by it; he wanted to be able to harmonize statutory legislation with the exigencies of historical development. Although he clearly ruled out immutable principles of natural law, he provided a working substitute, his "jural postulates" of the civilization of the time and place—later to be systematically reformulated by Roscoe Pound.[48] The key for Kohler is the Hegelian *Kulturentwicklung*, the evolution of civilization. But there is no practical guarantee that the civilization may not become retrogressive. The result of Kohler's thinking is a relativistic justification of power by the standards of the dominant civilization. The history of the twentieth century reveals how disastrous an idea that has been. Nevertheless, the Neo-Hegelians, despite some theoretical extremism, did suggest a proper and necessary role for history in putting the legal subject and the law in existential context.

H. Contemporary Synthesis

Jurisprudence, in the early twentieth century, despite the insights that had been added by the social-philosophical schools, was seriously fragmented, approximating unity only through a common positivist perspective. Without changing that perspective. Roscoe Pound (1870–1964), long-time Dean of the Harvard Law School, magisterially synthesized the major loose ends of legal thinking into his own grand plan, Sociological Jurisprudence, with its four components: historical, analytic, philosophical, and sociological. Incidentally, the key word, sociological, did not have for Pound the specialized meaning that it has today; rather, it was the "study of the system of law functionally as a part or phase of social control, and of its institutions and doctrines with respect to the social ends to be served."[49] His goal was to satisfy and harmonize social wants as skillfully and as completely as possible. However, he understood this goal positivistically without any other philosophical constraints. "If in any field of human conduct or in any human relation the law, with such machinery as it has, may satisfy a social want without a disproportionate sacrifice of other claims, there

48. Roscoe Pound, *Outlines of Jurisprudence*, 5th ed. (Cambridge: Harvard University Press, 1943), pp. 168, 179, 183–84.
49. Ibid., p. 4.

is no eternal limitation inherent in the nature of things, there are no bounds imposed at creation to stand in the way of its doing so."[50]

A look at Pound's law-making process reveals his pragmatic basis for determining legal values. There are four steps: observe all interests; synthesize general principles (jural postulates of the time and place); formulate a scheme of interests based on the principles; and harmonize conflicting interests. What is the basis of justice? Proximately, it is interests or felt needs; remotely, it is the system of postulates of the time and place. Such were his standards for decision making in a positivist state.

What precisely has Pound achieved in terms of the legal subject? Has he healed the dichotomy introduced by Descartes between reason and experience? Certainly he has identified the major categories of a complete jurisprudence; he has kept his focus on the subject, whose interests are paramount; nevertheless, he has left the subject almost as diminished as he found it, though admittedly provided for more skillfully. Within his positivist parameters, he has erected an integrated structure, transcending the special pleading of earlier schools. But it is a vulnerable structure, intrinsically conditioned by the exigencies of the civilization, its progress or decline; it is a function of the *status quo*.

For those who prescind from fundamental philosophic issues and the deepest of human concerns, Sociological Jurisprudence offers a productive technique or methodology for the institution of law in the body politic. But because its consumer is a diminished subject, Sociological Jurisprudence is itself diminished. Pound manifested this inner deficiency even when singing a paean to his system as a final end or realization of legal development:

I am content to see in legal history the record of a continually wider recognizing and satisfying of human wants or claims or desires through social control; a more embracing and more effective securing of social interests; a continually more complete and effective elimination of waste and precluding of friction in human enjoyment of the goods of existence—in short, a continually more efficacious social engineering.[51]

Despite the allure of this myth of progress, the revealing metaphor of "social engineering" breaks the spell; we realize that these dimin-

50. Idem, *The Philosophy of Law* (New Haven: Yale University Press, 1922, 1954), pp. 46–47.
51. Ibid., p. 47.

ished subjects are to be objectified and serviced, more like things than like persons, and that *l'esprit positif* of Comte still lives, now animating Sociological Jurisprudence.[52]

The Legal Realists, who flourished during the interval between the two World Wars, directed their critical talents against Sociological Jurisprudence as well as against the whole legal establishment. Pound said that they approached the science of law in terms of its ugly factors, and he labeled it "the cult of falling short." To a certain degree Realism was just that, for it concentrated on the discrepancy between "paper rules and working rules" (Llewellyn). Once it began to study what was actually happening—unfortunately limiting its critique almost exclusively to the judiciary—a demythologizing of the law was inevitable. Questions began to proliferate, and long-overlooked aspects of the legal subject came to light.

Inspired by Holmes, Realism was largely positivistic, but it lacked any coherent philosophy of its own; it was a movement rather than a school of jurisprudence. The members of this movement espoused many viewpoints—pragmatism, behaviorism, skepticism, logical positivism, economic determinism, and Freudianism, to name a few. This diversity or lack of philosophic consistency occasioned much criticism.

Karl Llewellyn, as late as 1961, was prompted to correct the record: "Where you all go wrong is in thinking that Realism was a theory. It was not. It was merely a methodology."[53] Although this appraisal was undoubtedly correct, it does not resolve all theoretical issues. For, as has been rightly observed: "The basic problem in method is to arrive at a cognitional theory."[54] Some of the Realists, like Frank and Hutcheson, did take some psychological factors into account; in doing so they relied generally on commonsense insights and made reference to Freud, Watson, Piaget, and others, but without developing an adequate cognitional theory. In the process, however, they lifted the veil and started

---

52. Note the remark of Roscoe Pound, in "Philosophy of Law and Comparative Law," *University of Pennsylvania Law Review* 100 (1951): 17: "In common with most Americans who had a scientific training in the eighties of the last century, I was brought up on Comtian positivism and turned thence to the Comtian sociology at the beginning of the present century."

53. Karl N. Llewellyn, "Legal Realism: Its Cause and Cure," *Yale Law Journal* 70 (1961): 1037.

54. Bernard Lonergan, "Questions with regard to Method: History and Economics," *Dialogues in Celebration,* ed. Cathleen Going (Montreal: Thomas More Institute, 1980), p. 290.

looking at the participants in legal events as concrete human beings instead of fungible abstractions.

Much of Sociological Jurisprudence and the Realist critique has been internalized by American legal thinkers. Despite earlier controversies, the two approaches have apparently blended together to form an important part of the public philosophy of law, though currently the emphasis is more political than jurisprudential. Significantly, the concern that the Realists had for the cognitional aspects of the law has continued, as psychology and psychiatry have played an expanding role in the intellectual world, yet the influence of these two fields on the philosophy of law, as contrasted with the science of law, has been largely peripheral. Nevertheless, Realism has fostered a reassessment of the role of the subject.

a leftist neo-realism

In the 1970's and 1980's a new version of Legal Realism has appeared, under the name of "Critical Legal Studies." It shares the iconoclastic approach of the older school, with its attack on the establishment, but has by and large adopted a radically left-wing political bias. Using the old realist weapons of rule skepticism and fact skepticism to further structuralist and neo-Marxist strategies, the new group confronts the legal institution as an illegitimate and exploitive system, which has established distributional inequalities only to divinize them through rituals of formalism. This leftist Neo-Realism has more in common with the student activism of the 1960's than it does with the Legal Realism of the 1920's and 1930's, which was a methodology without a philosophy; the current version has found its content in an ideological reductionism moving from law to power politics under the aegis of a yet undetermined utopianism. And yet, in the attack on formalism, the subject emerges here too. Roberto M. Unger, a leading exponent of Critical Legal Studies, devoted a chapter on the self in his *Knowledge and Politics:* "A theory of the self is needed to resolve the main problems posed by the argument of this book."[55]

During the last half of the twentieth century, there has generally been a renewed emphasis on values, as Critical Legal Studies obliquely

---

55. Roberto Mangabeira Unger, *Knowledge and Politics* (New York: The Free Press, 1975), p. 191. Although the philosophic underpinnings of the movement vary, a good presentation is Unger's major article, "The Critical Legal Studies Movement," *Harvard Law Review* 96 (1983): 561–675. Note, too, the critical analysis in John Finnis, "On 'The Critical Legal Studies Movement,' " *The American Journal of Jurisprudence* 30 (1985): 21–42.

evidences. Legal positivism has not been able to provide adequately for the needs that people have begun to articulate since the days of World War II. Victims of oppressive legal systems appeal to something beyond a societal basic norm or an organized system of power; for them justice is more than, in Kelsen's words, "an irrational idea."[56] Substance and content, not just formal validity, is a pressing concern. A species of Legal Positivism with neo-analytic and linguistic methods survives as a vested interest especially in academia, but it has passed its intellectual peak; it has proved to be inadequate for law.

The older schools of jurisprudence continue on, but now tend to emphasize concrete issues rather than philosophic foundations. Still divided, they often complement one another by focusing on different aspects of the same problem. The fact that the proliferating claims for human rights are ultimately based on a widely admitted perception of human values gives these various schools a start towards a working consensus, be it ever so contradictorily justified.

Although the name natural law is hardly a popular one, the underlying idea has been gradually emerging in bits and pieces. For example, Lon Fuller had in effect a procedural type of what he called "a variety of natural law"; Harold Lasswell and Myres MacDougal centered their own jurisprudence in human dignity. Robert Nozick based his libertarian state on a highly circumscribed set of natural rights. H. L. A. Hart, the English positivist, insisted that a minimum natural law content was needed for societal survival. Ronald Dworkin attacked the current "ruling theory" (Utilitarianism and Legal Positivism) in part by a "naturalistic" recourse to individual human rights.

What is happening is obviously not an attempt to revive natural law; but it is evidence of a growing recognition of the human person, though still largely a diminished one. The heart of a fully integral personalist jurisprudence, however, can be found in the voluminous works of Judge John T. Noonan, Jr., who has described with historical richness and moral sensitivity the many situations and contexts in which this depersonalization has occurred. He has analyzed explicitly and persuasively this juridic derailment in his book, *Persons and Masks of the Law*.

Noonan wrote of the need to "throw off the masks of the law," masks that tend to conceal human dignity through a formalism verging on reification: "By mask I mean a legal construct suppressing the

56. Hans Kelsen, *General Theory*, p. 13.

humanity of a participant in the process."[57] Since his book is an exercise in legal unmasking, it is helpful to know what to look for:

Masks of the law are of two kinds—those imposed on others and those put on oneself. "Property," applied to slaves, "sovereign," applied to lawmakers, are instances of the first kind. "The court" in the mouths of judges, "the law" in the mouths of judges and law professors are instances of the second. No doubt the extent to which these terms exclude humanity is a matter of context and degree.[58]

The mask accurately and dramatically symbolizes the abstract, mechanical, and theoretical approach to persons, which the law so easily and so often adopts. The mask affords a concrete reminder of the need for a jurisprudence of subjectivity. Only through the self-appropriation of one's own subjectivity can one fully respond to the subjectivity of others. Without this intersubjectivity there is no love, and, without love, the law congeals into a deadly formalism.

The turn to the subject has begun to prompt thinkers to look outside their abstract domains at the concrete data of human life. Now in the era of post-modernity, we are beginning to take an insider's view of our own subjectivity. We are, once again in Judge Noonan's phrase, throwing off the "masks of the law" to reveal the person, the existential subject and his mental operations. We are now truly approaching a jurisprudence of subjectivity and with it the promise of a new and fruitful dialogue.

III. THE INTERIOR MARKINGS

After three hundred years of preoccupation with the subject, modern jurisprudence has not yet adequately come to terms with subjectivity. As in the classicist era, it has remained by and large theoretical, with the subject considered something existing out there, to be observed, dissected, and put together again, one object among all the others in the world of our experience. Beyond theory, however, there is the realm of interiority or subjectivity, where we can meet the subject face to face

57. John T. Noonan, Jr., *Persons and Masks of the Law* (New York: Farrar, Straus, and Giroux, 1976), p. 20.

58. Ibid., p. 21. For a complementary personalistic approach, see Robert E. Rodes, Jr., *The Legal Enterprise* (Port Washington, N.Y.: National University Publications, 1976).

through our own inner experiences, through our consciousness. In the last two centuries, some major thinkers have so ventured; of those Kierkegaard, Newman, and Ortega serve well to point out, in an introductory way, salient features of this always accessible but strangely new realm.

A. The Subjective Focus

Søren Kierkegaard (1813–1855), in his *Concluding Unscientific Postscript* (1846), has dramatically described the role of subjectivity. He insisted: "Subjectivity, inwardness, is the truth."[59] Reacting against Hegel's absolute idealism or essentialism, he was convinced that to focus on concepts was to leave out the existing subject and to fail utterly in grasping reality. "What is abstract thought? It is thought without a thinker."[60] He distinguished two modes of reflection:

For an objective reflection the truth must become an object, something objective, and thought must be pointed away from the subject. For a subjective reflection the truth becomes a matter of appropriation, of inwardness, of subjectivity, and thought must probe more and more deeply into the subject and his subjectivity.[61]

Kierkegaard's rejection of speculative philosophy, at that time highly conceptualized, was not a rejection of philosophic thought. True philosophy for him looked to existence, life, freedom, commitment, and choice. "An existing individual is himself in process of becoming. . . . For as long as he is in existence he will never become eternal. In existence the watchword is always forward."[62] So he reacted against the conceptualized human being in favor of the concrete subject, dynamically actual: "The only reality that exists for an existing individual is his own ethical reality."[63] If that is the case, how relevant is the notion of dread, *Angst*, which was to be so topical some hundred years later: "Dread is the possibility of freedom,"[64] and "the alarming possibility of being able."[65] No longer secure in the calm of eternal concepts, we are challenged to act, knowing we may fail, but knowing that

59. Søren Kierkegaard, *Concluding Unscientific Postscript*, trans. D. Swenson and W. Lowrie (Princeton: Princeton University Press, 1974), p. 183.

60. Ibid., p. 296.   61. Ibid., p. 171.

62. Ibid., p. 368.   63. Ibid., p. 280.

64. Idem, *The Concept of Dread*, trans. W. Lowrie (Princeton: Princeton University Press, 1944), p. 38.

65. Ibid., p. 40.

we are able to act and that we have no other option, for the realm of abstraction does not offer enough reality to satisfy us.

Appropriation is what makes subjectivity attainable. That is why Kierkegaard spoke of an individual's "own ethical reality." For truth is not simply looking out at reality or simply allowing reality to shape our unresisting mind; it is the result of an energetic and vital function. Kierkegaard considered it a moral commitment. Going beyond intellectual apprehensions, however active, he demanded an additional ingredient. He believed that the stance of a detached observer made truth impossible, perhaps not in mathematics or the physical sciences, but certainly in theology, philosophy, ethics, and law. In these areas involving human existence, authentic choice alone can ground the acquisition of truth. "In the case of a kind of observation where it is requisite that the observer should be in a specific condition, it naturally follows that if he is not in this condition, he will observe nothing."[66] So Kierkegaard held that those Christians who were not true Christians did not know the truth of Christianity, for truth is not an academic accomplishment but a perceived transformation. Indeed, he might well have quoted the Bible: "He that keeps justice shall get the understanding thereof" (Eccl. 21:12), observing that neither the legislator nor judge nor lawyer necessarily has the truth about law, but only the just man or woman, not one who is reputed to know the law but only the one who lives the law.

Kierkegaard taught us to broaden the focus of our intentionality to include the inner arena so that our consciousness of legal reality can be total. Through self-appropriation we are personally involved in the search for truth, a truth that is not exclusively intellectual but is ethical as well, involving existential choice. He did not make truth a product of choice, but he did establish authentic existence and passionate commitment as conditions of truth.

In short, Kierkegaard prompted us to make the whole subject the focal point of our philosophy. Only from this viewpoint, he asserted, can truth be found, for only from this viewpoint can we experience our own concrete existence. Without that awareness, we never fully know reality; we can know about things, we can be very articulate, but we are pointed away from the center where truth is realized. Law, for,

66. Idem, *Concluding Unscientific Postscript*, p. 51.

Kierkegaard, is a field in which objective truth can be found only through authentic subjectivity.

B. The Real Assent

[handwritten: Kierk + Newman rejected mere conceptualism]

Real, and not merely notional, assent is the second requirement for a full experience of law. John Henry Newman (1801–1890) developed the distinction between the real and the notional in his *Grammar of Assent,* published in 1870. His work complemented that of Kierkegaard, for they were both reacting against the current conceptualism; but apparently they were unaware of one another. Their approaches, however, were different: Kierkegaard moved directly to subjectivity; Newman looked specifically at mental operations, focusing on real assent as the perfection of objectivity but locating it in subjective activities. Kierkegaard was more concerned with the philosophy and theology of subjectivity; Newman, with its underlying cognitional theory. The latter's descriptive explanation of the process of assent will, however, ultimately prove more valuable in experiencing the law, for it gives a preliminary sketch of the operations of the mind that constitute the subjective viewpoint.

The distinction that Newman made in the *Grammar of Assent* is important for legal reasoning. Here is how he distinguished the two types of assent.

In its Notional Assents as well as in its inferences, the mind contemplates its own creation instead of things; in Real, it is directed toward things, represented by the impressions which they have left on the imagination. These images, when assented to, have an influence both on the individual and on society, which notions cannot exert.[67]

Most of what we first think of as law involves notional assent. Thus, Newman classifies as notional, "legal judgments and constitutional maxims in so far as they appeal to us for our assent,"[68] and also "the assent to all reasoning and its conclusions, to all general propositions, to all rules of conduct, to all proverbs, aphorisms, sayings and reflections on men and society."[69] But these notional guidelines do not suffice

---

67. John Henry Newman, *A Grammar of Assent* (New York: Longmans, Green, 1947), p. 57.
68. Ibid.
69. Ibid., p. 56.

for knowing and handling the concrete singulars of the real world. Newman used ethics to illustrate this limitation:

An ethical system may supply laws, general rules, guiding principles, a number of examples, suggestions, landmarks, limitations, cautions, distinctions, solutions of critical or anxious difficulties; but who is to apply them to a particular case? Whither can we go, except to the living intellect, our own, or another's? What is written is too vague, too negative for our need.[70]

The same need for particularity is found in public law, though Newman recognized that public law is relatively "inflexible" compared to ethics. Indeed, all our thinking about singulars involves the same faculty. "The sole and final judgment on the validity of an inference in concrete matter is committed to the personal action of the ratiocinative faculty, the perfection or virtue of which I have called the Illative Sense."[71] This illative sense—developed along the lines of Aristotle's *phronesis* or practical wisdom—looks to real apprehension and real assent involving concrete persons or things. It enables us to deal with factual and historical matters by determining when the convergence of probabilities leads us to certainty. However circumscribed by natural and adventitious shortcomings a person may be, his own judgment here is indispensable. "Such as I am, it is my all; this is my essential standpoint, and it must be taken for granted; otherwise, thought is but an idle amusement not worth the trouble."[72] So, too, would any attempt to have a true experience of law without real assent be a vain endeavor.

Newman, of course, did not dispense with concepts. He well knew that concepts are necessary if we are to communicate with one another. For the very perfection of real assent is a function of the individuality of the person making it, whereas "notional apprehension is in itself an ordinary act of our common nature."[73] We have, he noted, the power of abstraction; we make logical inferences; and we exchange ideas. Our language is the medium of conceptual interaction. But Newman always insisted that we reach the truth about concrete beings, the persons and things of our experience, by means of real asset. His many references to law make it abundantly clear that for him a complete jurisprudence, while using both real and notional assents, depends on real assent for final, practical decisions.

70. Ibid., p. 269.   71. Ibid., p. 262.
72. Ibid., p. 263.   73. Ibid., p. 63.

C. The Concrete Ambiance

Contextual, rather than merely isolated or monadic, existence is the third dimension of the subjective perspective. This corollary, amplifying the implications of real assent through the accumulation of insights, is reflected in the writings of José Ortega y Gasset (1883–1955). His theory of perspectivism, however, seems at first to be too narrow: "Where my eye is, there is no other; that part of reality which my eye sees is seen by no other. There is no substitute for any of us, we are all necessary."[74] He appears to espouse not subjectivity but subjectivism: "Every life is a viewpoint on the universe."[75]

But Ortega did not isolate himself—far from it. He combined subjectivity and objectivity in a philosophy that he sums up in the memorable phrase: *Yo soy yo y mi circunstancia* ("I am myself and my circumstances").[76] His message is that the subject can realize himself only in terms of the circumstances that constitute his world. "The world is the sum total of our vital possibilities. It is not then something apart from and foreign to our existence, it is its actual periphery. It represents what it is within our power to be, our vital potentiality."[77] Our task, then, is to mediate the world through meaning: "Man reaches his full capacity when he acquires complete consciousness of his circumstances. Through them he communicates with the universe."[78] So man must try to personalize, to humanize the world of his experience, so that he can project his perfection through them. Ortega formulated this process as "the reabsorption of circumstances in the concrete destiny of man."[79]

In other words, the subject or self, uniquely focused by its own perspective, seeks the meaning of its circumstances—the realm of its possibilities—in order to achieve its own fullness of being. Man is an heroic project, partly in the real world and partly in the ideal world. Circumstances are "mute"—it is up to him to give them a voice—but they are "gifts" and "offerings," indispensable materials for the human

74. Ortega y Gasset, "Verdad y Perspectiva," *El Spectador* I (1916), *Obras completas,* 6 vols. (Madrid: Revista de Occidente, 1957–1958), 2:20.

75. Idem, "El Tema de nuestro tiempo," *Obras,* 3:200.

76. Idem, *Meditations on Quixote* (San Juan, Puerto Rico: University of Puerto Rico Press, 1957), p. 45. Cf. also note 4, p. 168.

77. Idem, *The Revolt of the Masses* (New York: Norton, 1932), p. 44.

78. Idem, *Meditations,* p. 41.

79. Ibid., p. 45.

project. We are intrinsically linked, even wedded, to this world of our experience. "I am myself and my circumstance, and if I do not save it, I cannot save myself."[80]

One may not disregard this contextual foundation if one hopes to comprehend the full range of law; such an attainment depends on an awareness of the relationship of subject and object, self and circumstance. We see specific, legal references to this need in the oath that a witness takes to "tell the whole truth" and in the Fourteenth Amendment due-process test for voluntariness, which involves the "totality of the circumstances." More fundamental is the recognition that all legal events are conditioned and can be appreciated only in full context; otherwise the administration of justice becomes an exercise in abstraction, precise but unreal.

CONCLUSION

The challenge of jurisprudence is to find meaning and value in the law. Since the seventeenth century, there has been a radical turn to the subject, which has shattered the classicist synthesis. This change of focus or new center of coherence eventually effected a progressive diminution of the subject and a positivist reduction of law. These unfortunate results prompted the absurdity response that characterized the thought of Holmes, Kafka, Camus, and so many others. But this very turn to the subject is also the key to a richer understanding of law, by which one can successfully transcend absurdity and achieve meaning and value in a new synthesis. This achievement requires participation in legal events, not just as an object but as a conscious subject, not just as a notional thinker but as one capable of real assents, not just as an abstract individual but as a concretely circumstanced person.

A jurisprudence of subjectivity continues to emphasize the subject, but does so from a subjective viewpoint, involving mental operations, conscious and intentional. By expanding an inner awareness of these operations through the various spheres of legal activity and by authentically appropriating them, we can reintegrate our legal knowledge and entertain the realistic hope of attaining ultimate meaning and value. Thus we begin our excursion through the Nomosphere in the clear light of the eyewitness perspective.

80. Ibid., pp. 45–46.

PART ONE

THE MONOSPHERE
THE INDIVIDUAL EXPERIENCE OF LAW

The Monosphere is the realm of the solitary thinker, all alone with the evidence of his senses and consciousness and with his questions about law. At the present stage of our cultural development, we would find it impossible to re-experience the innocence and ignorance of our earliest ancestors. The structures of language and thought that we inherit from the past are a communal achievement that we reject at our peril. Our question is: How much can one person—without expressly adverting to the fact that others share the same world—discover about the meaning and value of law?

Two ancient Greek symbols personify fundamental insights into legal experience: Eros reveals the positive dynamics of all action; Nemesis reveals the negative consequences of flawed action. For we experience a law moving us from within toward reality as true, good, and beautiful; and we experience, independently of ourselves, a law that sanctions our actions. Pondering about these two laws from the modern perspective of conscious intentionality, we are able to reach the center of ethical and legal decision making. To accomplish this goal, we must venture beyond the detached structures of theory to the personal realm of interiority. Only on a subjective foundation can we erect a fully comprehensive and communicable jurisprudence.

SUBJECTIVITY

CHAPTER 2

EROS: THE JURIDIC DAIMON

[handwritten: mas to know + to act]

[handwritten left margin: EPIGRAPH]

> *Just as the horse is born to run, the ox to plow, the dog to track, so man, as Aristotle said, is born for two things: to know and to act—to be as it were a mortal god.*—Cicero*

[handwritten right: Eros - the principle of the dynamism]

Law governs actions, which are dynamic. Plato calls the principle of their dynamism Eros, finding it in all man's strivings for truth, goodness, and beauty. The search for legal meaning begins with this common drive, for it is Eros that vitalizes our intentionality and our consciousness. If the cosmos lacked this energy, we would be mute and motionless—all actions, thinking too, would be impossible.

An appreciation of the role of Eros in legal matters has persisted through the centuries. Aristotle described its universal operation: "Every state is a community of some kind, and every community is established with a view to some good; for men always act to obtain what they think is good."[1] Scholastics of the Middle Ages, such as Aquinas, formulated this truth as the metaphysical principle of finality: Every agent acts for an end.[2] Justice Holmes shared this classical insight: "I have often thought of the superfluity of energy that makes it necessary for a man to act, as it makes a kitten play with its tail, as carrying with it a destiny to idealize, i.e., to persist in affirming the worth of ends—since every act has an end."[3] More recently, Harold Lasswell and Myres McDougal implicitly acknowledged Eros as the psychological postulate for their goal-oriented, jurisprudence of Law, Science,

---

* Marcus Tullius Cicero, *De finibus*, Bk. II, xiii, 40.

1. Aristotle, *Politics*, ed. W. D. Ross, trans. B. Jowett (Oxford: Clarendon Press, 1921), I, 1, 1252 a2–3.

2. Thomas Aquinas, *Summa theologiae*, I, q. 44, a. 4.

3. Oliver Wendell Holmes, Jr., *Holmes-Pollock Letters*, ed. M. Howe, 2d ed., 2 vols. (Cambridge: Harvard University Press, 1961) 1:261.

[handwritten: ASSIDIA - sloth / greatest of sins]

45

and Policy: "Men act to maximize their values, conscious and un-conscious."[4]

We need not go to the philosophers, however, to prove the existence of Eros. Each day reveals men and women seeking after power, wealth, fame, pleasure, health, knowledge, love, religion, beauty, happiness. And the media chronicle the conflicts that arise unceasingly over these same values, conflicts indicating the pervasive intensity of Eros and the necessity of control and guidance so that we who are so driven may live fruitfully and at peace. Thus we must look to ourselves to find in our own mental operations that fundamental law of our nature, which we symbolize as Eros, since familiarity with Eros is a prerequisite to a jurisprudence of subjectivity.

[margin handwriting: familiarity w/ Eros is a prereq. → subjectivity]

I. THE PLATONIC INTIMATIONS

Plato most perceptively described Eros and its necessary link with the institution of law. Of course, Greek myths had already personified this universal archetype; by Plato's time, Eros had long been recognized as "that ancient source of all our highest good."[5] His traditional genealogy explained his power and accomplishments, for Eros was the child of Resource and Need, begotten on the day beautiful Aphrodite was born.[6] His character thus stood revealed: he had an intense and unceasing love of beauty and whatever else seemed to be good or true; he was thoroughly resourceful in seeking, but was never long satisfied and so was ever in need.

The parentage of Eros may well strike a responsive chord in all of us, because, as we shall see, Eros is everyone's daimon, the well-spring of all human activity. Although the modern tendency is to limit the influence of Eros to romantic lovers, Plato found him active in all types—businessmen, athletes, and philosophers.[7] "For 'Eros that renowned and all-beguiling power' includes every kind of longing for

4. Myres S. McDougal and Associates, *Studies in World Public Order*, New Haven: Yale University Press, 1960), p. 998. For further analysis of this important jurisprudential theory on fostering human dignity and its parallels in Thomistic natural law, see David Granfield, "Towards a Goal-Oriented Consensus," *Journal of Legal Education* 19 (1967): 379–402.

5. Plato, *Symposium*, in *Collected Dialogues*, ed. E. Hamilton and H. Cairns (New York: Pantheon Books, 1961) 178C, p. 533.

6. See ibid., 203C, p. 555.

7. See ibid., 205D, p. 557.

[handwriting at bottom: daimon - the well-spring of all human activity]

happiness and for the good."[8] These two goals are intimately related: "The happy are happy inasmuch as they possess the good."[9] Self-reflection reveals the personal daimon in each one of us, relentlessly urging us to what appears to be good and beautiful—to happiness. We may be mistaken in the objects of our love; we may be conscious of making impetuous, selfish, short-sighted, and even wicked choices; but always in every choice, however ill-advised, "what we love is the good and nothing but the good."[10]

Nevertheless, we must eventually and sadly conclude that Eros—loving, passionate, energetic Eros—is not enough. Under the impulses of unrestrained daimonic powers, we may rush wildly and dangerously, even lawlessly, through life, unable to direct to fulfillment and happiness the power within us. The Greeks were aware of this daimonic ambivalence. For them, happiness was called *eudaimonia*—literally, the having of a good daimon. A critical question then arises: How do we get a good daimon or, more accurately, how do we get the daimon that we have, the Eros that animates us, to be good for us?

Before trying to answer that question, we might note that although some, like Hesiod and Parmenides, called Eros a god, Plato more properly and consistently called him a daimon. This change reflected a deepening psychological insight. The idea of gods afforded a primitive explanation of human conduct in terms of external influences; the idea of daimons did not openly contradict this position, but it did serve as a vehicle for a distinction between internal and external influences. The daimon was thought to be more intimately involved with the human person than a god usually was, almost to the point of identification. By 500 B.C. Heraclitus had actually made that move. "Character," he wrote, "is a man's daimon."[11] Opposing determinism, he implied that we are not coerced from without, but move ourselves from within; not external forces but our own system of value judgments or our own untamed passions account for our actions.

Who, then, is happy? One whose character, or daimon if you will, acts in harmony with the good. Aristotle later formulated this insight in defining *eudaimonia* as "an activity of the soul in conformity with

8. Ibid.   9. Ibid., 205A, p. 557.
  10. Ibid., 206A, p. 558.
  11. Heraclitus, quoted by Stobacus, *Florilegium*, iv, 40. 23. Hermann Diels, *Die Fragmente der Vorsokratiker*, 6th ed., ed. Walther Kranz (Berlin: Wiedmann, 1968), 22 B 119: Ethos anthropo daimon.

virtue, and if there are several virtues, with one that is best and most perfect."[12] Eros can lead us to happiness, because he enables us to love and to love freely. But this very freedom in loving means that Eros can also lead us to misery and ruin. So Euripides warned us that Eros and Sophia (Wisdom) should always be partners. His point is clear: Eros can choose between wisdom and folly, but only with wisdom can he be happy.

Accordingly, Plato's ideal man is daimonic, a *daimonios aner*. Such a person, like Eros, is neither a mortal nor a god; he lives in the in-between, in the Metaxy, to use Voegelin's term, moving between potentiality and actuality, between ignorance and truth, between mortality and divinity. He becomes perfect as, through detachment and wisdom, he participates in the life of God.

Wisdom, however, is not innate, as is Eros: we are born with intelligence, but we acquire wise directives slowly. The process of inculcating practical wisdom belongs to *paideia*, which, for the Greeks, meant education in the broad sense of cultural development. It has the task of guiding one's personal eros to that completion which is happiness. Werner Jaeger traced this development from the time of Homer to the end of the Classical period in the fourth century B.C. and concluded that of all the influences at work Plato's was the greatest and that nowhere was the insistence on the role of wisdom made more strongly than in the *Symposium*.[13]

Although one would expect to learn important legal truths in the *Republic* or the *Laws*, it is in the *Symposium*, where Plato discussed love and beauty, wisdom and happiness, that the profoundest psychological truth about law, in terms of these sublime realities, emerges. The point of insertion is the fact that Eros must be guided by wisdom. But note how Plato evaluated that guidance: "By far the most important kind of wisdom is that which governs the ordering of society which goes by the name of justice and moderation."[14] And he mentioned the great jurists, Lycurgus of Sparta and Solon of Athens, as two of the many who manifested, to their undying glory, the practical wisdom that channels the energy and love of Eros.

12. Aristotle, *Nicomachean Ethics*, I, 7, 1098 a16–18.

13. See Werner Jaeger, *Paideia: the Ideals of Greek Culture*, 3 vols. (New York: Oxford University Press, 1943) 2: ch. 8, especially pp. 176, 178, 194.

14. Plato, *Symposium*, 209B, p. 560.

It is not surprising that, for Plato, the experience of law should be an important stage in the ascent of the mind to the highest of all experiences, that of beauty's very self. He described the steps that must be taken to achieve this supreme consciousness. Beginning very concretely with the beauty of one individual body, the candidate for the inner experience of the sublime must then learn to love every beautiful body, not just this one or that one.

Next, he must grasp that the beauties of the body are as nothing to the beauties of the soul, so that whenever he meets with spiritual loveliness, even in the husk of an unlovely body, he will find it beautiful enough to fall in love with and to cherish—and beautiful enough to quicken in his heart a longing for such discourse as tends toward the building of a noble nature. And for this he will be led to contemplate the beauty of laws and institutions.[15]

This quest for "the soul of beauty" goes, of course, beyond law and institutions. The seeker of true beauty must be "ever mounting the heavenly ladder, stepping from rung to rung—that is, from one to two, and from two to every body, from bodily beauty to the beauty of institutions, from institutions to learning in general to the special lore that pertains to nothing but the beautiful itself—until at last it comes to know what beauty is."[16] Thus law is not our ultimate objective, but it ranks high in opening the mind and heart to ultimate reality.

To sum up Plato's insights into the relation of Eros and the law: this drive toward beauty is itself a law of our nature, a function of the life principle; the actions it energizes must be guided to fulfillment by the private laws of wisdom and the public laws of the community; and the contemplation of law and institutions forms an indispensable stage in the ascent to the awareness of transcendent beauty, to full consciousness of reality.

II. THE CONSCIOUS INTENTIONALITY

To understand the law, we must turn to the subject, that is, to one both conscious and intentional. Bernard Lonergan, in his magisterial work *Insight,* developed a discerning and comprehensive theory of human understanding to facilitate such a turn. The crucial issue of the book consists in "one's own rational self-consciousness clearly and

15. Ibid., 210B, p. 562. 16. Ibid., 211C, p. 563.

distinctly taking possession of itself as rational self-consciousness."[17] He called this approach both a "transcendental method," because it cuts across all categories and involves all mental operations, and a "generalized empirical method," because it rests on empirical data of sense and consciousness.

Through this method, we gradually become aware of our own dynamic, cognitional structure by personally appropriating our own experiencing, understanding, judging, and deciding. By the self-appropriation of our mental operations, we deepen our consciousness in every cognitive enterprise, including ethics and law. The originating principle, for Lonergan, is the detached, disinterested, unrestricted desire to know; this is the dynamism that moves the soul restlessly and relentingly towards a full awareness of reality: "The many levels of consciousness are just successive stages in the unfolding of a single thrust, *the eros of the spirit*."[18]

Beneath the metaphor, the eros of the spirit, are what Lonergan called abstractly the transcendental notions. Actually, they are not abstract at all but comprehensive—literally transcending all categories: "The transcendental notions are our capacity for seeking, and when found, for recognizing instances of the intelligible, the true, the real, the good. It follows that they are relevant to every object that we come to know by asking and answering questions."[19] Clearly the role of these notions in the inner experience of law is an indispensable one, for we are ever seeking to know and to do.

Although moved by an unrestricted desire for reality, our questions and answers may be specific. It is helpful, therefore, to note a fundamental distinction that Lonergan made concerning the sources of meaning, which he says are "all conscious acts and all intended content";

17. Bernard Lonergan, *Insight* (London: Longmans, Green, 1957; New York: Philosophical Library, Inc., 1958), p. xviii.

18. Idem, *Method in Theology*, 2d ed. (New York: Herder & Herder, 1973), p. 13. This work is not limited to Roman Catholic theology. Indeed, theology is also a vehicle for a presentation of his generalized empirical methodology from the perspective of cognitional theory as developed in *Insight*.

19. Ibid., p. 282. Lonergan noted further that when we objectify the content of the transcendental notions, we form transcendental concepts. "So if we objectify the content of intelligent intending, we form the transcendental concept of the intelligible. If we objectify the content of reasonable intending, we form the transcendental concepts of the true and the real. If we objectify the contents of responsible intending, we get the transcendental concept of value, of the truly good." Ibid., pp. 11–12.

he then divides these sources into the transcendental and the categorical:

The transcendental are the very dynamism of intentional consciousness, a capacity that consciously and unceasingly both heads for and recognizes data, intelligibility, truth, reality, and value. The categorical are the determinations reached through experiencing, understanding, judging, deciding. The transcendental notions ground questioning. Answers develop categorical determinations.[20]

The high points of this unfolding of these transcendental notions of the eros of the mind as they move into categorical questions and answers are two: factual judgment and authentic choice or, in subjective terms, rational consciousness and rational self-consciousness. Both are rational, the fruit of intelligence and reason, but they differ in that the rational self-consciousness takes a further step and effectively intends the good. Through authentic decision, the mind, having already judged with detachment about the true and the real, now experiences existentially its own subjectivity in choosing the good freely and responsibly. Let us now consider separately, first consciousness itself and then its two major forms, the better to achieve an inner experience of the law.

A. *Consciousness*

Consciousness gives us the empirical data for our quest, data that differs from what both science and philosophy currently take as their domain. Natural science embraces all sense data as its province and limits itself to what can be thus known empirically. Modern philosophy carries this process of generalization as far as theory allows, giving to metaphysics only the housekeeping function of analyzing and ordering the principles that science discovers or that philosophy derives from the findings of science. The question arises: Must philosophy remain in its new role as handmaiden to autonomous sciences? Perhaps so, unless there is another source of data not included in the natural sciences (the data of consciousness) and another realm of differentiation (the realm of interiority).

Lonergan's generalized empirical method differs radically from the more familiar method of the empirical sciences as well as from both

20. Ibid., p. 73–74. He made the same distinction earlier: "Categories are determinations. They have limited denotations. They vary with cultural variations. . . . In contrast, the transcendentals are comprehensive in connotation, unrestricted in denotation, invariant over cultural change." Ibid., p. 11.

the traditional and the current methods of philosophy. The change is from theory to interiority and involves the data of sense and consciousness. It does not neglect the goal of objectivity; indeed it expands its coverage of reality by approaching it through the new perspective of authentic subjectivity. Lonergan explained the special tasks of this new philosophical approach:

Philosophy finds its proper data in intentional consciousness. Its primary function is to promote the self-appropriation that cuts to the root of philosophic differences and incomprehensions. It has further, secondary functions in distinguishing, relating, grounding the several realms of meaning and, no less, in grounding the methods of the sciences and so promoting their unification.[21]

The effective use of conscious intentionality in trying to understand law requires that we distinguish both intentionality and consciousness, for only if they are in harmony do they bring full contact with reality: intentionality reveals the world to our mind; consciousness reveals our mind to itself. Things are made present to us through intentionality; we are present to ourselves through consciousness. In the words of Lonergan: "Just as operations by their intentionality make objects present to their subject, so also by their consciousness they make the operating subject present to itself."[22] This process does not consist in two separate actions—now I will think of myself; now I will think of objects—but rather in the very act of thinking of an object we broaden our range to include ourselves, we are aware of ourselves thinking of objects. In doing so, we understand not less sharply, but less narrowly and therefore more profoundly.

Our attention is apt to be focused on the object, while our conscious operating remains peripheral. We must, then, enlarge our interest, recall that one and the same operation not only intends an object but also reveals an intending subject, discover in our own experience the concrete truth of that general statement.[23]

What is consciousness? It is an awareness of both the subject and his acts, an awareness that is intrinsic to cognitional acts or immanent in them. We are aware of what we are doing and that we are doing it. It should be noted that this awareness is not achieved by treating the subject as an object; of course, it is possible to look at the subject introspectively, but this reflexive knowledge of the subject as object is not what is meant by consciousness.

21. Ibid., p. 95.   22. Ibid., p. 8.
23. Ibid., p. 15.

A few remarks on how to intensify consciousness will further clarify what is meant by consciousness itself. This heightening is most simply experienced just by trying to be aware of ourselves as we function. There are, however, three suggestions that will make the attempt more effective. First, focus awareness also on the act, not merely on its content. In that way, one's attention includes the subject intending as well as the object intended. Second, raise the level of activity. The more fully the mind is involved, the more the subject is self-aware; for example, more in getting engaged than in buying postage stamps. Third, objectify the data of consciousness. This objectification is not awareness of the subject as subject but of the subject as object; it does, however, help in identifying mental operations and appropriating them and thus in facilitating subsequent and more profound self-consciousness.

The appropriation of one's conscious intentionality is crucial if the legal subject is to have a full awareness of himself, his operations, and the legal events in which he participates. More than simply an experiencing of one's own experiencing—understanding, judging, and deciding—it is, as Lonergan insisted, also a further reduplication of this fourfold sequence, that is, an understanding (judging and deciding) of one's experiencing, understanding, judging, and deciding. Only by such a process is the legal act fully realized; this goal of objectified self-appropriation is achieved by "applying the operations as intentional to the operations as conscious."[24] Here is the perfection of conscious intentionality at the heart of a jurisprudence of subjectivity.

Consciousness not only makes the subject present to himself; it constitutes the subject as subject. Of course, a human being is objectively constituted as a substance independently of his consciousness; a sleeping man is still a man, but it is his consciousness that constitutes him a subject. He is a subject to the extent that he is conscious; so both the level and the quality of consciousness are determinative. In other words, we must distinguish two approaches: we may take a wholly objective and metaphysical approach to man by studying his soul or substance according to the same method that we might use to study any living being, moving from objects to acts to habits to potencies to essences. Or we may take an approach that is primarily subjective: "The study of the subject is quite different, it is the study of oneself

24. Ibid., p. 14.

inasmuch as one is conscious."[25] This process of experiencing and appropriating one's own subjectivity is an empirical process working with the data of consciousness as the scientist uses the data of sense. The two phases of this conscious intentionality are rational consciousness culminating in judgments of facts and rational self-consciousness culminating in decision making. We shall consider them separately as the major underpinings of a jurisprudence of subjectivity.

B. Rational Consciousness

The process of cognition involves, as we have seen, three operations—experiencing, understanding, and judging—that Lonergan explained thus:

There is a first step in attending to the data of sense and consciousness. Next, inquiry and understanding yield an apprehension of a hypothetical world mediated by meaning. Thirdly, reflection and judgment reach an absolute: through them we acknowledge what really is so, what is independent of us and our thinking.[26]

At first glance, this description hardly seems noteworthy, yet it does make an important contribution in objectifying and articulating an element usually overlooked in accounts of how we know. With good reason Lonergan centered on understanding, or what is more memorably called insight, a term for the mental operation linking the raw data and the judgment of reason. The world of our experience is mediated through meaning, and meaning is first grasped, tentatively and provisionally, in the insight. When this insight is sufficiently verified, the judgment issues forth, giving us a fact. Only then do we actually know.

What is an insight? It is a bright idea, a snap judgment, a shrewd guess, an tentative understanding. Insights ground every kind of knowledge. But an insight should not be considered to be like seeing something; it is not literally an intuition. The naive realist thinks that he looks at his experiences, the data of sense and consciousness, and then judges. But he leaves out an essential step, the insight, which occurs when the intelligence comprehends in the data some kind of coherence, when the data begins to make sense, to evidence a possibility, to suggest

25. Idem, *A Second Collection*, ed. W. Ryan and B. Tyrrell (Philadelphia: Westminster Press, 1974), p. 73.
26. Idem, *Method*, p. 35.

a meaning. An insight as such is unverified and unproved; it may be wrong but it is plausible. It is like love at first sight, perhaps an infatuation but perhaps the beginning of a lifelong commitment. "Insight," Lonergan told us, "occurs with respect to some schematic image"[27] and is "an intelligible organization that may or may not be relevant to data."[28] More precisely:

It occurs (1) in response to inquiry, (2) with respect to sensible presentations or representations including words or symbols of all kinds. It consists in a grasp of intelligible unity or relation in the data or image or symbol. It is the active ground whence proceed conception, definition, hypothesis, theory, system.[29]

The human mind is filled, even cluttered, with insights, these manifold first vestiges of meaning, these building blocks of truth; for we are always trying to make sense out of the constant influx of data that we receive from the world around us. Without insights we are numbed and overwhelmed by a meaningless flood of immediacy. Nevertheless, important though insights are, they still do not enable us to know.

Consequently, reflective understanding has a job ahead of it: to marshal and weigh the evidence in order to see whether or not an insight has been verified. This verification depends on the fulfilment of conditions. The judgment of truth is made when the reflective understanding grasps a virtually unconditioned insight; that is, unconditioned by virtue of having all its conditions fulfilled. Thus the fundamental principle in assessing the relationship between the conditioned and the conditions is that "an insight is correct if it is invulnerable and it is invulnerable if there are no further pertinent questions."[30] For, as Lonergan explained: "It is only through further questions that there arise the further insights that complement, modify, or revise the initial approach and explanation."[31] Hence, if the insight proves invulnerable, not susceptible to further inquiry, the proposed judgment has been adequately verified and rational consciousness has been achieved. Then and only then can we say that we know. This blend of inquiry and verification leading to knowledge obviously forms an essential part of the legal process. But it must be complemented by a decision-making function, the basic structure of which we will consider next.

27. Ibid., p. 86.
29. Ibid., p. 213.
31. Ibid., p. 284.

28. Ibid., p. 10.
30. Idem, *Insight*, p. 287.

C. Rational Self-Consciousness

Rational self-consciousness begins where rational consciousness leaves off. This level relies on the three earlier levels of consciousness—experience, insight, and judgment—but sublates them; that is, it goes beyond them, while in some way taking them along and perfecting them.[32] Although the virtually unconditioned is the end-product of reflective understanding and constitutes rational consciousness—in that we really know—it does not completely gratify the desire of Eros for reality, nor is it the fullest expansion of our consciousness. In actually knowing, we must transcend our own views and preferences to judge what the reality truly is. We try to be as detached and as disinterested as possible. Through self-appropriation we are conscious of our experiencing, understanding, and judging, but we ourselves are not the focal point.

On the fourth level of consciousness, however, by deliberating, evaluating, deciding, and acting, we at last become fully operative and fully self-conscious. Here the turn to the subject becomes complete and a jurisprudence of subjectivity becomes practicable. We know ourselves best in the decisions that we make; the more significant the decision, the more revealing the self-knowledge.

This intensification of consciousness occurs because the subject by his decisions is constituting himself and the world around him. Eros pushes him to this new level, when practical intelligence suggests what changes the subject's decision can make, what new things and events he can bring into existence.

The detached, disinterested, unrestricted desire to know grasps intelligently and affirms reasonably not only the facts of the universe of being but also its practical possibilities. Such practical possibilities include intelligent transformations not only of the environment in which man lives but also of man's own spontaneous living.[33]

The subject can change reality; he should do so, however, without jeopardizing his integrity. Although the subject now is both a knower and a doer, he still remains one subject. This unity of consciousness grounds the exigency that knowing and doing be consistent.[34] Clearly, the principle of consistency is at the heart of ethics and law, ideally

32. Idem, *Second Collection*, p. 169.
33. Idem, *Insight*, p. 598–99.
34. See ibid., p. 599.

determining the conduct of citizens, witnesses, police, lawyers, jurors, and judges. The legal process constantly relies on human good will—essentially the habitual tendency to keep one's doing in accord with one's knowing.

Each person must work out his role with the fullest rational consciousness and fullest rational self-consciousness; that is, each one should try to make as sound judgments as possible by being open to data and by verifying insights, and each one should make sure that all decisions are authentically in harmony with what is known. In brief, each subject, if he is to heighten his consciousness of the law, must adhere to four "transcendental precepts"—Be attentive; Be intelligent; Be reasonable; Be responsible.[35]

In the light of conscious intentionality, we take a second look at the relationship between fact, value, and norm. The following brief statements will summarize our position. (1) We begin with Eros—the dynamic thrust of the spirit toward reality—which moves us to truth and to goodness through various mental operations. (2) Through experience, insight, and judgment, we discover the ways that the self or the environment can be changed by our choices. (3) Through deliberation and evaluation, we determine which possibility is a value; that is, a concrete good as a possible object of rational choice.[36] (4) Through our exigency for consistency, we, who are already goal-oriented by Eros, experience the choice as obligatory. (5) The choice, though obligatory, is free owing to the radical contingency of the beings of our experience; that is, no concrete good so fulfills our desire for reality that we must necessarily choose it. (6) The failure to obey an obligatory choice of value is the frustration of Eros, the loss of integrity, and the advent of entropy and absurdity.

III. THE REALIST REDISCOVERY

Lest it seem that such problems of cognition have been of little concern to legal thinkers of the past, we shall note some parallel perceptions made by members of the Realist School of the first half of the twentieth century. We have already mentioned their place in the history of jurisprudence, their highly critical, trouble-shooting, iconoclastic approach to the institution of law and their vehement attacks

---

35. Idem, *Method*, p. 53.   36. See idem, *Insight*, p. 601.

on mechanistic notions of judicial decision making, whereby judges were thought to dig out pre-existing laws and then apply them syllogistically to concrete factual situations. Justice Holmes, sometimes called the "Father of Legal Realism," proclaimed one of their fundamental principles: "General propositions do not decide concrete cases. The decision will depend on a judgment or intuition more subtle than any articulate major premise."[37]

Although the Realists did not use insight as a word of art, they were empirically familiar with that mental operation, the idea of which they used to shock the legal establishment out of its mechanistic ways. None of them more enthusiastically objectified insight than did Joseph C. Hutcheson, Jr., Chief Judge in the Fifth Circuit Court of Appeals. Especially influential was his article "The Judgment Intuitive: the Function of the 'Hunch' in Judicial Decision." Here is his description of how he was accustomed to handle an involved and difficult case:

I, after canvassing all the available material at my command, and duly cogitating upon it, give my imagination play, and brooding over the cause, wait for the feeling, *the hunch—that intuitive flash of understanding which makes the jumpspark connection between the question and the decision,* and at the point where the path is darkest for the judicial feet, sheds its light along the way.[38]

Hutcheson did not limit the hunch to legal matters, contending that not only do the best gamblers, detectives, lawyers, and judges rely on hunches but the great scientists and mathematicians as well. Here are two of the many instances of the awareness of the role of insight: J. H. Poincaré (1834–1912), a French mathematician, spoke of four stages of the creative process: preparation, incubation, illumination, and verification;[39] and Simone Weil (1909–1943), another French intellectual, experienced art in a similar fashion: "Method for understanding images, symbols, etc. Not to try to interpret them, but to look at them till the light suddenly dawns."[40]

---

37. O. W. Holmes, Jr., dissenting in *Lochner v. N.Y.*, 198 U.S. 45, at 76.

38. Joseph C. Hutcheson, Jr., "The Judgment Intuitive: The Function of the 'Hunch' in Judicial Decision," *Cornell Law Quarterly* 14 (1929): 278.

39. Jules Henri Poincaré, *Science and Method*, trans. F. Maitland (London: Thomas Nelson & Sons, 1914), passim. Michael Polanyi wrote that "verification" in mathematics is closer to demonstration than it is to the "verification" of experimental science. *Personal Knowledge* (Chicago: University of Chicago Press, 1962), p. 121, note 3.

40. Simone Weil, *Gravity and Grace*, trans. A. Wills (New York: G. P. Putnam's Sons, 1952), p. 172.

Getting back to Hutcheson and the law, we should note a precise phrase of his, "the hunch which is the clue to judgment."[41] This linkage is critical; for the hunch is a clue, not a conviction, but if adequately verified it can lead to a certain judgment. Hutcheson described the steps to be taken: "The vital motivating impulse for the decision is an intuitive sense of what is right or wrong for the cause, and . . . the astute judge, having so decided, enlists his every faculty and belabors his laggard mind, not only to justify that intuition to himself but to make it pass muster with his critics."[42]

We can see, however, that Legal Realists might well be naive realists. The use of terms such as intuition, introspection, light, or sixth sense may have led others, if it did not lead Holmes and Hutcheson, into thinking that insight is a kind of seeing, a fleeting glimpse of reality, whereas it is essentially an endowing of data with problematic meaning, which must then be verified before we can really know. An insight is not an intuition of unity but a tentative imposition of unity on susceptible data, which understanding may or may not be verified by marshalling and weighing the evidence. The Realists recognized the mental operation that we call insight. They discussed its practical function in the common sense realm without, however, putting it in full theoretical context.

Jerome Frank, also a Federal Court of Appeals judge, was one of the most articulate of the Realists. Early in his career, following the lead of Hutcheson, he emphasized the importance of this mental operation which linked data and decision: "If the law consists of the decisions of the judges and if those decisions are based on the judge's hunches, then the way in which the judge gets his hunches is the key to the judicial process."[43] Frank identified three kinds of "hunch producers": the rules and the principles of law; political, economic, and moral prejudices; and, most importantly, the judge's personality.[44] In short, what actually sparks the hunch is the judge plus his circumstances. This conclusion suggests some recourse to interiority for, as Frank observed: "We shall not learn how judges think until the judges are able and ready to engage

41. Hutcheson, "The Judgment Intuitive," p. 282.
42. Ibid., p. 285.
43. Jerome Frank, *Law and the Modern Mind* (New York: Brentano's Inc., 1930; Doubleday Anchor Book, 1963), Pt. I, ch. xii, p. 112.
44. Ibid., pp. 113–20. See also: "To know the judge's hunch producers which make the law, we must know thoroughly that complicated congeries we loosely call the judge's personality." Ibid., pp. 119–20.

in ventures of self-discovery."[45] Only by "searching self-analysis"[46] can this knowledge be arrived at. He quoted Piaget approvingly; "The less a mind is given to introspection the more it is the victim of the illusion that it knows itself thoroughly."[47] Accurate self-knowledge is especially necessary in a judge because of the awesome scope of judicial discretion. Frank does not reject discretion—that would be tantamount to eliminating judicial creativity—but he does insist that judges know themselves well enough to be aware of what produces their hunches in these discretionary matters.

> The honest, well trained judge with the completest possible knowledge of the character of his powers and of his own prejudices and weaknesses is the best guaranty of justice. Efforts to eliminate the personality of the judge are doomed to failure. The correct course is to recognize the necessary existence of this personal element and to act accordingly.[48]

To speak too narrowly of the insight would be to underrate the sophistication of Realist jurisprudence. Insight does more than give a clue to a concrete case; it is the subject matter of a concept—the abstract formulation of the understanding captured by the insight. Rules are composed of concepts, and therein lies the possibility of legal formalism.

Karl Llewellyn was concerned about "the tendency of the chrystallized legal concept to persist after the fact model from which the concept was once derived has disappeared or changed out of recognition."[49] He admitted the indispensability of concepts, but voiced skepticism over the adequacy of many of these received categories. His solution was sensible: "The counsel of the realistic approach here, then, would be the constant back-checking of the category against the data, to see whether the data are still present in the form suggested by the category-name."[50] He wanted to avoid what Lonergan called "an oversight of insight."[51] Concepts give understanding, but that understanding ever needs need to be verified by recourse to data, especially in a field such as law, where circumstances change so rapidly. On the other hand,

---

45. Ibid., p. 123.   46. Ibid.
47. Ibid., p. 126, from Jean Piaget's *The Child's Conception of the World*, trans. A. and J. Tomlinson (New York: Harcourt, 1929), p. 239.
48. Ibid., p. 148.
49. Karl Llewellyn, "A Realistic Jurisprudence—The Next Step," *Columbia Law Review* 30 (1930): 453–54.
50. Ibid., p. 454.   51. B. Lonergan, *Insight*, p. xxvii.

lawyers tend to be conservative and resistant to changes in the intellectual structure of their working capital. For many, conceptuality is most agreeable for the very reason that, in Jung's words, "it promises protection from experience."[52]

The same justifiable concern about the rigidity of conceptual thinking is found in Edward H. Levi.[53] In his analysis of legal reasoning—the basic pattern of which, he contended, is reasoning by example—Levi discussed the moving classification involved in the life cycle of legal concepts. There are three stages: (1) the creation of concepts is the result of a determination of a similarity or difference, which is labeled by a word and emerges as a concept; (2) the meaning of the concept is more or less fixed and is used almost deductively; (3) due to social change, however, new similarities or differences are noted, the concept begins to break down and is eventually replaced by another word and another concept.

In this circular process, Levi noted, there is the presentation of competing versions or examples of the factual situation, which are eventually formulated as competing propositions. More precisely, we would describe what happens as the presentation to the fact finder of competing insights; the outcome depends on how effectively the parties to this adversarial interaction communicate and verify their insights, thus enabling the fact finder to make, in accord with proper standards of proof, a sound judgment.

IV. THE JUDICIAL APPLICATION

How Eros operates in criminal law through conscious intentionality is evident in *Terry v. Ohio* (1968), where the Supreme Court established the Fourth Amendment legitimacy of "stop and frisk" procedures. This case clearly illustrates the four levels of consciousness—experiencing, understanding, judging, deciding—in the concrete context of an emerging probability.

The defendant Terry was convicted of carrying a concealed weapon. At a pretrial hearing on a motion to suppress that evidence, a plain-

52. Carl Jung, *Memories, Dreams, Reflections*, ed. A. Jaffé and trans. R. and C. Winston (New York: Random House, 1961), p. 144.

53. See, Edward H. Levi, *An Introduction to Legal Reasoning* (Chicago: University of Chicago Press, 1948) and "The Nature of Judicial Reasoning," *University of Chicago Law Review* 32 (1965): 395–409.

clothes Cleveland police detective stated that his attention had been attracted by two men. He had never seen them before and could not say exactly why he first noticed them.

However, he testified that he had been a policeman for 39 years and a detective for 35 and that he had been assigned to patrol this vicinity of downtown Cleveland for shoplifters and pickpockets for 30 years. He explained that he had developed routine habits of observation over the years and that he would "stand and watch people or walk and watch people at many intervals of the day." He added, "Now in this case when I looked over they didn't look right to me at the time."[54]

This first insight of Officer McFadden was made with a minimum of new data and simply reflected his understanding that a deviation from accustomed conduct was occurring. His insight owed much to an habitual attitude of attention and inquiry and to a fund of accumulated experience with criminals. His decision, proportioned to the insight, dictated closer attention and further inquiry: "I got more purpose to watch them when I seen their movements."[55] So he took up an observation post in the entrance of a store some 300 to 400 feet away. He noticed that each man acting in turn looked in the store window, walked on a short distance, turned back and looked in again. When they had done this about a dozen times, they were joined by a third man, who spoke with them briefly. After he left, they continued their looking, walking, and conferring. Ten or twelve minutes later, they walked off together in the direction of the third man.

By this time the officer's original insight had been more specifically, though only partially, verified. "He suspected the two men of 'casing a job, a stick up,' and he considered it his duty as a police officer to investigate further. He added that he feared that 'they may have a gun.' "[56] Although he was far from certain of this unlawful possession, he believed that he had reasonable grounds for action; so he moved beyond passive surveillance to a limited but very real intrusion on their personal privacy. He went up to the men, stopped them, and asked their names. When they mumbled something in response, he grabbed Terry and spun him around so that he was facing the other two. Patting down his outer clothing, he felt what he thought might be a weapon. He eventually removed a pistol from Terry's overcoat pocket and found another pistol after frisking the second man.

54. *Terry v. Ohio,* 392 U.S. 1, at 5 (1968).
55. Ibid., p. 6.   56. Ibid.

On discovering the guns, the officer had reached a new stage of verification, justifying an even greater intrusion. He then had sufficient evidence to verify the insight that a felony, the possession of concealed weapons, was being committed. So he was legally correct in arresting the defendants, searching them thoroughly, and taking them into custody. Aside from testifying at the trial, Officer McFadden's job was over.

After the court denied a motion to suppress the evidence, Terry waived a jury trial and pleaded not guilty. The judge made a full verification of the charge, finding Terry guilty, and he made a decision about punishment, sentencing him to two to three years imprisonment. Terry appealed his conviction to the Federal Court of Appeals and to the Supreme Court of Ohio—both times unsuccessfully. The Supreme Court of the United States granted a writ of certiorari, but later affirmed the conviction, finding this "stop and frisk" procedure to be constitutional under the Fourth Amendment, "where the police officer observes unusual conduct which leads him reasonably to conclude in the light of his experience that criminal activity may be afoot and the person with whom he is dealing may be armed and presently dangerous."[57]

This case illustrates how the emerging probability of criminal conduct progressively validated four types of official activity. (1) Mere suspicion, the officer's original insight, justified only more surveillance. (2) Reasonable suspicion, however, the officer's more fully verified insight based on his observation of the men "casing" the store, justified the investigative stop for questioning and the pat-down for weapons, since robbery suspects can reasonably be believed to be armed and dangerous.[58] (3) Finally, probable cause, resting on the reasonable belief of a prudent officer that the suspects were committing a crime, here possessing firearms, justified the arrest. (4) Proof beyond a reasonable doubt, when the verification had been completed at the trial, justified the conviction and punishment.

So from mere suspicion to proof beyond a reasonable doubt, we see

---

57. Ibid., p. 30.

58. On the relation between hunch and verification, see the remark of Justice Marshall (part of the *Terry* majority) as he dissented in a later "stop and frisk" case, *Adams v. Williams*, 407 U.S. 143, at 158: "Terry did not hold that whenever a policeman has a hunch that a citizen is engaging in criminal activity, he may engage in a stop and frisk. It held that if police officers want to stop and frisk, they must have specific facts from which they can reasonably infer that an individual is engaged in criminal activity and is armed and dangerous."

the gradually emerging probability of criminal conduct. Each stage—
part of a continuum of questions and answers—has rules governing
official conduct and determining the defendant's rights. Each stage
depends on the particularized facts derived from an assessment of all
the circumstances, the differences between stages being the degree of
insight verification. Chief Justice Earl Warren, speaking for the Court
in *Terry v. Ohio,* said: "This demand for specificity in the information
upon which police action is predicated is the central teaching of this
Court's Fourth Amendment jurisprudence."[59]

Consequently, for a stop and frisk or an arrest and search to be valid,
the Supreme Court requires articulable reasons amounting respectively
to reasonable suspicion or probable cause. Moreover, the police officer
is not permitted to act unless he is certain of his justification to intrude
upon a citizen's right to privacy and freedom. This psychological requirement of certainty seems to pose a contradiction, since the officer
in performing his duties usually relies only on probabilities of varying
degrees.

Here we must make a distinction: the officer need not be certain
about the defendant's guilt, but he must be certain that he has the
requisite probability to justify his actions—hence his need for articulable reasons. If the frisk, arrest, or search is challenged, the court must
look at the data and assess the officer's judgment of probability—
whether before taking action he had sufficient data to make a certain
judgment that he had reasonable suspicion for a stop and frisk or
probable cause for an arrest. The underlying justification for the paradoxical requirement of certainty in matters of probability is: "Every
judgment rests on a grasp of the virtually unconditioned, and the
probability of a probable judgment is a certainty."[60]

The criminal law thus illustrates simply but vividly the cognitive
paradigm at work in all areas of law. Its two stages, the ascertaining
of facts and the making of decisions, operate in the context of antecedent norms, constitutional or simply legal. But whether the point of view
be that of the legislator, judge, or police officer, on the one hand, or
that of the citizen consumer, on the other, the process is one of conscious intentionality, with its roots in Eros and its fruits in consistency
between knowing and doing.

59. Ibid., p. 21, note 18.
60. Lonergan, *Insight,* p. 550.

CONCLUSION

Our acquaintance with the juridic daimon, Eros, has led from the dialogues of Plato, who objectified this basic drive, to the decisions of the Supreme Court, which gives it normative shape. The perspective of the Monosphere is that of a solitary person hoping to arrive at true knowledge and authentic choice and seeking a principle of direction. Eros is part of the answer, for Eros teaches that we are programmed for good things and for happiness. Only by focusing on the dynamism that reveals itself on many levels of consciousness can we determine what a legal event really is. We deepen our awareness of the first law of life as it unfolds in rational consciousness and rational self-consciousness.

A jurisprudence of subjectivity begins with a profound and existential awareness of this inner law that programs us without destroying our freedom. This energetic drive makes us seek always what appears good to us. We can direct this desire and perfect it through education and through trial and error, but the desire itself is a given; it constitutes us as human beings; it is the wellspring of our mental life and moral life. All our thinking about law presupposes this vital exigency. An inner experience of law, indeed, every experience of law and life, must begin, thematically or not, with the Eros of the mind.

Unfortunately, willing what appears good may not be enough to make us happy. Eros symbolizes one law, but Eros is not the only law in our life, not even in the Monosphere.

CHAPTER 3

NEMESIS: THE AVENGING GODDESS

*Judgment Day is not a day; it is a court in perpetual
session.—Franz Kafka**

Nemesis, like a dark shadow, counterbalances Eros. For Eros, though
energetic and creative, needs wisdom to guide it to a rich maturity.
When Eros acts unwisely, however, Nemesis matches its misdeeds with
deprivations.

Eros and Nemesis characterize developing legal awareness and constitute the Monosphere. Both symbolize laws of life: Eros, by directing
us to what appears good; Nemesis, by correcting us if that good is only
apparent. All the while, reason tries to distinguish the difference. Plato,
understanding justice to be conformity to virtue, called Nemesis, "the
messenger of justice"[1] and "the penalty of injustice . . . a penalty that
cannot be escaped."[2] Sometimes by sobering hints, sometimes by ter-
rifying evidence, Nemesis warns us against irresponsible attempts at
fulfilment, for we live in a world of manifold norms, where wrong
choices, no matter how well-intentioned or how wicked, how clandes-
tine or how flagrant, will without fail incur proportionately harmful
results. Nemesis, all-seeing and unforgiving, makes the promise of
getting one's just deserts sound like a guaranty.

The name Nemesis is Greek, but the idea of a moral universe that it
implies transcends Hellenic culture; other contemporary cultures had
personified a similar complexus of ideas, feelings, norms, actions, and
sanctions. I will briefly describe three major manifestations, the Greek,
the Hindu, and the Christian, as evidence of the widespread belief in
the existence of a cosmic conscience. Then I will suggest a philosophic
clarification by examining how Nemesis functions socially in the break-

---

* Franz Kafka, *Letters*, ed. Max Brod (New York: Schocken Books, 1958).
1. Plato, *Laws*, 717D.
2. *Theaetetus*, 176E–177A.

down of civilization due to the failure of self-determination and individually in the loss of psychic integrity due to basic sin, both processes being entropic manifestations of Nemesis in modern garb. Together they bring us to the ethical core of law.

I. THE PROTECTOR OF NOMOS   *Greek notion*

The Greeks personified Nemesis as the goddess of exact retribution, inexorable and inescapable, meting out to each person what is due him or her for crimes and even for mistakes. The two words *nemesis* and *nomos* are closely related etymologically, sharing as they are the same root, *nem*, which means to allot. It was believed that just as Zeus and the other gods originally gave laws to mankind, allotting duties to each state of life, so Nemesis allots to each one who violates the legal order a proportionate punishment. At first, Nemesis was thought to distribute both rewards and punishments, positive and negative sanctions, but the good that she did was gradually overlooked or attributed to other gods and she was identified only with chastisements.

Many other images of retribution were popular in Greek culture. For example, the Erynyes—diplomatically referred to as Eumenides (Well-wishers)—were spirits with the form of snaky-haired women of horrible mien, who were described by Aeschylus in the *Oresteia*, as "the disturbers of sleep." They aptly signified the biting and tormenting conscience that drove murderers to madness. Of course, individual gods, too, as the *Iliad* vividly and abundantly shows, were ready to punish erring mortals, but Nemesis remained the major symbol of divine retribution in a culture firmly convinced of the paramount need of order.

divine retrib in a culture firmly convinced of need of order

Aristotle, in the *Politics*, succinctly described the work of nemesis, by this time an abstract noun: "He who violates the law can never recover by any success however great what he has already lost in departing from virtue."[3] His two ethical works mention nemesis only briefly in discussing virtues, the earlier *Eudemian Ethics* having the fuller treatment.

Envy means being pained at people who are deservedly prosperous, while the emotion of the malicious man is itself nameless, but the possessor of it is shown by his feeling joy at undeserved adversities; and midway between them is the

3. Aristotle, *Politics*, VII, ciii, 1325, b5–7.

righteously indignant man (*nemesetikos*), and what the ancients called righteous indignation (*nemesis*)—the feeling pain at undeserved adversities and
prosperities, and pleasure at those that are deserved; hence the idea that
Nemesis is a deity.[4]

The most dramatic way to stir up the anger of the goddess was
through hubris, an act of insolence or arrogance, a contemptuous and
reckless violation of the boundaries established by moral laws; but
hubris also includes immoderate rejoicing in good fortune, together
with an irreverent and ungrateful taking things for granted. A memorable example of hubris was the act of the Titan, Prometheus, in stealing
fire from the gods for the sake of mankind. For his transgression,
impious from the viewpoint of Olympus, he was chained to a rock,
where by day an eagle gnawed at his liver, which grew back during the
night, so that his torment never ended. But the Greeks did not confine
hubris to flamboyant, monstrous, or sacrilegious deeds; any violation
of the law sufficed, for at the heart of each violation was a revolt against
cosmic order. Even when there was no specific law, Nemesis punished
that most fundamental of all faults—sensitivity to which is so charac-
teristically Greek—the disproportionate action. In *The Laws,* Plato
wrote:

If one sins against the laws of proportion and gives something too big to
something too small to carry it—too big sails to too small a ship, too big meals
to too small a body, too big powers to too small a soul—the result is bound
to be a complete upset. In an outburst of hubris, the overfed body will rush
into sickness, while the jack-in-office will rush into the unrighteousness which
hubris always breeds.[5]

Retribution followed from every deviation, whether intentional, neg-
ligent, or even innocent. A look at a few of the words that the Greeks
used for sin indicates how the critical factor is the unsuitability of the
action itself. A wilfully evil act will have the greater punishment; but
a wrong done reasonably and in good faith will not escape punishment.
The words used are not abstract terms, but rather concrete indicators,
as would be expected at this early stage of language formation. The
commonest word is a term in archery, *hamartia,* a missing of the mark,
a failure to hit the target. *Parabasis* is the overstepping of a boundary;
its Latin equivalent is *transgressio;* the French has *trépasser;* and the

4. Idem, *Eudemian Ethics*, III, vii, 1233, b20–27.
5. Plato, *Laws,* 691C.

English has both transgression and trespass. *Paraptoma,* a stumbling or falling from the path, also came to include both sins and errors. Finally, *agnoia* encompassed not only crass and vincible ignorance, but even merely not knowing some fact critical to right action.

All these terms denote an action that, regardless of the subjectivities, is radically defective and incurs punishment. Plato explained the inevitability of retribution by referring to the two patterns of life: divine happiness and godless misery. Whatever we do moves us in the direction of one or the other of these patterns. The wicked do not realize what they are doing to themselves, "unaware that in doing injustice they are growing less like one of these patterns and more like the other. The penalty they pay is the life they lead, answering to the pattern they resemble."[6]

The subtlest appreciation of what nemesis means comes from Greek tragedy, where the audience becomes aware of itself through vicarious participation in decision making. Ideally, the tragic hero, with whom the subject identifies, is not a moral monster beyond hope of redemption; rather, as Aristotle pointed out, his character (*ethos*) is true to life, like our own (*homoion*), and generally speaking is a good one (*chreston*).[7] Of course, differences abound. The tragic hero outshines the ordinary subject, for he is well-born, intelligent, courageous; his powers are greater, his status more prestigious, his achievements more admirable—and his downfall more shocking. Nevertheless, his excellence as an artistic creation is that we can see ourselves in him; we can by a reasonable stretch of the imagination envisage ourselves in similar circumstances and similarly tested.

Only if we are attuned to the tragic hero can we undergo a psychological catharsis or purification; for this experience is rooted in pity (this could happen to me) and in fear (how terrible that would be). We can understand and sympathize with him, because, although he is not a perfect man, he is not an utterly wicked one. What distinguishes the hero as tragic is that he finds himself in a situation in which his vincible ignorance, failure of judgment, moral error, passionate excess, or sinful decision leads to destruction. Had circumstances been different, his fatal flaw might never have borne such bitter fruit.

Why does the hero's fate move us so deeply and even begin to change

6. Idem, *Theaetetus,* 176D.
7. Aristotle, *Poetics,* 1454 a16–17 and a24–25.

our character? Perhaps because we recognize in him our own imperfect personalities, now imagined by us as seeded with doom. In the wrong situation, our blind spots, rigid ways of thinking and acting, shallow and selfish goals, rash or timid responses, could effect our moral and physical ruin. Having suddenly become aware of our manifold vulnerability through the explosive potentiality of our familiar or forgotten weaknesses, we find ourselves terrifyingly at the mercy of the changing circumstances of life. Although previously our lives may have been favorably balanced between happiness and misery, we begin to suspect that the reason is not because we deserve it morally, but because fate has been kind to us by not putting us to the test. This realization of precariousness must inspire in most hearts a "lead us not into temptation" response.

The catharsis effected by tragedy consists, at least ethically, of a clear recognition and an initial rejection of flaws. Nemesis points a warning figure at an audience that is not yet fully awake to its contingency and temporality. The drama has objectified the weakness hidden from the hero so that the audience can objectify and abjure its own similar and unexamined weaknesses. The dramatist shared his vision of the integrity and authenticity of action by highlighting the defects that could, with a shift of circumstances, shatter it. His moral aim was to offer a safeguard against nemesis by healing the flaws that might occasion retribution. No dramatist grasped the role of nemesis more profoundly than Aeschylus, of whom Werner Jaeger wrote: "His whole conception of fate is summed up in the tension between two ideas—his faith in the perfect and uninterrupted justice of God's government of the world, and his horrified realization of the daemonic cruelty and perfidiousness of *ate* [the spirit of infatuation], which leads man to violate the world order and inevitably to be punished for his violations."[8]

II. THE LAW OF KARMA

While the Greeks were working out the implications of their belief in a moral universe, farther east, the Hindus—faced with a realm of experience in which change seemed continuous and all-embracing and in which good and evil seemed ever in conflict—tried to show how

justice — ultimately prevails.

8. Werner Jaeger, *Paideia: The Ideals of Greek Culture*, 2d ed., 3 vols. (New York: Oxford University Press, 1943–45), 1:259.

justice ultimately prevails. In gradually mediating the empirical data through meaning, more constitutive than cognitive, they were able to create a cosmology that has perdured to the present. The Hindus, like the Greeks, discovered Nemesis to be fully operative in their world. Its role can be best seen in the relationship between four major ideas: *samsara, karma, moksha,* and *dharma,* which, as R. C. Zaehner noted, reflect how the Hindu world view, though preeminently mystical, is rooted in the notion of law.[9]

Samsara comprises the endless world of cyclic change, the whole process of cause and effect, of time and place, in which human beings are almost inextricably caught up. Day follows night; the seasons and years repeat unceasingly; human beings are born, mature, generate, grow old, and die—these experiences reveal the wheel of *samsara,* the empirical data that all peoples share.

The law of *karma,* however, is at work in this changing world. Already perceptible in the cosmic regularities, it takes on a new precision as the rule and measure of actions in the moral and physical universe. The law is found throughout the Upanishads: "The doer of good becomes good, the doer of evil becomes evil. One becomes virtuous by virtuous action, bad by bad action."[10] The effects of all actions are automatic; one becomes what one does.[11] In the *Bhagavad-Gita,* Krishna describes graphically the karmic process of decline: "The evil doers turn not to me: these are deluded, sunk low among mortals. Their judgment is lost in the maze of Maya, until the heart is human no longer: changed within to the heart of a devil."[12]

Theory, however, did not always comport with experience. For the wicked often prospered while the good suffered. Individuals frequently found themselves, independently of their actions, to be radically unequal in wealth, social status, health, beauty, pleasure, and intelligence. To explain this discrepancy, the Hindus developed, as did Greeks like Plato and Pythagoras, a doctrine of reincarnation. With that new com-

---

9. See R. C. Zaehner, *Hinduism* (London: Oxford University Press, 1962, paperback 1971), *passim.* His works have been helpful.

10. *Brhad-Aranyaka Upanisad,* trans. Radhakrishnan (London, 1952), 4.4.5.

11. Speaking specifically of one of the ways of liberation, Mircea Eliade wrote: "In Yoga, every sin produces its consequences immediately." *Yoga: Immortality and Freedom,* trans. W. R. Trask, Bollingen Series LVI (New York: Pantheon Books, 1958), p. 49.

12. *Bhagavad-Gita,* trans. S. Prabhavananda and C. Isherwood (New York: New American Library, Mentor Books, 1958), p. 72.

ponent, the law of *karma* was more consistent: one's past life determines the present; and the present life, the future. They could have easily adopted Freud's statement: "Anatomy is fate," but they would have given it moral significance, as they did in evaluating economic conditions: "Poverty is a state of sinfulness."[13] Whether one's life and circumstances are good or bad, however, the wheel of *samsara* is ever spinning; even with reincarnation, and more fundamentally because of it, the future is problematic and grim.

Moksha or liberation from the wheel of *samsara* turned by *karma* is possible, though arduous. Theoretically, one lifetime suffices; in practice, countless rebirths may not. Good *karma* improves one's chances, but good *karma* is not liberation in possession, but liberation in prospect. *Moksha* means liberation from all *karma,* good and bad; it occurs only when one unites oneself with Brahman, the eternal and unchanging reality beyond the phenomenal world of experience.

The means of liberation is the perfect fulfilment of duty, *dharma.* To accept one's state of life and to perform all one's duties constitute the sole means of escaping the everlasting bondage to change. Through fidelity to *dharma,* the subject is able to transcend the evil of his past and the exactions of Nemesis and to achieve that union with the divine in which liberation consists. The etymology is revealing: the root is *dhr,* which means to hold, uphold, support, sustain, maintain.[14] Zaehner pointed out that the Latin words *forma* and *firmus* come from the same root. "*Dharma* is, then, the form of things as they are and the power that keeps them as they are and not otherwise."[15]

In its most general sense, *dharma* is that which sustains and holds together the physical and moral universe. At its core, *dharma* is the sacred and eternal word given to the *rishis* and preserved in the *Vedas.* Through many mediators and with numerous elaborations, it comes to the individual Hindu, as he seeks to fulfill his own personal duty, his *svadharma,* which he determines in the concrete context of his caste and state of life, his *varnashrama.* Hence, there arises the inevitable

13. *Mahabharata,* trans. P. C. Roy, 18 vols. (Calcutta: Baharata Press, 1884–1894), 12:8.

14. See Pandurang Vaman Kane, *History of Dharmasastra* (Ancient and Medieval Religious and Civil Law in India), (Poona: Bhandarkar Oriental Research Institute, 1968), Vol. I, Pt. I, p. 1; and Austin Creel, *Dharma in Hindu Ethics* (Columbia, Mo.: South Asian Books, 1977), p. 3.

15. R. C. Zaehner, *Hinduism,* pp. 2–3.

tension between authority and freedom, between law and conscience. This tension is aggravated by the hermeneutic difficulties that stem from the complexities, ambiguities, and even contradictions in Hinduism itself.

On the practical and normative level of human activity, Hinduism simplifies life as a balanced use of possessions (*artha*) and pleasures (*kama*) dictated by duty (*dharma*).[16] The fulfillment of the duties of this group of three (*trivarga*) ideally leads to liberation (*moksha*) from the endless round of change and rebirth (*samsara*). This longed-for release or emancipation is by no means an inevitable achievement; for the subject, until he is actually liberated, is held exactingly under the law of *karma,* with its nemesis-like retribution. But even *karma* can be overcome by conformity to *dharma.* Despite the tensions, difficulties, fears, and uncertainties clouding their religious vision, the Hindus still call it *Sanatana Dharma,* the Eternal *Dharma,* the Eternal Law. Through this central and existential idea, they hope, though threatened with the absurdity of endless change, eventually to realize meaning and fulfillment in the perfection of *nirvana.*

Some ambiguity clouds the relationship between *dharma* and *moksha.* The precise issue, van Buitenen indicated, is that the realm of *dharma* is *samsara* and that *dharma* upholds this established order, but that *moksha* abandons it "to achieve a self-realization that is precluded in the realm of *dharma.*"[17] What then is the relationship? Most Hindus take it for granted that fulfilling one's *dharma* is a necessary preparation for liberation, although they recognize that *moksha* is a transdharmic state. It seems that even perfect fulfillment of *dharma* does not lead automatically to *moksha,* but such perfection certainly facilitates the renunciation that actually does liberate and bring self-realization through union with Brahman.

16. The Hindus have codified the detailed requirements for the realm of *samsara* in respect to each of the three parts of the *trivarga.* These include *Arthasastras,* the *Kamasutras,* and, most important, the *Dharmasastras* and *Dharmastras* or "Books of the Law." The latter cover, with their social, legal, ritual, and sacrificial norms, the whole of orthodox Hindu religious life. These guides go back to the *Vedas,* but the *shruti* (texts) were insufficient for this purpose and had to be complemented by *smriti* (traditional memory), *sadacara* (good customs), and *atmatusti* (concordant developments). See P. V. Kane, *History of Dharmasastra;* Heinrich Zimmer, *Philosophies of India,* Bollingen Series XXVI (Princeton: Princeton University Press, 1971), p. 40 and passim; and A. Creel, *Dharma in Hindu Ethics,* pp. 11–15.

17. J. A. B. van Buitenen, *"Dharma and Moksa," Philosophy of East and West* 7 (1957): 37. See also pp. 38–39.

As might be expected in a religion with a plurality of gods, the personification of the law of *karma* as a kind of Hindu Nemesis would emerge in the popular consciousness even before the concept of *karma* and its cognates had been formulated. This personal symbol was the god Varuna, described in the *Rig Veda* and "generally regarded as the highest ethical creation of the Vedic Indians."[18] He was the universal monarch of the gods, the preserver of the cosmos, and the guardian of law, justice, and truth—the last three ideas contained in the word *rita,* which in post-Vedic times developed into the idea of *dharma.* Varuna was the cause, the protector, and the restorer of order, *rita,* in the physical and moral universe.

Like Nemesis, Varuna punished sinners, even for sins committed in ignorance or by mistake. His fetters of sin were feared: "O Varuna, untie the upper fetter, untie the middle, untie the lower, for we would be sinless in [carrying out your] ordinances."[19] Yet, unlike Nemesis, who was simply and inexorably just, Varuna was compassionate, even forgiving. The myth reveals how the human beings, wondering at the order of the cosmos, humbly expected punishment for sinful disorders, yet yearned for the possibility and assurance of forgiveness. Although other gods, especially Indra and Shiva, were to eclipse Varuna and take over his functions, his spirit continued to animate Hindu thinking. Varuna, through law, ruled a moral universe: "By virtue of the law, the Son of Aditi [Varuna] is possessed of the law."[20] His continuing appeal and contribution was that, in safguarding law and order, he did not overlook the basic human need for mercy.

III. THE WRATH OF GOD   *— The Christian Notion*

A principle of exact retribution, paralleling the Greek *nemesis* and Hindu *karma,* also operates in Christianity. Though found in both the Old and the New Testaments, it is nowhere more strikingly present than in the writings of St. Paul, for example: "Be not deceived, God is

---

18. Ibid., p. 19, and see also pp. 26–33. For a fuller discussion, see Mircea Eliade, *Images and Symbols,* trans. P. Mairet (New York: Sheed and Ward, 1952), pp. 92–99; and T. R. Organ *The Hindu Quest for the Perfection of Man* (Athens, Ohio: Ohio University Press, 1970), pp. 349–52.

19. *Rig-Veda,* 1.24.15.

20. *Rig-Veda,* 4.42.

not mocked; as a man sows so shall he reap. For he that sows in his flesh, of the flesh he shall reap corruption, but he that sows in the spirit, of the spirit shall reap everlasting life" (Gal. 6:7–8).

Paul's major concern is not retribution, but righteousness. The word he uses, *dikaiosune,* can be translated as either justice or righteousness. The latter is preferable, for it includes both the punitive and the forgiving aspects of God's dealings with mankind, whereas the word justice seems to imply disproportionately the legal processes of retribution.[21] Actually, when Paul wants to speak of divine retribution, the negative aspect of divine righteousness, he uses the idea of the wrath of God.

RIGHTEOUS-
NESS

The *Epistle to the Romans* contains Paul's fullest exposition of the wrath of God. In the very first chapter, he sets up the cause-and-effect relationship; he accuses both Jews and Gentiles—the whole known world—of being sinful and subject to divine punishment: "For the wrath of God is revealed from heaven against all ungodliness and unrighteousness of those men who detain the truth of God in unrighteousness" (Rom. 1:18). The reason Paul gives for the divine wrath is the twofold despising of God as revealed both in His creation and in His law. This negative action on man's part consists in holding back, detaining, hindering God's truth. "All have sinned and have fallen short of the glory of God" (Rom. 3:23). Being wicked, they have not manifested in themselves by their actions the goodness of God and thus have failed to glorify him; they have balked at that self-actualization which is the human side of divine glorification.[22]

This injustice provokes their doom; indeed, it is their doom. Three times Paul describes how, by letting their wickedness run its own course, God has delivered up (*paredoken*) sinners to their fate: "to the lusts of their hearts" (Rom. 1:24); "to dishonorable passions" (1:26); and "to a reprobate mind" (1:28). By this triple use of *paredoken,* "Paul tries to establish the intrinsic relationship between sin and punishment: impiety brings its own punishment."[23] How this process of

21. See John L. McKenzie *Light on the Epistles* (Chicago: Thomas More Press, 1975), p. 88.

22. See Mat. 6:16: "So let your light shine before men that they may see your good works and glorify your Father, who is in heaven."

23. Joseph A. Fitzmyer, "The Letter to the Romans," *The Jerome Biblical Commentary* (Englewood Cliffs, N.J.: Prentice-Hall, 1968), Vol. II, 53:26, p. 297.

moral disintegration follows from the scorning of God and His law can be seen in the full text of the third condemnation, where the final punishment is death:

And as they liked not to have God in their knowledge, God delivered them up to a reprobate mind to do those things which are not proper. Being filled with all iniquity, evil, avarice, wickedness; full of envy, murder, strife, deceit, malignity; whisperers, detractors, haters of God, insolent, arrogant, boasters, inventors of evil things, disobedient to parents, foolish, faithless, heartless, merciless, who, knowing the ordinance of God, did not understand that they who do such things are worthy of death, and not only they that do them but they also that consent to them that do them (Rom. 1:28–32).

The notion of divine wrath, though a commonplace of Greco-Roman and Jewish culture, is sometimes disquieting for those who believe in a God who is Love. Paul seemed aware of apparent incongruity and so made careful choice of words. He used the phrase "the wrath of God" only three times, and he never has God as the subject of the verb "to be angry."[24] C. H. Dodd's conclusion was that Paul used this notion of wrath "not to describe the attitude of God to man, but to describe an inevitable process of cause and effect in a moral universe."[25] Dodd clearly labeled the process: "This is the Nemesis of Sin: the revelation of 'the Wrath,' "[26] as if he were to say that "man is punished by his sins, not for his sins." The fearsome aspect of the wrath of God is that it makes punishment virtually self-inflicted. Dodd picked up the intimations of existential dread:

The act of God is no more than an abstention from interference with their free choice and its consequences. . . . "It is an awful thing," says the Epistle to the Hebrews (x. 31), "to fall into the hands of the living God." Paul, with a finer instinct, sees that the really awful thing is to fall out of His hands, and to be left to oneself in a world where the choice of evil brings its own moral retribution.[27]

Three points concerning the wrath of God should be noted. First, "There is no respect of persons with God" (Rom. 2:11). Jews and Gentiles are equally subject to punishment. That no one can sin with impunity is said repeatedly throughout the Epistle. Second, "We are plunged into what to human logic seems to be a vicious circle of guilt-

24. See C. H. Dodd, *The Epistle to the Romans*, The Moffatt New Testament Commentary (London: Hodder and Stoughton, 1932), p. 21.
25. Ibid., p. 23.   26. Ibid., p. 29.
27. Ibid.

punishment which is one of the most terrible insights of the Bible."[28] For each punishment leads to further sin, with further punishment, again and again. But, third, there is the possibility of forgiveness. The punitive aspect of righteousness is complemented by the forgiving one. Man can respond to grace and through repentance be made whole. However, it is not his work alone, but his cooperation with the free and unmerited gift of God. Terminal nemesis, the truly fatal effect of sin, is to become so hard-hearted as to refuse the grace of repentance that God is ready to give. If, in His wrath, God allows our self-destruction, in His love, He offers total reconciliation.

IV. THE PHILOSOPHIC CLARIFICATIONS

The widespread cultural acceptance of the notion of nemesis prompts us to examine it more closely. Both on the societal level, where it is most visible in the breakdown of civilizations, and on the individual level, where it reveals its radical cause in so-called basic sin with its inevitable psychological sequelae, we shall see nemesis as the negative consequence of flawed decision making.

The historian Arnold Toynbee, in analyzing the breakdown of civilizations, gives nemesis a major role.[29] For him, breakdown is not simply the termination of the period of growth: civilizations do not die of natural causes, as do aging human beings; nor do they expire as murder victims, although a dying civilization may be dispatched by an alien enemy. Civilizations cease to exist essentially through a kind of social suicide—a failure of self-determination.

Toynbee lists three main categories of the failure of self-determination; each reveals nemesis as sanctioning an improper response to the challenges facing a civilization. The first one, the "mechanicalness of mimesis," is paradigmatic and is based on the observation that a civilization is composed of a creative minority that is imitated more or less mechanically by the majority. That relationship is an ideal one for progress. But when the mechanical attitudes of the majority so affect the minority that the creative minority ceases to be creative, the civili-

28. Gerhard Kittel and Gerhard Friedrich, trans. W. Bromiley, 10 vols. *Theological Dictionary of the New Testament* (Grand Rapids, Mich.: Wm. B. Eerdmans, 1964), 5:443.

29. I have relied here on Arnold Toynbee's *A Study of History* (London: Oxford University Press, 1939), vol. 5.

zation has been arrested. The desperate tendency of the threatened minority is to try to retain its leadership role, if not by attracting the majority by its creativity, then by controlling it by its power. The former creative minority now becomes merely a dominant minority, and the civilization, already arrested, begins to disintegrate. Nemesis has punished both the failure of creativity and the recourse to power.

Secondly, the "intractability of institutions" is also a failure of creativity, although only a partial one. For even when the minority remains generally creative, it may not be able to fashion institutions that are proportioned to the new social forces it has released. And so it tries somehow to use the old institutions, ill-suited though they may be. The result is either a total explosion in the form of a revolution or a radical distortion of the old institutions so that they become a "social enormity." In either case, the civilization has broken down, sanctioned by nemesis.

Thirdly, speaking of more typical instances, Toynbee analyzed nemesis, in its narrow sense, "the nemesis of creativity." The focus is still on the failure of the creative minority—not that it stops being creative and becomes coercive, or that it does not continue to fashion institutions to make its creations work, but that, after an initial success, it commits some crime or blunder and vitiates the very use of creativity itself. This nemesis of creativity is of two kinds: the active type of Greek hubris, in which success leads to arrogant presumption and, in turn, to outrageous behavior, for example, the suicidalness of militarism and the intoxication of victory; and the passive type, in which success is followed by complacently resting on one's oars, because of the idolization of an ephemeral self, an ephemeral institution, or of an ephemeral technique. Nietzsche once said, "The snake that does not shed its skin will die." So too that civilization which does not move beyond its earlier successes will destroy itself as truly as one that, puffed up by its accomplishments, recklessly disregards the boundaries of prudence and right reason.

Bernard Lonergan pushed more deeply than did Toynbee in his quest to understand this breakdown, both societal and individual, which nemesis produces. For him, the crucial factor was "basic sin." Here we have to be precise. Lonergan was speaking as a philosopher; he was not simply implementing a religious code, but was validating the very possibility of ethics. Toynbee spoke of the failure of self-determination;

Lonergan spoke similarly: "By basic sin I shall mean the failure of free will to choose a morally obligatory course of action or its failure to reject a morally reprehensible course of action."[30] Essentially, basic sin is a shattering of the organic relationship between knowing and doing. Only when both are in harmony has a person moved from rational consciousness to rational self-consciousness. Since it is one and the same person who both knows and acts, there comes from this identity of consciousness an exigence for self-consistency; and "the dynamic exigence of rational self-consciousness for self-consistency unfolds into a body of moral precepts concretely operative in moral conscious-ness."[31] The willful frustration of this exigency can be a deadly decision. Mircea Eliade elaborated this crucial point:

In Goethe's conception, Mephistopheles is the spirit who denies, protests, and, above all, halts the flux of life and prevents things from being done. Mephi-stopheles' activity is not directed against God, but against life. Mephistopheles is the "father of all hindrance." What Mephistopheles asks of Faust is to stop. "Verweile doch!" is the essential Mephistophelian formula. Mephistopheles knows that the moment Faust stops he will have lost his soul. Mephistopheles does not directly oppose God but his principal creation, Life. In place of movement and Life he tries to impose rest, immobility, death. For whatever ceases to change and transform itself decays and perishes. This "death in life" can be translated as spiritual sterility; it is, taken all in all, damnation.[32]

Basic sin is an irrational saying "no" to life; the action that follows from this negation is only derivative. "For basic sin is not an event; it is not something that positively occurs; on the contrary, it consists in a failure of occurrence, in the absence in the will of a reasonable response to an obligatory motive."[33] It is a narrowing of the mind, a limiting of the field of consideration whereby pleasures are preferred to values, short-term benefits to long-term costs. The motivation for this myopic choice is egoism, whether of the individual or of the group. Teilhard de Chardin expressed the attitude thus: "He is spiritually impure who, lingering in pleasure or shut up in selfishness, introduces,

30. Bernard Lonergan, Insight (London: Longmans, Green, 1957; New York: Phil-osophical Library, 1958), p. 666.
31. Ibid., p. 99.
32. Mircea Eliade, The One and the Two (New York: Harper and Row, 1969), p. 79.
33. B. Lonergan, Insight, p. 667.

within himself and around himself, a principle of slowing-down and division in the unification of the universe in God."[34]

It is as a principle of disorder that egoism not only motivates basic sin but accounts for the inevitable retribution. What follows from basic sin is a progressive decline or breakdown in the individual and in the community to the extent that his decision affects others or is shared by them. Even when the egoism remains individual, not yet combining into group egoism, the effects on the community are great. Society uses law to try to counter this divisive force, yet the power of the law is limited. Lonergan showed how formidable an enemy, how pernicious a contagion, this egoism can be, and how inexorable the process of decline:

Egoism is in conflict with the good of order. Up to a point it can be countered by the law, the police, the judiciary, the prisons. But there is a limit to the proportion of population that can be kept in prison and when egoism passes the limit, the agents of the law and ultimately the law itself have to become more tolerant and indulgent. So the good of order deteriorates. Not only is it less efficient but also there is the difficulty of exercising even-handed justice in deciding which injustices are to be winked at. The practical question is apt to be whose social sins are to be forgiven, and whose are to be punished, and then the law is compromised. It is no longer coincident with justice. In all likelihood it becomes to a greater or less extent the instrument of a class.[35]

Egoism easily becomes the driving force of a group; when it is so amplified, the rate of decline increases. The reason is that egoism effectively skews the process of self-determination, and, as Toynbee observed, "A loss of self-determination is the ultimate criterion of breakdown, for . . . it is the inverse of the criterion of growth."[36] In describing this individual and social decline, we can identify two fundamental components, alienation and ideology.[37] Alienation is the denial or disregard of the transcendental precepts; in other words, it results when bias and egoism cause a failure to be fully attentive, intelligent,

34. Pierre Teilhard de Chardin, *The Divine Milieu* (New York: Harper and Row, 1960), p. 113. See also St. Paul's references to "those men who detain the truth of God in injustice" (Rom. 1:18) and to those who, "when they knew God, have not glorified him as God or given thanks" (Rom. 1:21).

35. B. Lonergan, *Method*, 2nd ed. (New York: Herder and Herder, 1973), p. 54.

36. Arnold Toynbee, *A Study of History*, revised and abridged by A. Toynbee and J. Kaplan (London: Oxford University Press, 1972), p. 166.

37. See B. Lonergan, *Method*, p. 55 and also Eric Voegelin, *Science, Politics and Gnosticism* (South Bend, Ind.: Gateway, 1968).

reasonable, or responsible. Ideology is the attempt to justify alienation by rationalizing preferences into an articulate counter-position,
whereby the inconsistency between knowing and doing becomes a
covert inconsistency within knowing itself. Together the egoistic disregard and the tendentious construct continue to bring about that
cumulative and progressive retribution that is nemesis.

The psychological dimension of the intrinsic efficiency of nemesis is
manifest in the impact that basic sin or the failure of self-determination
has on the nervous system. Conscious action leaves its mark on the
psyche. As the great Canadian neurosurgeon Wilder Penfield observed;
"The engram of experience is a structured record within the brain."[38]
Of course, it would be comforting to imagine that flawed choices are
only momentary, like smoke that blows away without a trace, like a
ship leaving no sign of its passage. The illusion here is that if one is not
discovered or apprehended, one suffers no harm. Yet, in fact, even
hidden sins are declarative of themselves, not just as the stigmata of
iniquity, a kind of psychic disfigurement, but also as dysfunctional
potentialities biasing future decision making. Dr. Penfield explained
how we become what we do:

The imprint of memory's engram is somehow added during neuronal action.
Conscious attention seems to give to that passage of neuronal impulses permanent facilitation for subsequent passage of potentials along the neuronal
connections in the same pattern. Thus a recall engram is established. This, one
may suggest, is the real secret of learning.[39]

One who has made an unauthentic choice is disposed to make further
unauthentic choices, for he has developed an abiding tendency to act
the same way. With repetition, this type of activity becomes easier and
easier. After a bad action it is not enough to say, I am sorry, I repent,
I will not do it again. These attitudes are a beginning, but they do not
restore a person to a state of innocence. What is needed in addition is
a restructuring of neuronal pathways, a long and difficult task. The
scars from earlier falls may always remain as points of vulnerability;

38. Wilder Penfield, M.D., *The Mystery of the Mind* (Princeton: Princeton University
Press, 1975), p. 8.

39. Ibid., p. 66. For a complementary study involving the psychological scope of
nemesis, see John F. Kihlstrom, "The Cognitive Unconscious," *Science* 237 (1987):
1445–1452; he stated: "Research in subliminal perception, implicit memory, and hyp-
nosis indicate that events can effect mental functions even though they cannot be consciously perceived or remembered" (p. 1445).

they may, however, also become badges of courage for weaknesses overcome.

The experience of nemesis is the experience of disorder. The primitive notion of nemesis is simply that flawed actions, whether innocent or wicked, bring negative results. The moral dimensions of this objective assessment come from the consciousness of making a free but knowingly wrong choice. Morally, nemesis reveals to the subject the psychic division and disorder that comes from knowing what is good and doing what is bad. Guilt is the name that we give to this experience of freely caused mental fragmentation. Guilt has both an emotional and an intellectual component; the affect, however, is secondary to the subject's realization that he willingly forfeited his own spiritual and mental integrity. He recognizes, in Shakespeare's words, "If I lose mine honor, I lose myself."[40] Nemesis makes the subject conscious of that loss, or, if the subject has a hardened conscience, nemesis bears witness to his moribund state of blind intransigence.

The Latin helps to clarify these points by distinguishing *culpa, reatus culpae,* and *reatus poenae. Culpa* (fault) causes the *reatus* (the state or condition of being guilty), which incurs punishment (*poena*). *Reatus culpae* is the guilt that indicates that the subject is a wrongdoer. *Reatus poenae* is the guilt that indicates that the subject deserves punishment. Both are the effects of *culpa;* they differ in that a person may disaffirm his wrong by repentance and conversion, thus restoring his moral equilibrium, but still need to compensate for the disorder or to balance it by the loss of a proportionate good. This punishment, the deprivation of a good consequent on fault, may or may not be extrinsically imposed by God or man, but it nevertheless always involves an intrinsic deprivation: the loss of personal order and integrity. Even physically, as we have seen, the neuronal structures of the brain are proportionately disordered by fault, which engenders an habitual tendency to unauthenticity. This kind of objective guilt with its self-destructive biases reveals nemesis at its most intimate and inexorable.

Underlying all these other manifestations of nemesis, however, there remains the dread reality of entropy, the tendency of all things to move to a state of random disorder. This happens because order is improbable. Indeed, of all beings, man is the most improbable, and man has within himself the power to bring order or disorder into his life. His is

40. William Shakespeare, *Antony and Cleopatra,* III, 4.

the awesome burden of freedom of choice and action. Unfortunately, this freedom can foster entropy, "the principle of diminishing potential."[41] So man lives precariously, not only because entropy is at the heart of matter and man is an embodied spirit, but because the spirit, abdicating its responsibility, can bring about in itself an entropic condition of disordered and diminished potentialities, over which dismal state Nemesis ever presides.

CONCLUSION

Eros and Nemesis work together in the Monosphere to give us a fundamental understanding of legal experience. They focus our attention on the law within and without. Eros symbolizes the inner law that directs our actions to concrete existents. Nemesis reveals the outer laws, by showing us the sharp edges of reality and thus teaching us the hard way that misdirected actions have counterproductive and even painful results. Even so, the distinction between inner and outer as so expressed may oversimplify their relationship for Nemesis also affects our inmost being, but it stands apart from or over against the inner law of Eros. It signifies a reality not subject to our will.

The lesson of Nemesis is twofold: actions have consequences; so actions involve standards. We cannot simply follow our desires or execute our choices and expect inevitable fulfillment. The results of our actions, even if initially satisfying, may ultimately turn out to be disappointing, frustrating, painful. We soon learn that some actions are good for us and some are bad. With an accumulation of insights and a self-correcting process of verification, we discover an emerging predictability concerning our commonsense relations with the world of our experience. Living takes on a more and more nuanced normative character, eventually to be institutionalized in part as law.

In a jurisprudence of subjectivity, we find an inner experience of law first in the authentic unfolding of Eros, whereby the mind exercises its own dynamic integrity. Nemesis then leads us obliquely to this same inner realization, for we confront reality as it impinges on our drives and actions, making us aware of norms outside ourselves and of norms within us but independent of us. We speak readily of guilt feelings; we

[handwritten marginalia: Eros - inner law → good + beautiful   Nemesis outer laws whereby some are good & some bad.]

41. Kenneth Boulding, *The Meaning of the Twentieth Century* (New York: Harper and Row, 1965), p. 138.

do not as precisely identify or sound our feelings of authentic decision making. The latter are more than an absence of the guilt that comes from being a house divided against itself; they are rather the positive experience of a mind at peace, functioning in harmony with itself. This joy comes from a heightened awareness of authentic subjectivity, flushed with the conquest of Nemesis.

PART TWO

THE ISOSPHERE
THE BILATERAL EXPERIENCE OF LAW

The Isosphere is the realm of equals. We continue to use the data of sense and consciousness in our quest for the full meaning of law as a rule and measure of acts. But now we add something new—our interaction with another subject. The basic question is then: What difference does it make in our understanding of law to include another subject in our decision making?

To answer this question, we study the implications of intersubjectivity: the bonds it forges and the claims it makes. For justice is a response to the fact of intersubjectivity, and rights are a response to the possibility of justice. But what catches the essence of intersubjectivity? A dog fight? An armed truce? A zero-sum game? A shared value?

Our method of understanding justice and rights from the perspective of interiority depends on ascertaining the mental operations performed. Objectively, justice and rights involve proportionate reciprocity; subjectively, however, they reflect conscious intersubjectivity. Both take their stand on the notion of human dignity and human equality; both appeal to reason rather than to force in handling the ever-present conflict situations of life: interaction, claim, and decision, in an arena of limited resources. Both justice and rights, when wholeheartedly endorsed and faithfully pursued, reveal the beauty of human bonding and the possibility of temporal happiness.

INTERSUBJECTIVITY

CHAPTER 4

JUSTICE: THE BOND OF
INTERSUBJECTIVITY

If you want peace, work for justice.—Paul VI[*]

Justice becomes a question when plurality becomes a fact. Interaction with another human being brings one out of the Monosphere into the Isosphere, the realm of equals. In the Monosphere, there can be no justice, because there is no interaction. If only one person is involved, however mistakenly, foolishly, or wickedly he may act, he cannot act unjustly; but when another, God or man, enters one's world, justice and injustice become possible. Moreover, the struggle for good things by many persons in a world of limited resources easily results in conflicts,[1] and conflicts must be resolved by force or by reason. Justice follows reason, so that in recognizing and implementing equality it can guide Eros without arousing the wrath of Nemesis.

From the viewpoint of a jurisprudence of subjectivity, I examine justice as theory and justice as interiority. We are all familiar with the commonsense manifestations of justice, knowing, for example, what it is to be dealt with fairly or to be cheated, deceived, assaulted, betrayed. Even a dog, it is said, can tell the difference between being stepped on and being kicked.

To know justice more fully, we look beyond these everyday instances and venture, first into theory, where, with the help of Aristotle, we understand justice as proportionate reciprocity, and then into interiority, where, under the guidance of Del Vecchio, we understand justice

---

[*] Paul VI, *The Teachings of Pope Paul VI*, 11 vols. (Vatican City: Libreria Editrice Vaticana, 1971), 5:330.

1. Carl G. Jung remarked: "A sane and normal society is one in which people habitually disagree, because general agreement is relatively rare outside the sphere of instinctive human qualities." C. J. Jung, "Approaching the Unconscious," *Man and His Symbols* (Garden City, N.Y.: Doubleday, 1964), p. 59.

as conscious intersubjectivity. Together, these two aspects reveal the intellectual and moral beauty of this indispensable human bonding.

I. THE PROPORTIONATE RECIPROCITY

Aristotle (384–322 B.C.) was the first to formulate a full theory of justice; he was not, of course, the first to philosophize about justice. For example, the Pythagoreans in the sixth century had already conceived of justice as equality (*isotes*) and reciprocity (*antipeponthos*)— and Aristotle owed much to them and to many other thinkers.

The major influence on Aristotle was Plato, his teacher, who had worked out the implications of justice as a general virtue. In the *Gorgias,* Plato had distinguished justice and injustice from pain and pleasure; he showed that justice is not a matter of superior power and that it is better to be done an injustice than to be unjust. Later, in the *Republic,* to understand this virtue more perfectly, he studied its full-blown presence in the body politic, which derived its form (*eidos*) and excellence (*arete*) from the justice of its individual members. Justice as a general virtue was at the heart of political life. As Jaeger put it, "Plato's conception of justice transcended all human institutions: it went back to the origins of justice in the soul. What the philosopher calls justice must be based in the most inward nature of the human spirit."[2]

Aristotle did not follow this lead into interiority; rather, he tried to systematize justice. Rethinking the accumulated wisdom of the past, he articulated two major developments: he moved the idea of justice from the realm of common sense into the realm of theory, and in so doing he made a radical distinction between justice as virtue and justice as fairness. Here, by and large, jurisprudence has faithfully remained. Contractarians, utilitarians, rationalists, positivists, naturalists: all have seemed content to be legal theoreticians and to take Aristotle, even as they differ from him, as establishing the common language of juridic discourse.

One may, of course, take issue with various aspects of the Aristotelian corpus, and one may explore new dimensions, but one can hardly disregard his major insights and still communicate intelligibly about

2. Werner Jaeger, *Paideia: the Ideals of Greek Culture,* trans. G. Highet, 3 vols. (New York: Oxford University Press, 1943–1945), 2:202.

justice. In this section, then, we shall consider justice theoretically: the method of investigation that Aristotle used; the variety of forms that he distinguished; and, finally, the overarching idea of equality on which he grounded this central virtue.

A grasp of Aristotle's method used in the fifth book of the *Nicomachean Ethics* enables us to evaluate his theoretical conclusions. His starting point was the community, with its fund of accumulated wisdom, traditional and current, about justice and injustice. These *endoxa*, reputable opinions, Aristotle analyzed and developed, consolidating and integrating them.[3] He worked inductively, relying on contingent assumptions rather than on *a priori* propositions or self-evident principles. For him, the ultimate test was whether or not there had emerged a coherent corpus, a logically consistent whole substantially in harmony with community insights and satisfactorily responsive to the questions those insights occasioned.

The initial insights into justice were on the commonsense level. They were practical observations and directives, bringing standards of balance and proportion and reciprocity into the interactions of human beings. Justice was a norm of practical living, to enable people to get along well. The fact that some form of the golden rule has appeared in all human societies indicates a perception of the value of justice and even the necessity for it. These guidelines of common sense are sometimes too narrow, sometimes too abstract, and sometimes even in conflict with one another. For example, "An eye for an eye and a tooth for a tooth" (Ex. 21:24), and "Love your enemies, do good to those who hate you" (Mat. 5:4).

Of course, theory swiftly outstrips the limitations of common sense. Principles of justice can now be looked at not simply as they relate to practical goals involving persons and things, but rather as these principles, their terms and relations, relate to one another.[4] Aristotle has provided more than a collection of efficacious guidelines or even a reclassification of normative statements; he has fashioned a body of knowledge answering questions that reach beyond the competence of common sense.

3. Aristotle made wide use of *endoxa* in, for example, *Prior Analytics, Topics, Ethics, Politics,* and *Metaphysics.*

4. For a discussion of the various realms of meaning: common sense, theory, interiority, and transcendence, see Bernard Lonergan, *Method in Theology* (New York: Herder and Herder, 1973), pp. 81–85.

The method that Aristotle used is immediately evident. He began Book Five with what might seem insufficient material—the common notion of what justice is: "Now we observe that everybody means by justice that disposition which renders men apt to do just things and which causes them to act justly and to wish what is just; and similarly by injustice that disposition which makes men act unjustly and wish what is unjust."[5] This statement is almost an *idem per idem* definition, but we do learn something from it: that the idea of justice springs from the community; that this common assumption points to something real; that the reality involved is the disposition to will and to act as well as the action itself; and that both disposition and action can be characterized as just or unjust. Despite this advance, further questioning is needed for an analysis of what thinkers have actually meant by the terms "just" and "unjust." Acknowledging that the usage encompasses several meanings, Aristotle discovered by careful scrutiny that the just refers both to what is lawful and to what is fair. On this simple but fruitful distinction between lawfulness and fairness, Aristotle erected his theory of justice. I will consider each aspect separately.

Justice as lawfulness, Aristotle called general justice. For him, the law-abiding man is just and the lawbreaker is unjust; that is because "in one sense we call those acts just that tend to produce and preserve happiness and its components for the political society."[6] The community both formally and informally enunciates its norms: it does so formally by law, which establishes rules of conduct; it does so informally by education, which provides regulations fitting one for a good social life. To obey these rules and regulations is to be virtuous and just, for justice is perfect virtue, not absolutely but as it relates to another (*pros heteron*). Justice, as a general virtue, might more properly be called righteousness than justice, for although it necessarily looks to another, it essentially encompasses all the virtues. Plato and St. Paul used the term in this broad sense. Aristotle recognized both the antiquity and the validity of general justice, but he was seeking greater precision—not a synonym for virtue, but a particular species of virtue.

Justice as fairness, which Aristotle called particular justice, is significantly different from justice as lawfulness. Aristotle picked up this difference when he noted that the synonyms for unfair are grasping,

5. Aristotle, *Nicomachean Ethics*, V, 1, 1129 a6–10.
6. Ibid., V, 1, 1129 b17–19.

overreaching, avaricious. This unfairness is called *pleonexia*, a taking of more than one's share of good things or less than one's share of bad things; Aquinas phrased it neatly: *Plus de bonis, minus de malis.*[7] For example, an unjust politician through graft may take more than his share of benefits and through tax evasion bear less than his share of burdens. Here the profit motive operates, for the unfair man acts "because of the pleasure of gain."[8] The focal point is precise: "For an unjust act by which a man has profited is not attributed to any vice except injustice."[9] This unfairness involves a plus or minus relationship to others, but to speak of more or less is to imply a standard. That standard is the fair share, the mean, the equal. Justice as fairness, then, is a species of general justice existing in its own right. When Aristotle spoke of justice, without qualification, it is usually this particular justice that he meant.

Aristotle distinguished two main types of justice as fairness or particular justice: the distributive and the corrective (the latter often called rectificatory or compensatory). He described them as follows:

> One kind is exercised in the distribution of honor, wealth, and other divisible assets of the community, which may be allotted among its members in equal or unequal shares. The other kind is that which supplies a corrective principle in private transactions ... those which are voluntary and those which are involuntary.[10]

Each form reveals an equality of some kind, but equality need not always mean identity. In fact, Aristotle criticized, perhaps mistakenly, the Pythagoreans for holding that "simple reciprocity is justice," a *lex talionis* oversimplification.[11] More subtly, he argued for "a reciprocity on the basis of proportion not equality."[12] It is proper then to speak of the proportionate reciprocity of particular justice, though the proportion differs with each of its two major forms.

Distributive justice uses geometric proportion, for the persons involved may be unequal in merit or demerit and therefore unequal in the shares allotted, extracted, or denied. For example, the military hero

---

7. Thomas Aquinas, *Commentary on the Nicomachean Ethics,* trans. C. I. Litzinger, 2 vols. (Chicago: Regnery, 1964), 1:430 (*Sententia libri Ethicorum,* V. Lect. X, 993). See also the distinction between general and particular injustice in *Summa theologiae,* II–II, q. 59, a. 1.

8. Aristotle, *Nicomachean Ethics,* V. 2, 1130 b4.

9. Ibid., V, 2, 1130 a31–32.   10. Ibid., V, 2, 1130 b31–1131 a3.

11. Ibid., V, 5, 1132 b21.   12. Ibid., V, 5, 1132, b32–33.

and the ordinary soldier will receive different degrees of honor or amounts of money according to their relative contributions to victory, but will be proportionately on a par. Distribution is according to merit (*kat'axian*), but the standard for determining what activates the process remained for Aristotle problematic: it is merit or its equivalent; it is positive or negative; it may even be, though Aristotle did not so envisage it, poverty, ill-health, basic human nature.

Corrective justice uses arithmetic proportion: the persons involved are treated for the purposes of conflict resolution as equals: "For it makes no difference whether a good man has defrauded a bad man or a bad man a good one . . . the law looks only at the nature of the damage, treating the parties as equal, and merely asking whether one has done and the other has suffered injustice, whether one has inflicted and the other sustained damage."[13] The issue is the determination of the just mean by balancing loss and gain, using those terms broadly.

Aristotle divided the subject matter again, not altogether satisfactorily, into transactions in which the parties voluntarily establish a rule for themselves, such as a contract, and transactions in which liability is involuntarily incurred, such as a tort. He called the first commutative justice and the second judicial, because the mean requires some determination by a judge. The judicial type is further divided into actions occurring by stealth and by violence; there is no explicit consideration of criminal law.

After a detailed analysis of the two major types of justice, Aristotle noted that what was being investigated was not only justice in the absolute sense but also political justice. Not satisfied to speak of justice merely abstractly, he wanted to see it in the context of the moral and social life that is the *polis*. "Political justice means justice as between persons who are free, equal proportionately (*kat'analogian*) or numerically (*kat'arithmon*), and living a common life for the sake of self-sufficiency."[14] In so defining political justice, Aristotle bypassed the hard questions—who are equal? and by what standards? He was able to do that without controversy, because his subject matter was the *polis,* an active organization with fixed views on what constituted equality and citizenship. Given that context, his fundamental principle

13. Ibid., V, 4, 1132 a1–6.
14. Ibid., V, 6, 1134 a24–28. For other persons, justice is present only by analogy. 1134 a29–30.

dictated the equal treatment of equals and the unequal treatment of unequals.

Aristotle, however, realized that political justice may also involve questions of justice in the absolute sense. The problem arose in his discussion of the components of political justice: that which is just by nature (*dikaion physei*) and that which is just by law (*dikaion nomo*):

A rule of justice is natural that has the same validity everywhere and does not depend on our accepting it or not. A rule is legal that in the first instance may be settled in one way or the other indifferently, though having once been settled it is not indifferent.[15]

The section of the *Ethics* from which these two sentences have been taken has occasioned some disagreement, primarily because of its lack of clarity. Frequently, it has been interpreted as a declaration of the unchangeability of natural law. This does not seem to be what Aristotle meant. Although he acknowledged that among the gods the rules of justice may be immutable, he held that among human beings these rules, whether natural or legal, are mutable.[16] He recognized degrees of mutability, depending on whether or not the subject matter was indifferent or natural. The rules of justice for indifferent things, the *adiaphora,* such as weights and measures, fines or ransoms, are determined by agreement, convention, law.

But the rules of justice concerning natural things must take those natural things into consideration; one is not free to make the determination arbitrarily, for there are relevant facts that must be marshaled and weighed. Thus, the date that taxes are due may be chosen freely, but the minimum age for marriage may be ascertained only by considering the mental and physical maturity of males and females. But, convinced that nature itself can change, to say nothing of changes in our knowledge of nature, Aristotle concluded about the rules of natural and legal justice that "both sorts alike are variable."[17]

Even the most prudently made laws may fail on occasion by reason of their generality, for it is not usually possible to cover all the singular situations that may arise. In other words, the law may be valid for the majority of cases, but fall short of justice, due to special circumstances in this or that particular case. Equity (*epieikeia*), then, becomes nec-

15. Ibid., V. 7, 1134 b19–21.
16. See ibid., V, 7, 1134 b27–33.
17. Ibid., V, 7, 1134 b32.

essary to correct the law. So equity is greater than legal justice but not greater than justice simply because it is justice.[18]

One makes this equitable exception to the general law "by deciding as the lawgiver himself would decide if he were present on the occasion and would have enacted had he been cognizant of the case in question."[19] This attempt to read the mind of the lawgiver has been the traditional approach to equity, although more recently some—realizing the difficulty, if not the impossibility, of knowing what the actual ruler or legislative majority would do—seek rather to determine what a reasonable lawgiver would decide under the circumstances. This more liberal approach is consonant with Aristotle's remark: "We do not allow a man to rule but a rational principle."[20] At any rate, equity is proper whether the rule of justice under consideration is natural or conventional or mixed, for the fact that generalizations are man-made, that circumstances are complex and changing, and that even nature is mutable makes equity indispensable to a legal process.

Underlying the analysis of the forms of justice and its equitable corrective is the recognition of the importance of equality. Implicitly referring to the *endoxa,* the reputable opinions found in the *polis,* Aristotle said, "All men think justice to be a sort of equality."[21] From this insight follows the general norm: "Equality consists in the same treatment of similar persons and no government can stand which is not founded on justice."[22] He spoke strongly of the political necessity of justice: "The very existence of the state depends on proportionate reciprocity; for men demand that they shall be able to requite evil with evil—if they cannot, they feel they are in the position of slaves—and to repay good with good—failing which no exchange takes place, and it is exchange that binds them together."[23]

Despite his grasp of the crucial role of equality, Aristotle's appreciation of the dimensions of justice is not wholly satisfactory. First of all, he fails to establish the criteria of equality. He is well aware of the problem: "There still remains a question: equality or inequality of

Criticisms
① fails to estb
criteria of
equality.

18. See ibid., V, 10, 1137 b24–27.
19. Ibid., V, 10, 1137 b19–24.
20. Ibid., V, 6, 1134 a35. N.B. Oxford text has *logon* (rational principle); Loeb has *nomon* (law).
21. Idem, *Politics*, III, 12, 1282 b18.
22. Ibid., VII, 14, 1332 b27–29.
23. Idem, *Nicomachean Ethics*, V, 5, 1132 b33–1133 a2.

what? here is a question that calls for political speculation."[24] It is a question that he did not fully answer; certainly, he never managed to ground equality squarely in human nature or in human dignity. He could accept, not without some qualms, the institution of slavery; he believed that Athenians should not be slaves, but that some others might need masters for their own good. Secondly, perhaps as a consequence of the first failure, he seemed to think of justice as primarily political. He mentioned that a kind of justice obtains between master and slave, parent and child, husband and wife—but after the fashion of a metaphor.

 ② justice is primarily political

Nevertheless, Aristotle's basic insights remain valuable for justice in the Isosphere as well as in the Koinosphere. He did not work out all the implications of his insights; he, too, was conditioned by his culture. He did clarify and integrate basic truths about justice that others would bring to a more personalistic fulfillment: the central role of equality was to bear fruit in Stoic as well as in Christian philosophies; the notion of proportionate reciprocity was to expand the coverage of justice to all types of bilateral decisions; and the corrective power of equity was to bring the delicate adjustments necessary to general laws in a world of concrete goods, multiple circumstances, and singular events.

An important question remains: can our idea of justice be grounded on more than the opinions of the wise and the prudent? Must our methodology initially be that of the pollster trying to discover what people think about things? Or can we also ground the notion of justice on our own interiority and then, by objectifying this self-appropriation, return ever more soundly into the realm of theory?

II. THE CONSCIOUS INTERSUBJECTIVITY

To base a theory of justice on an analysis of reputable opinions, as did Aristotle, provides a sound beginning. It suggests, on the basis of accumulated insights and informal, trial-and-error verifications, that the resultant structure of ideas will comport well with reality. It does not, especially in an age that challenges traditions and patronizes the past, answer a crucial question: How did the first thinkers arrive at their opinions? Consequently, unless we are content with an infinitely

24. Idem, *Politics,* III, 12, 1282 b21–22.

regressive series that never gives a final answer, we may want to discover how anyone, ancient or modern, arrives at principles of justice.

A psychogenesis of justice involves at least two major focal points: the social and historical one, whereby cultural communities formulate a notion of justice; and an individual or psychological one, whereby a person attains a sense of justice for himself. These two processes inter-penetrate, converging on a time-space continuum; for individuals, as parts of a social tradition, perceive the world in a personal but condi-tioned way.

In our analysis of Aristotle, we sketched out a major advance in the long course of juridical development. Now it is important for us to examine the mental process at work. Here also two different methods can be followed: one may try to discover how, along the lines of Piaget's work on the development of the moral judgment of the child, human beings first form a notion of justice; or one may try to discern the mental steps that an adult must take in order to comprehend and authenticate his notion of justice. Of course, the individual process does to some extent parallel or recapitulate certain aspects of the cultural and historical processes, but it should be able to stand on its own in accounting for an individual's firm grasp of justice as a personal experience. It is this conscious pattern of operations that we now consider.

Giorgio Del Vecchio (1878–1970), an Italian legal philosopher, worked in the realm of theory and talked the language of subjectivity. For him, justice was essentially a mode of consciousness reflecting a special kind of relationship between persons, one which he character-ized as "a principle of coordination between subjective beings."[25] He proposed two tasks: the grasping of this essential coordination; and the derivation of its logical elements. Incidentally, there still remains a third task, one that actuates the full experience, namely, that of con-sciously doing justice. Del Vecchio proposed to account for the pe-rennial presence of the conception of justice throughout the history of mankind. "The explanation is that this conception proceeds directly from the inner nature of consciousness and represents one of its nec-essary and fundamental attitudes or modes of behavior."[26]

25. Giorgio Del Vecchio, *Justice: An Historical and Philosophic Essay,* ed. A. H. Campbell, trans. Lady Guthrie (Edinburgh: Edinburgh University Press, 1956), p. 2.
26. Ibid., p. 77.

His main steps, though perhaps not the concepts and the process itself, are fairly simple. First, the subject by becoming self-aware also becomes aware of that which is not the subject; that is, the non-self or the world of objects. But that is not yet a basis for justice; the subject still remains isolated in the Monosphere. Therefore, a second step is taken when the subject perceives that some of the objects are themselves subjects like himself and he learns too that, though he is a subject, he may be perceived by others as an object. From this twofold relationship arises the notion of intersubjectivity. Each person has this subject-object role in the world of intersubjectivity; the recognition of this fact is the foundation of justice: "We find then the essence of justice in the *objective positing of subjectivity* and in the *intersubjective coordination* which results therefrom."[27]

Del Vecchio next described the logical elements of this subjective coordination; *bilaterality* (the subjects are placed on the same plane, the one being the function of the other); *parity* (the subjects are presupposed to be initially equal); and *reciprocity* (the subjects are functionally correlated).[28] In bilaterality and parity the static predominates, whereas in reciprocity it is the dynamic; together, however, they form an integrated operation that evidences the categorical imperative of Kant: "Act as if the maxim of your action were to become through your will a universal law of nature."[29]

We see that, as with Aristotle, reciprocity is pivotal, virtually authorizing corresponding treatment when roles are reversed. Not only requital, in the negative sense, but reward too is mandated. "That is so because the self here posits itself *sub specie alteritatis,* and the self and the other become, so to speak, fungible entities, because of the essential objectivity of the relation which binds them."[30] Cain's reaction after murdering Abel manifests an implicit awareness of this reciprocity: "I shall be a vagabond and fugitive upon the earth. Everyone that finds me shall kill me" (Gen. 4:14). Through reciprocity, nemesis operates both psychologically and socially; the sinner virtually authorizes his own punishment; he has willingly treated another subject as a thing, so he cannot logically complain of proportionately similar treatment for himself.

27. Ibid., p. 83.   28. See ibid.
29. Immanuel Kant, *The Moral Law: Kant's Groundwork of the Metaphysic of Morals,* trans. and ed. H. J. Paton (New York: Barnes and Noble, 1963), p. 89.
30. Del Vecchio, *Justice,* p. 84.

Del Vecchio's summary statement about the conception of justice involves a twofold evaluation, recognitive and attributive: "Every subject shall be recognized (by others) for what he is worth" and "to everyone shall be assigned (by others) what belongs to him."[31] Here we are back again to the traditional definition of justice—to give to each his own—but this time it is erected, not on a Biblical or Stoic foundation, but on a Neo-Kantian one. Before looking more closely and critically at Del Vecchio's philosophic underpinnings, let us, keeping in mind Del Vecchio's insights, see how two other thinkers dealt with the subject-object relation: Buber, who leads us to more than justice; Sartre, who leaves us with much less.

Martin Buber (1878–1965), like Del Vecchio, was strongly influenced by Kant, and he elaborated the distinction that Kant had made between beings that exist for their own sake (*propter se*) and beings that exist for the sake of another (*propter alium*).[32] Kant wrote: "Act in such a way that you always treat humanity, whether in your own person or in the person of any other, never simply as a means, but always at the same time as an end."[33]

As a consequence, Buber's thought is structured in terms of two types of human relationships: the I-Thou and the I-It. In other words, we can treat a person as another self or treat him as a thing. In the I-Thou relationship, each subject is recognized as existing in his own right, for his own sake. In the I-It relationship, although we may be dealing with another person, we treat him as a thing to be used, even used up, for our benefit. If we treat persons as things, we never get to know them as persons. As the Sufi story has it: a great saint came to the village of a thief, but the thief never saw the saint—he was too busy looking at his pockets. Only in an I-Thou relationship is the subject adequately revealed; only in that way is there full intersubjectivity and justice, enabling the subject to transcend the world of objects, where he is selfishly and necessarily alone, and bringing him into the realm of other selves, subjects like himself, where he can love and be loved.

Jean-Paul Sartre (1915–1979) rejected intersubjectivity for anarchic individualism.[34] He spoke of an irreducible tension between the con-

31. Ibid., p. 85.
32. See especially, Martin Buber, *I and Thou,* trans. R. G. Smith, 2d ed. (New York: Scribner's, 1958).
33. I. Kant, *The Moral Law,* p. 96.
34. See Jean-Paul Sartre, *Being and Nothingness,* trans. H. E. Barnes (New York: Philosophical Library, 1956).

scious subject (*l'être pour soi*) and the non-conscious thing (*l'être en soi*): the former is active, the latter passive. Human beings, he said, are ever trying to assert their own consciousness by denying the consciousness of others, by considering them as objects. As a consequence, personal relationships were for Sartre sadomasochistic, a question of dominance or submission.[35] There is an interplay between two antagonistic experiences: that of being a subject, *pour-soi*, because one is able to perceive the other as an object, *en-soi*; or that of being an object because one is perceived by the other as an object.

A determining perspective, *le regard*, silently but inevitably establishes a vertical relationship. Every look is a challenge; the result is a conquest or a capitulation. So there can be no justice because there is no possibility of intersubjectivity. The relationship is an inevitable power struggle between subject and object, consciousness and thing, or I and it. Morality never gets out of the Monosphere; it is a morality for oneself and by oneself. It is not surprising, therefore, that Sartre promised, but did not produce, a work on morals—the ethical responsibilities arising from the confrontation with "a human reality in situation." He was thwarted by his own ontological and psychological views on human beings and their interactions. His aphoristic conclusion about intersubjectivity was: *L'Enfer, c'est les Autres* ("Hell is other people").[36]

To return again to Del Vecchio for a closer look at his method of establishing intersubjectivity, we find him using here the formulation of Fichte, a disciple of Kant. He began with a conscious subject who, in positing himself, posits the external world and, also by an equally pure act of thought, posits other subjects. This positing is highly conceptual: it is an *a priori* deduction from the self, "an immanent and irrepressible mode of behavior."[37] Moreover, it does not depend on facts for it "is not bound at all to the empirical perception of this or that individual."[38]

Farther on, Del Vecchio acknowledged a real relation to the empirical: "Of course, it is phenomenal experience which provides the matter

---

35. Ibid., Part III, chap. 3, "Concrete Relations with Others." Sartre described a person's two basic attitudes: "First Attitude Toward Others: Love, Language, Masochism," pp. 364–79; "Second Attitude Toward Others: Indifference, Desire, Hate, Sadism," pp. 379–412.

36. Idem, from the play, *Huis Clos* (Paris: Gallimard, 1947), p. 62.

37. Del Vecchio, *Justice*, p. 78.   38. Ibid., p. 79.

to be subsumed into the *a priori* forms of the spirit, which in fact manifest themselves *in concreto* only in their application to objects of the external world and to other subjects."[39] This conceptualism comes unexpectedly from one who was a master in both law and history, two disciplines where singular events and concrete facts are indispensable. Indeed, so taken up with the conceptual was Del Vecchio that he made no adequate provision for value. He asserted that this mode of consciousness or behavior encompasses practical as well as theoretical values, but he did so cursorily: "Psychologically, it proclaims itself in us not only as an *idea* but as an imperious and irrepressible *sentiment*."[40] True but hardly adequate. We, however, have already seen that the underlying basis for this conclusion rests in the general concomitance of insight and feeling.

In short, Del Vecchio had clearly taken a jurisprudential turn to the subject; he is a profound and erudite witness to the unfolding of the experience of justice. Nevertheless, I find him constrained by his Neo-Kantianism and even verging on innate ideas and a return to rationalism. Almost forty years after his book *Justice* and some six years before his death, Del Vecchio could still write: "This idea [of justice] is a real category (*a priori*) of the mind and is not undetermined or undeterminable, as some have claimed; rightly understood, it contains precise prescriptions for all intersubjective or social relations."[41]

This ambitious formulation helps us assess the contribution of Del Vecchio. He did recognize the central role of the subject, but not the full importance of the existential subject. Empirical facts and concrete values were unfortunately relegated to second-class status in his theory of justice through "an oversight of insight." Though deeply concerned with subjectivity, he never moved philosophically from the realm of theory to the realm of interiority. For him, subjectivity and intersubjectivity always remained abstract concepts. Nevertheless, Del Vecchio's understanding and formulations highlighted profoundly the key role of the subject in jurisprudence.

---

39. Ibid., p. 80.   40. Ibid.

41. Idem, *Man and Nature: Selected Essays,* trans. A. H. Campbell (Notre Dame, Ind.: Notre Dame University Press, 1969), pp. 27–28. This essay was written in 1962; his book *Justice* was first published in 1924. See also his discussion on this point and his conclusion in *The Philosophy of Law,* trans. T. O. Martin from 8th ed. (Washington: The Catholic University of America Press, 1953), p. 255: "The logical form of Law is a datum which is *a priori*, that is, not empirical and it constitutes precisely the condition-limit of juridical experience in general."

Intersubjectivity does not rest exclusively on the elaborate articulations of Neo-Kantian metaphysics. Indeed, we may find this prime social fact more accessible through the door of conscious intentionality, where the grasp of subjectivity in oneself and in others has an empirical basis. As we have seen, consciousness is intrinsic to our actions, but many of our actions are interactions; these interactions with others, whether spontaneous or deliberate, supply the data of intersubjectivity.

We are literally born into an ongoing intersubjective situation; our involvements with nutrition and health, language and education, norms and rituals, culture and religion, work and play, the pursuit of truth and beauty, the need to love and be loved—all expose us to the immediacy of intersubjectivity. The purity of our awareness may be blurred by biases; it may never be fully thematized; but, given the reality of ordinary living, we spontaneously understand and affirm a human commonality.

The response to intersubjective data through understanding, judging, and deciding enables us to know the fact of intersubjectivity and to act in harmony with that knowledge. Moving into the Isosphere involves sublating what has been realized in the Monosphere and applying it to a plurality of subjects; we bring personal integrity to bear on social interaction. Thus beginning with empirical data, our mental operations establish the bond of intersubjectivity, from which emerges the idea of justice.

III. THE AESTHETIC BALANCE

Plato, as we have seen, considered "the beauty of laws and institutions" to be an indispensable stage in the ascent of the mind to the sublimity of beauty. An appreciation of the beauty of justice is, therefore, necessary to that ascent, for if justice holds no beauty for us, laws and institutions will also appear empty and ugly.

Without losing ourselves in the complexities of aesthetics, we can profitably apply to justice the no-nonsense aphorism about beauty taken from the English sculptor and social philosopher Eric Gill, who wrote: "Look after truth and goodness, and beauty will take care of herself."[42] Translating that advice into terms more appropriate to law,

---

42. Eric Gill, *Beauty Looks After Herself* (New York: Sheed and Ward, 1933), p. 245.

we may say: look after meaning and value, and the beauty of justice will take care of itself. Or, more technically: look after rational consciousness and rational self-consciousness, and the inner experience of law will take care of itself.

Approaching beauty as a byproduct makes good sense in legal matters, where it would be monstrous for anyone to aim at aesthetic symmetry and let the merits of the case fall by the wayside. As a matter of historical fact, of course, in philosophy, science, and law, symmetry has often proved to be a fruitful source of insights; but law in action is more than knowing, it requires responsible decision making. The ancients distinguished art and prudence, skill in making beautiful things and skill in doing virtuous acts. But they recognized, too, that virtue had its own beauty, transcending the world of artifacts.

Beauty, in Santayana's phrase, is "pleasure objectified."[43] Thus when the Psalmist rejoiced: "How good and pleasing it is when brethren dwell together as one" (Ps. 133:1), what touched his heart and moved it to song was not just the working out of problems of social interaction, but the loveliness of human bonding.

This same beauty is possible on a global scale as well. Dante, who wrote both political tracts and epic poetry, envisaged the unity of the human race in a world ruled by justice. In his *Monarchia* he described the idea of *jus* or right in aesthetic terms as: *Hominis ad hominem proportio* ("The proportion of man to man").[44] Since man is sacred, as Dante certainly believed, then this proportion, which Dante sought, would indeed shine forth with supernal beauty. Note too how the vision of beauty is shattered by the Hobbesian perspective: *Homo homini lupus* ("Man is a wolf to man").[45] Yet Hobbes too had his dream; above all, he wanted a political community, where through the absolute power of the "mortal god," the state, there would be peace, allowing beauty to shed at least a dim and flickering light.

At its core, the beauty of justice is subjectivity writ large. In the *Republic,* Plato tried to determine what is justice for the individual by turning, as we have seen, to the political community, where justice,

---

43. George Santayana, *The Sense of Beauty* (New York: Scribner's 1936), p. 41.

44. Dante Alighieri, *Monarchia,* L, II, Cap. V, I: "Jus est realis ac personalis hominis ad hominem proportio, quae servata societatem servat, corrupta corrumpit."

45. Hobbes, *The English Works of Thomas Hobbes,* ed. W. Molesworth (London: John Bohn, 1841), vol. II, p. 11.

being magnified, might more easily be analyzed. This procedure may not simply have been a literary device to facilitate a study of the *polis*. Plato may well have been suggesting that it is in community that we learn not only how to treat others but how to understand ourselves, for we need intersubjectivity in order to be fully and knowledgeably human.

But Plato aside, we naturally find true intersubjectivity to be emotionally and intellectually pleasing. Justice, realized in the concrete, manifests an essential element of beauty—unity amid variety, complementing philosophy's concern with the one and the many. Consider, for example, the timeworn patriotic phrase, "one nation indivisible with liberty and justice for all." Here are individuals, groups, communities, cities, territories, states—a multitude of different persons politically unified. And this social artifact can evoke one's deepest feelings, including the willingness to die for what it signifies. Should patriotism wane, as it often does, intersubjectivity bonded by justice still reveals its strength and beauty abundantly—in marriage and the family, in local communities, in institutions, professions, and churches. Even the *ad hoc* fleeting unity of a protest or demonstration, of a charity fund-raiser, a flood emergency, a prayer meeting, may evince a sense of human solidarity, and on occasion a real experience of the beauty of justice. But we must be especially in awe when we contemplate the steady stream of decisions that flow unceasingly from our courts. With all the inefficiencies, venalities, and outright injustices, the legal institution remains a great and beautiful achievement in the history of mankind's continuing hunger and thirst after justice.

Since justice operates in a world where interests are in conflict, its beauty has many flaws. Universal justice would not remove all conflicts; it would rather handle them according to right reason. Even then, tensions would still remain. Tension is not necessarily something bad, suggesting undue stress or a personal cold war. Legitimate tensions are intrinsic to all levels of existence. In the legal and political arena, for example, they exist between authority and autonomy, majority and minority, common good and personal good, law and equity, justice and mercy, church and state, men and women. We all live in what Voegelin called the Metaxy (*metaxu*), the "In-between." He rightly censured the utopian mentality that tries to improve life by denying its polarities. We do not resolve the struggles between men and women by a unisex compromise; nor do we remove majority-minority differences by a demand for unanimous decision making or a dictatorship.

Tensions result necessarily from the fact that our Eros can move each one of us divergently. Take an example from criminal law: we want the police to protect us against criminals, but we also want the courts to protect us against the police. The Fourth Amendment is a guide to balance the justifiable right to intrude and the reasonable expectation of privacy; but neither the police nor the citizens are entirely happy with the results of the compromise. Such tensions, necessary though they are, are apt to befog the vision of beauty, which is already disfigured by the evils of a less than ideal world. If we are discouraged at this lack of fulfillment, it may be because our hopes are unrealistic. We forget that, in Goethe's words, "beauty is a promise, not a performance." A glimpse of the beauty of justice is already possible without having experienced apocalyptic perfection. But we have to look perceptively with open minds.

CONCLUSION

Justice is rooted in the existential subject. When it functions in a political community, it does not lose its essential bilaterality, its subject-to-subject orientation. One who is truly just not only does right actions for the right motives, but accepts the standard of justice as a dominant value in all social interactions. This commitment to value that constitutes the just man and woman rests on a vision of human dignity and equality. The just have a way of looking at the world that differs radically from that of the unjust. In a word, it is respect, respect for the world, respect for one another.

The depth and intensity of this emergent respect reveals the compelling beauty of justice as the well-proportioned and mutually harmonious ordering of conscious persons. To appreciate its splendor, we must be aware of the legal subjects achieving that order, the bond of intersubjectivity uniting them, and the conduct bringing that linkage to fulfillment. Justice is both recognition and attribution; it knows and it does—a blend of rational consciousness and rational self-consciousness, whereby knowing and doing complement one another with genuine consistency in personal interactions.

Symbolically, grasping the beauty of justice is more like appreciating a ballet than a statue, for it is dynamic, not static. Indeed, it is more like dancing with someone than watching someone dance; it is an enlightened sharing, a consciousness of reciprocity. The vision is not extinguished by human failures; nor is it measured by the sum total of conflict resolutions; it is far greater than that; it is the creative bonding of all persons in the unity of the spirit. In the words of the Psalmist: "Justice and peace have kissed" (Ps. 85:10). The traditional "kiss of peace," the Pax, reflects the intimate joy that is born of justice and love. Augustine linked these two sources: *Justitia—amor soli amato serviens*, "Justice is love serving only the beloved."[46]

46. Augustine, *De moribus ecclesiae catholicae et de moribus Manichaeorum*, I.15, 125 (Migne, *Patrologia latina*, 32:1322).

CHAPTER 5

RIGHTS: THE CLAIMS OF INTERSUBJECTIVITY

*If the act of justice is to give to each man his due, then the act of justice is preceded by the act whereby something becomes his due.—Thomas Aquinas**

Justice forges the bond of intersubjectivity; rights declare its claims. The terms are correlative: a person cannot be just without granting another his rights; a person claiming rights demands that another act justly. But a right is not simply justice turned inside out. In addition to what we have already discussed about justice, there remain questions specifically concerned with rights: What are the alternative approaches to rights? What are the inner experiences of the possessor of a right? What is the crucial function of participated value in the rights arena? Only by trying to answer these questions can we fully incorporate rights into a jurisprudence of subjectivity.

I. THE ALTERNATIVE APPROACHES

Underlying justice and rights is a basic conflict situation: interaction-claim-decision in a world of limited resources. Each participant in the interaction is driven by Eros toward concrete goods; competition over these goods arises whenever scarcity enters into the calculations—a usual occurrence. Most material goods cannot be shared indefinitely without depleting the supply, population and resources being inversely proportional; even intellectual and spiritual goods may have a material and thus exhaustible context. For example, ideas can be shared by all with no loss to anyone, but schools, teachers, libraries do have drastic time-place, cost-benefit, logistical limits. Scarcity makes the rights issue

unlimited wants or limited resources [handwritten margin note]

* Thomas Aquinas, *Summa contra gentiles*, Bk. II, ch. 28.

critical, since it fosters zero-sum competition, a situation aggravated by the prevailing adversary system of law. Consequently, a clear understanding of the jural relationship is necessary if we are to grasp what rights involve and what governs allocations of goods and restrictions on liberty.

The conflict over competing claims can be resolved in two fundamentally different ways: by an appeal to reason or by recourse to some non-rational expedient; in other words, by trying to discover principles that, looked at objectively, can convince reasonable minds, or by bypassing reasonableness for the short-term effectiveness of force, stealth, deception, or breach of contract.

The civilized consensus, despite flagrant institutionalized violations, is that reason should establish the norms of conflict settlement. Positivists, too, although they rely ultimately on power, recognize the entropic character of its mindless use; both Holmes and Kelsen look to a rule of law, and, although they envisage law as a coercive order of human behavior, they do not subscribe to the unqualified principle that might makes right. Reason, however, for positivists plays a subordinate role, giving form rather than content.

Reason, as a norm for ordering actions in terms of content, can work from the perspective of either rational self-interest or conscious intersubjectivity. Looking first at rational self-interest, we find its basic weakness in that each party by definition considers his own good paramount and uses others for his own advantage. In the last analysis, he treats the other party as a being *propter alium*, but treats him reasonably, for he depends on him for his own well-being.

Rational self-interest is usually an unstable basis for one-to-one relationships, where the inequalities may be more obvious, the conflicts more personal, and the safeguards less strong. On the communal level, however, with greater protections owing to institutional pressures and a shared though selfish concern for the common good, there may be more balanced stability. Social-good theories, such as Utilitarianism, Sociological Jurisprudence, and the Rawlsian theory of justice illustrate with mixed success attempts to give a rational justification for human rights based on self-interest.

Intersubjectivity, on the other hand, goes beyond the egoistic biases of individual and group self-interest and looks to a recognition of the equal and reciprocal status of the subject as a being *propter se,* with his own human dignity and destiny. Where rational egoism sees mutuality of interests, intersubjectivity perceives a fellowship of persons. Intersubjectivity transcends self-centeredness through a more profound appreciation of human equality; it acknowledges human interdependence, not as an exclusive determinant of norms but as a necessary condition for mutual flourishing. In short, the difference between the two perspectives, rational self-interest and conscious intersubjectivity, is the difference between the diminished subject and the transcendent one.

II. THE JURAL RELATIONSHIP

In examining the jural relationship from the perspective of intersubjectivity, I shall look briefly at a concrete area of human rights as illustrative of the need to harmonize conduct and interest—the core of the jural relationship. Justice William O. Douglas often spoke of the Constitution as a means of keeping the Government off the backs of the people.[1] The Fourth Amendment is a helpful example. It reads: "The right of the people to be secure in their persons, houses, papers, and effects, against unreasonable searches and seizures, shall not be violated, and no warrants shall issue, but upon probable cause, supported by oath or affirmation, and particularly describing the place to be searched and the persons or things to be seized."

The Fourth Amendment, however, only points to an ideal; it does not work out the concrete details; these are the work of the legislature and the courts. In balancing individual and community interests, the Fourth Amendment relies generally on a standard of reasonableness but more concretely on warrants, oaths, probable cause, particularity. The cases deal with issues such as arrest, stop and frisk, expectations of privacy, search and seizure, bodily examinations, warrants and exceptions to the warrant rule, wiretapping and electronic surveillance, as well as standing and motions to challenge the admissibility of evidence.

This last item involves the so-called "exclusionary rule," by which, in the words of Justice Cardozo, then a New York appellate judge: "The criminal is to go free because the constable has blundered."[2] The Warren Court, in *Mapp v. Ohio* (1961), began the "criminal law

1. William O. Douglas, *The Court Years: 1939–1975* (New York: Vintage Books, 1981), p. 383.
2. Benjamin N. Cardozo, in *People v. Defore*, 242 N.Y. 13, 21 (1926).

revolution" by using the Fourteenth Amendment to apply this Fourth Amendment "exclusionary rule" to the states.[3]

Since many murderers, rapists, robbers, burglars, and spies have benefited from this rule, there has been a sharp split in the community's perception of the proper balance of interests. Accordingly, Herbert Packer distinguished two current models of the criminal process, which may afford an insight into the conduct-interest relation found not only in criminal law but in all cases involving rights.

Packer contrasted the crime control model with the due process model: the first operates like an assembly line and emphasizes the right of the community and the police to take action in protecting societal interests against criminal conduct; the second operates like an obstacle course and emphasizes the rights of the suspected criminal in protecting his interests from unconstitutional conduct by police and judges.[4] What complicates the interaction is that suspects, police, and judges have interests, perform actions, and have rights and duties. Moreover, in the larger context, the whole community has interests and the right to protect them. Suspects, of course, are part of that community; to deprive them of their rights indirectly makes all citizens vulnerable.

Putting together the various components gives us the following formulation: *A right is a relationship between the conduct of one subject and the interests of another, protected by law and grounded in equality.*[5] Clearly, a right is not a thing, or even an interest in a thing, though it is frequently defined as an interest protected by law; this shorthand expression targets a critical issue—the interests the law does in fact protect—but it takes the issue out of context. A right is not the parcel of land or the high-school education; it is not my interest in land or education; it is not another's conduct in respect to land or education. A right is a relationship between another's conduct and my interest in the land or education. I say interest, because that term refers to a desire, demand, or claim for things (boats, stamps) or actions (voting, mar-

---

3. *Mapp v. Ohio*, 367 U.S. 643 (1961).

4. Herbert L. Packer, *The Limits of the Criminal Sanction* (Stanford: Stanford University Press, 1968), ch. 8, especially p. 163.

5. Ludovicus Bender, O.P., developed a definition of *ius* as a relationship between person and operation based in equality, though it needed further development: "Ius est relatio inter personam et operationem vel ommisionem alterius, qua haec persona se habet ad hanc operationem vel omissionem tamquam ad rem sibi debitam ex fine formaliter sumpto ad aequalitatem." *Philosophia Iuris,* 2d ed. (Rome: Officium Libri Catholici, 1955), p. 67.

rying someone of another race); and I say conduct because that term includes positive and negative action, commission and omission.[6]

The common notion of a right as an interest protected by law works well enough in practice as long as it does not serve as a principle. Indeed, in practice right is usually formulated as a *two-termed* relationship; that is, a relationship between a person and a thing (or action): I have a right to an automobile (or I have a right to practice medicine). Hohfeld analyzed right as essentially *three-termed,* a person-action-person relationship.[7] This step is important because it recognizes bilaterality and focuses on action. And action is the subject matter of law, for the law operates by commanding, forbidding, permitting, or punishing actions. Even *in rem* proceedings (against property itself) control human actions.

What Hohfeld leaves out is what the popular notion of right never forgets: the role of interests. So an adequate notion of right must be *four-termed;* that is, person-interest-action-person; that is, two persons in conflict over the relation between the interests of one and the conduct of the other. It leaves us with the task of harmonizing interests and conduct through the principled determination of a shared value (we shall examine the key notion of shared value later in this chapter).

It might be possible to reduce the complexity by overlooking the parties and concentrating on the harmonization of conduct and interest. To do so, however, would be to fall into the formalistic trap of envisaging rights without claimants, justice without just men and women, as if the jural relationship were a mechanistic calculus—a perspective suitable only for diminished subjects. Again, in John Noonan's imagery, it would be putting masks on persons, that is, "classifying human beings so that their humanity is hidden and disavowed."[8]

Only from the viewpoint of subjectivity can the jural relationship be

6. Charles Fried, in *Right and Wrong* (Cambridge: Harvard University Press, 1978), spoke of one first order positive right as "a right to a fair share" (p. 82), of negative rights as "a constraint upon the pursuit of fair shares" (p. 215), and of a general negative right as "a right to be let alone" (p. 132).

7. W. N. Hohfeld's jural relations as *jural* imply the idea of right; in terms of Anglo-American law, however, Hohfeld gave right a more limited definition in his *Fundamental Legal Conceptions,* ed. W. W. Cook (New Haven: Yale University Press, 1966), pp. 36–38. John Finnis rightly valued this more correct formulation, but did not take fully into account the distinction between actions and interests and its effect on the notion of rights; see his splendid *Natural Law and Natural Rights* (Oxford: Clarendon Press, 1980), pp. 199–204.

8. John T. Noonan, Jr., *Persons and Masks of the Law* (New York: Farrar, Straus and Giroux, 1976), p. 19.

fully intelligible: two subjects moved by Eros to apparent goods, who are in conflict unless their conduct and interests become reasonably commensurate through mutual participation in a common value.

Rights rest on the existential character of legal subjects. These subjects are found in a state of being and becoming, possessing both existence and the potentiality for change. More personally, they have human dignity and human destiny; that is, they are worthwhile in themselves and they can perfect themselves through their actions. Without the freedom to act, they cannot reach fulfillment; that is why H. L. A. Hart said that "if there are any moral rights at all, it follows that there is at least one natural right, the equal right of all men to be free."[9]

But liberty can be exercised only in a suitable context, one with adequate base values: *resources* such as food, clothing, shelter, tools, books; other *persons,* with whom to interact; and finally *institutions* for the shaping and sharing of values.[10] Freedom without resources, persons, and institutions would be that of a sailor marooned on a barren rock and left to starve, free only in thoughts and in futile actions.

To speak meaningfully of justice and rights, we must include freedom as a basic human interest. Liberty is in possession, and law must be justified; but the first limitation on individual liberty is the equal liberty of others.[11] Rights are the fruit of the tension between liberty and equality. Indeed, the very law that limits liberty also protects rights as it justly balances interests and conduct.

The legal protection component in the notion of rights lifts the relationship between conduct and interests to the level of a duty. Von Jhering considered this definitional insight crucial to his jurisprudence.[12] As a Social Utilitarian influenced by Bentham's theory of interests and by Austin's analytic and imperative approach, he was in turn to contribute to Pound's Sociological Jurisprudence. As a result, the

9. H. L. A. Hart, "Are There Any Natural Rights?" *The Philosophical Review* 64 (1955): 175.

10. H. Lasswell and M. McDougal so classified base values—used to achieve scope values or objectives—as a structural part of their goal-oriented jurisprudence, Law, Science, and Policy. See analysis by David Granfield in "Towards a Goal-oriented Consensus," *Journal of Legal Education* 19 (1967): 379–402.

11. See David Granfield, *The Abortion Decision* (Garden City: N.Y.: Doubleday, 1969), pp. 140–44, for a discussion of the relation of law and liberty.

12. Rudolf von Jhering, *Law as a Means to an End,* trans. I. Husik, Modern Legal Philosophy Series, vol. 5 (Boston: The Boston Book Co., 1914), preface, p. iii.

limited view of a right as an interest protected by law was widespread among thinkers in the first half of the twentieth century and is still common today. Llewellyn's formulation is typical: "Statements of 'rights' would be statements of likelihood that in a given situation a certain type of court action loomed in the offing."[13]

The notion of rights pruned of moral overtones was most congenial to Sociological Jurists and Legal Realists, who were largely positivistic. Indeed, H. L. A. Hart stated that the main characteristic of positivism was this separation of law and morals.[14] Rights, however, even as an interest protected by law, need not be construed so narrowly. Law is an analogous concept, applicable to many spheres of activity. A claim of right is an appeal for protection to whatever laws—not just positive laws—cover the event, although the sanctions may differ in character and predictability, and indeed may be cumulative. One may dispute the existence of a given law or legal system, but the notion of rights involves some law or legal system—at least one, usually more than one.

A right, moreover, is not only protected by law, it is grounded in equality. In examining justice, we noted the role of intersubjectivity, with its bond of proportionate equality; in discussing rights, we look at this same factor, but from the perspective of the claimant, for if justice is rooted in equality, so are rights.

Certain insights about equality from Aristotle's *Politics* may prove especially revealing, if in reading them we keep our mind on rights. Aristotle, however, did not understand rights as we do; he spoke more concretely of "the right thing," which is the object of justice; nevertheless, his observations are still able to shed light on the jural relationship as we understand it today. I shall mention briefly five points.

First, equality has a radical role in constituting justice. "Justice is a sort of equality,"[15] that is, "what is just or right is to be interpreted in the sense of what is equal."[16] Note that the Greek more closely connects justice (*dikaiosune*) and right (*to dikaion*) than does English. A right is a just thing; a right is understood as the object of a just man's actions.

Second, the principle of justice is to treat equals equally and to treat

13. Karl Llewellyn, "A Realistic Jurisprudence—The Next Step," *Columbia Law Review* 30 (1930): 431.

14. H. L. A. Hart, *The Concept of Law* (Oxford: Clarendon Press, 1961), pp. 181–82, and 253 note.

15. Aristotle, *Politics*, 1282 b18.   16. Ibid., 1283 b40.

unequals unequally. This is not a justification of unfairness but a recognition of difference. The key is proportionate equality, a political necessity. "Equality consists in the same treatment of similar persons and no government can stand which is not founded on justice."[17]

Third, the dynamism surrounding equality is historically evident: "Inferiors revolt that they may be equals and equals that they may be superior."[18] Eros, the daimon in each person, moves him to greater and greater fulfillment. Equality achieved becomes superiority craved. Rights delineate the boundaries of this dynamic escalation.

Fourth, a twofold fallacy often results from the thrust toward equality. "Some think that if they are equal in any respect, they are equal absolutely; others that if they are unequal in any respect, they should be unequal in all."[19] Aristotle added that governments that are based on these attitudes, democracy and oligarchy, are perversions of justice; we should carefully note, however, that he is speaking of common denominator egalitarianism and vested-interest elitism. His ideal is proportionate equality, which would be found in a constitutional democracy.

Fifth, the standard for equality is problematic: "But there still remains a question: equality or inequality of what? Here is a difficulty which calls for political speculation."[20] The problem is not yet resolved in current controversies over human and civil rights. Aristotle failed to ground equality in human dignity and destiny; nevertheless, he did articulate its basic implications, however grounded.

To summarize in one sentence these observations of Aristotle, we would say: (1) Equality is a necessary basis for justice and rights, (2) for all should have proportionately the same treatment, (3) although conflicts inevitably arise due to the drive for upward mobility, (4) especially through a fallacious attempt to get an unfair advantage from equality or inequality, (5) all of the above being operative whatever the ultimate standard.

At present there is a growing emphasis upon what people have in common rather than upon how they differ individually, on non-discrimination rather than on merited privilege, on social mobility rather than on rigid stratification. These developments, however, are frequently skewed by a lack of emphasis on duties and by a reliance on

---

17. Ibid., 1332 b27–29.
18. Ibid., 1302 a29–30.
19. Ibid., 1301 b37–39.
20. Ibid., 1282 b21–22.

the fallacious premise of egalitarianism—a simplistic but dangerous answer to the question of standards.

Understandably, when confronted with *de facto* oligarchies of wealth, power, and rank, people often react with an overcompensating swing of the social pendulum. But fallacies are not the answer to fallacies. Egalitarianism, in rejecting proportionate equality, radically distorts the jural relationship among members of the community by falsifying the relevant facts. For individuals do differ in manifold ways—in intelligence, skill, virtue, motivation, industry, strength, and health. Having basic human dignity and being politically equal does not obliterate those differences and their consequences.

Egalitarianism is self-defeating. Theoretically, it may aspire to lift everyone to the same status; actually, it is a social leveling to the lowest common denominator. And it is as old as envy. Heraclitus, writing in about 500 B.C., reacted bitterly against the stupidity of egalitarian injustice: "The Ephesians had better go hang themselves, every man of them, and leave their city to be governed by youngsters, for they have banished Hermadorus, the finest man among them, declaring: 'Let us not have anyone among us who excels the rest; if there should be such a one let him go and live elsewhere.' "[21] More recently, Caspar W. Weinberger, when Secretary of Health, Education, and Welfare, concerned over the loss of freedom in an expanding welfare state, insisted: "Equal opportunity means the right to compete equally for the rewards of excellence, not to share its fruits regardless of effort."[22] He did not, however, overlook human need: "Of course, we must protect and help the most vulnerable members of society, but if we do not persevere in the quest for excellence, then our reward will be a death of excellence."[23]

III. THE PERSONAL RESPONSE

After considering the notion of a right theoretically, we are in a position to examine it subjectively, to experience it from within. It is crucial, first of all, to distinguish the experience of right from that of justice. The just person in social interaction must make sure that his acts or omissions are compatible with another's legitimate interests.

21. Quoted by Strabo, XIV, 25.
22. Casper W. Weinberger, "My Turn: On Losing our Freedom," *Newsweek,* August 18, 1975, p. 11.
23. Ibid.

He fulfills a duty; whether it is pleasant or burdensome, he is not free, ethically or legally, to act otherwise; he must, where proper, conform his conduct to the interests of others.

The possessor of rights stands in a very different position; he does not suffer the constraints of the just person. Where the just person has an obligation, the rights-claimant has freedom; where the just person is compelled, the rights-claimant is empowered. Two values, then, make rights desirable: freedom and power. The possessor of a right, to the extent of its coverage, is free to do what he wants and can also oblige others do what he wants. To have a right is to have one's special interest positively fostered or at least protected from interference.

[margin note: 2 values which make rights desirable]

Clearly, rights are not experienced only by victims. We speak also of royal rights and privileges, the rights of multinational corporations, the rights implicit in the doctrine of *laissez faire*. Rights may connote a vibrant freedom and power far removed from the vulnerability of a soul crying for the redress of wrongs. Nevertheless, because so many moral claims arising out of exploitation have attained, after a long power struggle, the status of legally protected interests, we still think of "civil rights" as the rallying cry of the downtrodden.[24]

To speak of rights, however, whether of the establishment or of the oppressed, exclusively in terms of power and liberty, is to confine rights in terms of the *libido dominandi* to the realm of the impoverished subject. The aspect of free control is present in all rights, but is hardly their full flowering.

Hobbes, as we have seen, formulated this limited notion most memorably; he envisaged a winner-take-all struggle between law and liberty, with rights existing only when the law is silent. For him the "right of nature," a description of Eros untrammeled, is constrained by the "laws of nature," prudential decisions to ensure security. Indeed, the cause of security makes every individual expendable. The sovereign or the government alone possesses the full complement of rights, the subjects retaining only those portions of the "right of nature" that the political organization allows to filter through to them. To that extent only are their interests protected by law. This way of conceptualizing rights, however, programs an adversarial legal structure attuned to positivism but not fully consonant with the exigencies of the existential subject. Nevertheless, there is the widespread assumption that rights

24. See Horace, Sat., i, 3. III: *Iura inventa metu injusti fateare necesse est.*

are best understood in terms of the lust for power. The result is a built-in bias that distorts the administration of justice.

For an appreciation of what a more profound notion of rights entails, it is helpful to survey briefly the historically changing content of the ends of law. Roscoe Pound sketched out the major phases, which we shall consider from the point of view of rights.[25] In primitive society, Pound wrote, the paramount end was keeping the peace, with a basic right against aggression providing for the security of the citizens. Every society requires this minimal public order.

More developed societies also have as an end the preservation of the *status quo,* the precarious balance that constitutes the social structure. The *Bhagavad Gita* spoke of a person's becoming perfect only if he devotes himself to the work that is natural to him.[26] For the Hindus, the caste system institutionalized these role differentiations. This two-stage development was also evident in Classical Greece and Rome and again in Europe during the Middle Ages, culminating in the stable complement of reciprocal rights and duties called feudalism.

With the Renaissance, a new spirit emerged, emphasizing individual freedom and equality protected by a theory of natural rights. Economic change, religious fragmentation, devastating plagues, and new methods of warfare had undermined the old order; the feudal lords were over-come by national kings; there was a renewed interest in classical phi-losophy, in art and technology, in trade and exploration. The resulting sense of unleashed potentialities and expanding horizons had its impact on the notion of rights, which was now cloaked with the mystique of personal power.

Suarez and Grotius in the seventeenth century established the new perspective: Suarez defined a right as "a kind of moral power which every man has over his own property or with respect to that which is due him."[27] Grotius, derivatively, called a right "a moral quality of the person enabling him to have or to do something justly."[28] The end of the law now became free and individual self-assertion. Inspired by the idea of natural rights and equal opportunity, the political myth envis-

25. Roscoe Pound, *An Introduction to the Philosophy of Law* (New Haven: Yale University Press, 1954), ch. 2, esp. pp. 33–47.

26. *Bhagavad Gita,* ch. 18.

27. Francisco Suarez, *Tractatus de legibus ac Deo legislatore* (Venice: Coletus, 1740), I, ii, 5.

28. Hugo Grotius, *De jure belli ac pacis,* trans. F. W. Kelsey, Classics of Interna-tional Law, vol. 3 (Oxford: Oxford University Press, 1925), I, I, iii.

aged a *laissez-faire* interaction guided by an "invisible hand": if the people are free to will their conscious goals, society too will inevitably flourish.[29]

This libertarian policy flourished from the seventeenth century to the end of the nineteenth, when a fourth and new understanding of the end of law emerged, one that would eventually prove very significant for a theory of rights. Pound spoke of a shift from the harmonization of wills to the satisfaction of wants, the core of his new jurisprudence:

I am content to think of law as a social institution to satisfy social wants—the claims and demands and expectations involved in the existence of civilized society—by giving effect to as much as we may with the least sacrifice, so far as such wants may be satisfied or such claims given effect by an ordering of human conduct through politically organized society.[30]

With Pound, as with many of his fellow jurists, there began a retrieval of the older relational idea of right—relational in that both parties are related not just to one another but—and this is often overlooked—to a just thing (*ius* or *to dikaion*), the one party to claim it, the other party to provide it—without going back to the stratified status of pre-Renaissance societies. Also at this time, states started first to limit then to move beyond the freewheeling libertarianism that long impeded the full realization of justice.

It is not surprising that Pound noted: "Difficulties arise chiefly in connection with the criteria of value."[31] He tried unsuccessfully to resolve the problem by a more or less neutral focus on interests and the need of harmonizing them for the greatest good to the greatest number with the minimum of friction and waste. His philosophic base was the pragmatic philosophy of William James: since every *de facto* claim sets up an obligation,[32] we should satisfy every claim as it makes for the best whole.[33] Nevertheless, these two principles do little more than give a direction; they are hardly an adequate ethical or legal foundation.

This is not the place to discuss Pound's utilitarian ethics, his analytic

29. Adam Smith's full remark is: "Every individual intends only his own gain, and he is in this, as in so many other cases, led by an invisible hand to promote an end which was no part of his intention," in *Wealth of Nations,* ed. E. Cannan (New York: G. P. Putnam's Sons, 1904), Vol. I, 421.

30. R. Pound, *Introduction,* p. 47.   31. Ibid., p. 45.

32. Cf. William James, *The Will To Believe and Other Essays in Popular Philosophy* (New York: Longmans, Green, 1917), p. 194.

33. See ibid., p. 204.

mentality, his positivistic philosophy. What is important is his clear-sighted perception of the need of fundamental change in the process of shaping and sharing values. Unfortunately, the very adversarial structure of the legal process has impeded the theoretical and practical working out of the relational dimension of rights. For full clarification, what was needed was the added light that would radiate from a grasp of authentic subjectivity.

In scrutinizing rights from a subjective viewpoint, we necessarily include the mental operations that constitute the relationship between the conduct and interests of the subjects. We have seen already the need to move beyond the popular two-termed relation of person and thing and even beyond the Hohfeldian three-termed relation of person, action, and person, to a four-termed relation of person, conduct, interest, and person. Lest the latter relation seem like a proliferation of entities, we recall that for rights, the conduct of one person is specified by the interest of the other. Even so, a problem remains, for the desired harmony or commensuration between conduct and interests appears to be elusive because of the very difference that exists between the two. Are we really comparing things of the same class? In order to answer this question satisfactorily, we must study the interaction more deeply.

Underlying the conduct-interest aspects of the jural relationship, there is a decision-making process at work: we are comparing two decisions, each based on a separate value judgment about the same situation—judgments based on data, understood and verified. Ideally, if both parties are adequately and equally informed, intelligent, and good-willed, they will approximate a harmony in their decisions, a true commensuration.

Unfortunately, not all conflict situations are so readily resolved, even between the wise and the virtuous. Pertinent laws—divine, natural, positive—help in the determination, but not all laws are clear in themselves or in their application. Moreover, the relevant data may be incomplete, ambiguous, or disputed. Nevertheless, the subject matter to be balanced is clear: two judgments of value—involving persons, their actions, and their interests—culminating in responsible decision-making.

The idea of harmonizing value judgments might not seem to cover a situation where no judgment at all is made by the party whose rights are in jeopardy, for example, a fetus, an infant, a retarded, insane, or comatose person, or even an absent one. Since, however, justice and right are correlatives, implying one another, rights may be substantially preserved when one person tries to judge the situation as justly as the other would, if able. Usually, however, no one else appreciates and weighs our own interests as perceptively and as conscientiously as we do ourselves, so there is a need to hear the rights-claimant, if at all possible; an *ex parte* judgment may not quite measure up. Hence the practice of appointing a guardian *ad litem* to protect an incompetent's interests, even though he may not be a litigant, as in a divorce case when a child's custody is contested.

In matters of justice and right, the obvious goal is to be fair to all concerned. "That action alone is just," said Mohandas Gandhi, "which does not harm either party to a dispute."[34] The process of harmonizing value judgments aims at the discovery of a common value that the parties can share, a mutually participated value composing justice and right into an integrated whole.

IV. THE PARTICIPATED VALUE

Looking at rights from the perspective of subjectivity, we can appreciate how central the notion of participated value actually is. A brief consideration of what value means will help clarify its participated form. It should be noted at the outset, however, that value is not simply a synonym for interest, good, claim, felt need, demand, or desire— terms related to value but not constitutive of value. Value implies much more.

To appreciate the paramount role of value, we distinguish three levels of the good: the good of appetite, the good of order, and finally the good of value.[35] The first level is familiar enough; from the beginning we are all aware of appetites and inclinations, whether natural or acquired; we recognize the manifestations of eros in our lives. The second level is almost as obvious; through nemesis, we quickly learn that desires are not always fulfilled, and when fulfilled are not always good for us; we then gradually learn that there are higher orders of good, which must be taken into account: the good of the body, the whole person, the family, the group, the political society, the religious

---

34. Mohandas N. Gandhi, *The Collected Works* (Delhi: Government of India, Ministry of Information and Broadcasting, 1958 and following), XIV, p. 233.

35. See Bernard Lonergan, *Insight* (London: Longmans, Green, 1957; New York: Philosophical Library, 1958), pp. 596–98; and *Understanding and Being*, eds. E. A. and M. D. Morelli (Lewiston, N.Y.: Edwin Mellen Press, 1980), pp. 277–78.

community, the human race, the universe—to name the major ones. Note, too, that cooperation between persons, though most illustrative, is not the only kind of good of order.

Let us consider these two levels further. Clearly, a given order or system may be good or bad, sovereign or subordinate, so the fact that an order exists does not mean it is necessarily worth promoting; it too must be assessed. For example, we easily distinguish the Cosa Nostra from the Red Cross. But even in a good order, tensions are inevitable, as Holmes bluntly pointed out in *The Common Law*: "Justice to the individual is rightly outweighed by the larger interests on the other side of the scale."[36]

Interests include both the good of appetite and the good of order. Roscoe Pound gave this inclusive definition: "An interest is a demand or desire which human beings either individually or in groups seek to satisfy, of which therefore the ordering of human relations in civilized society must take account."[37] Pound followed the lead of James and considered all interests to be "self-legitimizing" but not without, in Rawls's phrase, a utilitarian "higher order administrative decision."

The precise balance, in a concrete case, between the good of appetite and the good of order is often complex and troublesome. Obviously, not all goods of appetite or goods of order are values; for example, we should not assume automatically that what is good for our taste buds is good for our bodies, or what is good for our family is good for the community. It is clear that the good of appetite should be subordinated to some kind of order, and that lesser orders should be subordinated to higher orders, preserving, of course, the role of subsidiarity.

The satisfying of desires, involving both the good of appetite and the good of order, does not by itself constitute an ethical good. Ultimately, the tension in the choice of a concrete good is resolved only by a value judgment, an authentic decision, which is the fruit of rational self-consciousness. Precisely defined, a value is a concrete good as the possible object of rational choice.[38] This decision-in-context, effecting

36. Oliver Wendell Holmes, Jr., *The Common Law* (Boston: Little, Brown, 1938), p. 48.

37. Roscoe Pound, *Outline of Lectures on Jurisprudence*, 5th ed. (Cambridge: Harvard University Press, 1942), p. 96.

38. See Bernard Lonergan, *Insight*, p. 601. To his definition from *Insight*, I have added the word "concrete" for the sake of explicitness; see his *Method in Theology*, 2nd ed. (New York: Herder and Herder, 1973), p. 36: "By the good is never meant some abstraction. Only the concrete is good."

self-fulfillment and self-transcendence, reveals an objective aspect (a concrete good) and a subjective aspect (the possible object of authentic choice); together they give us a fully dimensioned good, a value.

Moral excellence is realized in this authentic choice of value; here is the ongoing union of a human person (an originating value) with a concrete good (a terminal value); that is, the person through an inner dynamism starts to move toward the reality in which that motion, in a limited way, terminates. The good of value is a perfection of the person, precisely because it is an opening of the person to the concrete world of reality. Values expand the mind; disvalues contract it.

This intending through our eros is primary and indispensable. Lonergan described it, as we have noted earlier, in terms of transcendental notions, by which the mind is able to intend—that is, seek and recognize—the intelligible, the true and the real, and the good.[39] In so intending, we attend to our desires; we impose upon them an intelligible order; we verify this order through a judgment of value; and we effectuate that judgment through a decision to act. We properly reach the concrete good only through this ethical process of rational self-consciousness. It involves the self, not only because it stems from this inner dynamism, but also because through our decisions we are changing ourselves and our world. It is not a mere satisfaction of desires, but a perfection attained through a decision with objective and subjective components, an ethical decision that is truly normative, grounded as it is on transcendental value.[40]

39. See also Chapter Two on Eros, *supra.* The transcendental notion of value, implicitly a part of Lonergan's ethical position in *Insight,* was not made fully explicit until his lecture on "The Subject" (1968) now in *A Second Collection* (Philadelphia: Westminster Press, 1974), especially pp. 79–86, and his book, *Method in Theology* (New York: Herder and Herder, 1973), especially in the chapter on "The Human Good," pp. 27–55.

40. John Finnis, in his *Fundamentals of Ethics* (Washington: Georgetown University Press, 1983), pp. 32, 42–45, 48, 54, criticized Lonergan's ethical theory, although he acknowledged Lonergan's contribution to the analysis of the structure of human understanding. The roots of the misunderstanding are as follows: (1) Finnis did not recognize the good as always concrete; (2) he narrowly limited the good of order to interpersonal cooperation; (3) he did not realize that the good of appetite and order become fully moral only through a decision of value and that Lonergan thus avoided an "unequivocal empiricism" that bases ethics on a positivist satisfaction of desires; (4) and most fundamentally, he did not distinguish attending and intending from understanding and so could not appreciate the role of feelings or how Lonergan could preserve, as Finnis rightly held necessary, the difference between the good as experienced and the good as understood.

In the jural situation—an interaction involving conduct and inter-ests—both parties ideally make rational and responsible decisions about value. Note, too, that both parties are concerned with the same conduct-interest unit. Their preferences and existential circumstances may differ, but they can both make a mutually consonant choice in terms of some higher principle such as personal integrity, human in-tersubjectivity, political community, or divine sovereignty. Then they can begin to experience, if only in a microcosm, the unity of mankind, as they step toward the realization of one world bonded together in justice and love.

In other words, social unity requires the good of order to which the goods of appetite are subordinated. To act in harmony with the overall order is to live in essential union with the just members of that order. The justice and rights conflict is resolved when both parties agree about their proper relationship to the just thing or the right thing (the two words reflecting only the differences in viewpoint). When, through their judgments of value, they achieve this harmony, the true proportion between human subjects is achieved. This proportion is a participated value, whereby two very different human beings, on that issue at least, have perfected intersubjectivity.

In the less than ideal but more frequent cases, the subjects cannot or will not work out this bonding through their own responsible decisions; the law then steps in to adjust the relationship. "The nature of the judge," Aristotle wrote, "is to be a sort of animate justice; and they seek the judge as an intermediate, and in some states they call judges mediators on the assumption that if they get what is intermediate they will get what is just."[41]

The judge, then, makes a value judgment in which both parties can and must participate. He gives them a value to share, although it may not be the preference of both of them or either of them. The positive law does not always do a good job; it may lack the fine tuning that a mutually cooperative and responsible judgment could achieve, but, rough and fallible though it may be, it does establish order by resolving a divisive conflict. Despite problems over facts and rules, and perhaps in view of them, the judge determines the participated value that the parties and the larger community require to maintain the overarching goal of the political order.

41. Aristotle, *Nicomachean Ethics*, V, 4, 1132 a19–24.

The jural relation, thus viewed subjectively, is a mutual participation in a concrete value through the complementary decisions of partners in a intersubjective event. Ideally the level of interaction is between persons, each regarding the other as another self. Both are ethically bound to be just: one in making claims, the other in performing duties. As a consequence, power and liberty prove to be subordinate to participated value. The tension between power and liberty becomes critical only when the value is not mutually participated in, when something is claimed or refused with the *plus de bonis, minus de malis* that constitutes *pleonexia*. For justice is impaired by either party if their decisions deviate from the concrete norm of participated value.

Since the aim of justice is an enduring bond between changing human beings in changing circumstances, the jural relation must be an ongoing and flexible one. Concretely, many values are emergent probabilities, owing to the generally uncertain character of facts and rules. Nevertheless, participated value is the link consciously binding persons together in justice, persons who are fundamentally related through intersubjectivity. Even just people are not always conscious of the participated values, upon which the inner experience of justice depends. Awareness often depends on whether one personally finds the situation such that the rights issue challenges one's assumptions and one's preferences.

When an obligation dictates that we do something for another in a positive way, we are most aware of the demands of justice, all the more so if we would rather forbear than act. To act justly, we often have to transcend our private interests for the sake of a higher order good. Even when the standard of positive justice involves a liberal or distributist interpretation of what is meant by a fair share, an awareness of the participated value, perhaps acknowledged reluctantly, becomes present.

A negative obligation—involving the right to be let alone—is more or less taken for granted in civilized society by what Hume referred to as "the human party." A sense of decency and respect enjoins us to live and let live and to mind our own business. These maxims reflect a commonsense approach to human intervention, not a philosophic first principle. It is not the whole truth, but it is by and large a sound practical directive, indispensable to our cherished right to privacy. Incidentally, although some libertarians may try hard to make negative rights the exclusive principles of political society, they face the difficult task of overcoming the positive implications of intersubjectivity.

Returning, however, to the experience of negative rights already largely internalized, we find our awareness of them minimal unless we are tempted or provoked or shocked in a particular case. When dealing with others, most people are not consciously repressing the urge to lie, to cheat, to steal, to rape, or to kill. Yet, if for a moment we envisage the total absence of negative rights, we can begin to appreciate how justly in harmony with others we now are. Without the obligation to let others alone, everything would be ripe for the taking, given the opportunity and the strength. We would be back in the Hobbesian state of nature with no moral impediment to the maximizing of our own selfish interests at the expense of everyone else.

The fact that we daily respect the person and the liberty and the property of others, usually without giving it a second thought, shows us how deeply ingrained our sense of negative rights has become and how bound we are to others in the harmonious mutuality of participated values. We experience, though imperfectly, a solidarity with the rest of mankind. To advert to this experience of negative rights, to heighten our consciousness of this mutual respect, is to grasp in large measure the intersubjective bonding that is justice.

This subjective insight into rights, resting as it does on participated value, prompts the lawyer to focus his efforts on harmony rather than on power. Despite the adversary system that divisively characterizes Anglo-American law, many have begun to make provision for negotiated settlements. Instead of having the parties confront one another as warriors in a battle to the death, there is an effort to discover a common ground for agreement. Lawyers are then functioning more as "peacemakers" than as "hired guns." Not only does this approach lessen the expanding caseload of the courts, but it saves the parties the time, energy, stress, embarrassment, and expense that litigation involves. Judge Learned Hand candidly expressed an insider's view: "I should dread a law suit beyond almost anything else short of sickness and death."[42]

The very word "litigation," going back to Roman law, sets the tone of the legal interaction: it is a struggle to conquer rather than an effort

---

42. Learned Hand, *Lectures on Legal Subjects,* Association of the Bar of the City of New York (New York: Macmillan, 1926), 3:105.

to reconcile. The goal of a just interaction should be the discovery of the right thing—the *ius* or *to dikaion*—assuring fair value for both parties. Competing claims imply a victor and vanquished; a negotiated settlement looks to an intersubjective balance that is bilaterally just. Obviously such a resolution often requires some compromise and adjustment, some give and take, some mutual sacrifice for the greater good of a sound intersubjectivity.

During the last few decades there has been a great increase in litigation and more recently an emphasis on mediation, conciliation, and arbitration as complementary alternatives. Former Chief Justice Warren E. Burger, speaking to the American Bar Association in 1982, noted that civil case filings in Federal courts had increased fivefold from 1940 to 1981, creating a "litigation explosion during this generation."[43] He strongly recommended arbitration as a time-tested and relatively inexpensive means of helping lessen the burden on the courts. The move towards arbitration has been underway for some time. Most states already permit its use as an alternative to lawsuits, but both the bench and the bar, he stated, have opposed arbitration in order to preserve their vested interests. The Chief Justice, however, did not intend to displace the courts but simply to give them additional tools with which to work. He mentioned a number of areas that could be successfully dealt with administratively or by voluntary, binding arbitration: divorce, child custody, adoption, personal injury, wills, and landlord and tenant problems.

Currently, much is being written and is being done about extra-legal or para-legal conflict resolution. Lectures, articles, study groups, professional associations, civic organizations, and university projects—all are focusing on the employment of these same negotiating skills. Roger Fisher and William Ury, in a recent book, have suggested a psychological basis to explain the ground swell toward negotiation: "Everyone wants to participate in decisions that affect them; fewer and fewer people will accept decisions dictated by someone else."[44] What is fundamental to a sound negotiated settlement is the living awareness of participated value, for only on such terms are people going to agree freely.

43. Warren Burger, in a speech to the American Bar Association in 1982, *American Bar Assn. Journal* 68 (1982): 275.

44. Roger Fisher and William Ury, *Getting to Yes* (Boston: Houghton Mifflin Co., 1981), p. xi.

CONCLUSION

Since the Enlightenment—most appropriately called the Age of Absolutism—the notion of right as a moral power has afforded a philosophic justification for institutionalizing the power struggle. On the other hand, dealing with right as just and equitable, as did an earlier tradition, affords the parties the possibility of a common good, however different the initial formulations of their preferences might be. The respective task of the parties would then be not antagonistic but mutually heuristic—they would be seeking to find the value that binds them together. The legal institution and the greater political community must never lose sight of this idea of a shared value, if they aspire to realize in the concrete the perfection of justice. They must preserve the vision of intersubjectivity—two persons both trying, despite their conflict, to judge authentically about a value in which they can both share, a value grounded in proportionate equality and fulfilled in the sublimity of justice.

PART THREE

THE KOINOSPHERE
THE COMMUNAL EXPERIENCE OF LAW

The Koinosphere is the realm of citizens. The legal subject, who achieved ethical meaning and value in the Monosophere and intersubjective meaning and value in the Isosphere, now looks for meaning and value in a political community that has authority over its members. The question arises: Does the legal subject forego ethical integrity and reciprocal justice when he enters the body politic, or does he rather protect and foster these same fundamental values by cooperating in a communal endeavor toward self-sufficiency?

In our analysis of the Koinosphere, we examine the body politic, its external and internal structure as well as its authoritative core. The body politic does not have a life of its own, independent of its constituting subjects. So if we wish to understand the organization itself and the power it wields, we must understand its members subjectively, for their mental operations constitute the roles that they play, and their roles, in turn, constitute the political community.

The Koinosphere, in its truest sense, is a practical participation in legal meaning and legal value for the enhancement of the personal dignity and destiny of all the members of a civilly organized community.

Koinonia - fellowship, community.

CHAPTER 6

THE DIMENSIONS OF COMMUNITY

The state exists for the protection and forwarding of human
interests, mainly through the medium of rights and duties.
*—John Chipman Gray**

A classic tension exists between the individual and the community
or, more abstractly, between freedom and law. Each person, the center
of his own universe, perfects only with difficulty what Tillich called
"the courage to be a part." This problem of the one and the many
becomes acute in political society, where by sacrificing autonomy for
the sake of authority we render ourselves vulnerable. To put ourselves
in the hands of others is to make our objectification possible. Even
when we participate in political decision making, we usually play a
minor role. Recognizing both the need for community and its high cost,
we experience a profound tension.

Nevertheless, this tension, resolve it as we may, is a permanent part
of being human; we can never live completely individual lives; our own
life story and the history of the human race attest to our state of
continuous interdependence. But mere association with others, even if
all activities are inspired by justice, is hardly sufficient. A world of *ad
hoc,* I-Thou relationships would eventually fragment under the burden
of social complexity. The pandemic reality of injustice adds to this
instability. So a broader principle of social harmonization is necessary
to protect and supplement justice, if full human development is to
succeed.

The move to the Koinosphere necessitates an adaptation of the role
of justice. In the Isosphere, the intersubjective relationship provides, to
the extent that each party is knowledgeable, wise, and virtuous, the
basis for a fairly exact determination of complementary rights and

* John Chipman Gray, *The Nature and Sources of the Law,* 2nd ed. (New York:
Macmillan, 1921), p. 103.

duties through the search for participated value in a concrete legal event. The Koinosphere, however, not only encompasses the legal events taking place between diverse persons but has the immense task of trying to harmonize the private and the common good.

As a consequence, this broader coverage does not always meet the exigencies of the singular case, for it is inconceivable that any one person or even the whole group in a complex society could know all the pertinent facts and could fashion general laws attuned to every possible change in circumstances.[1] But the need for community is such that even less than perfect legal justice is, in this less than perfect world, a mandate for survival.

The Koinosphere sublates the justice of the Isosphere, but in incorporating earlier insights it adjusts them to the demands of communal living; thus the rules of general applicability emerge. People civilly united may still interact on a one-to-one basis, but in a new context. Ways of acting take on a normative character as more and more members of the community begin to act similarly and eventually expect others to do likewise. These customary norms coming from the Isosphere, even before they become official policy, establish community expectations.

Moreover, since this social interaction gives rise to a great variety of legal events, which spawn many different and even conflicting rules, the community finds itself structured legally—not just because some individual or group has intentionally imposed a legal system but because the community itself has sublated the operative principles of justice, worked them out in practice, and sanctioned them corporately.

The process at work is the commonsense accumulation of insights and decisions forming centers of order in the chaotic and fluctuating arena of human events. When these normative insights are verified in practice, they gain acceptance by the wider community. Minds readily respond to the results of the practical insights of others, as the longevity of proverbs illustrates. If the insights make sense and the decisions based on them prove beneficial, they become part of the tradition of practical wisdom. Eventually, the community puts its stamp of ap-

1. See Friedrich A. Hayek, *Law, Legislation and Liberty,* Vol. 1: *Rules and Order* (Chicago: University of Chicago Press, 1973), pp. 11–15.

proval on many of these expectations, with clusters of insights and decisions developing into the major areas of law.

No longer is justice an *ad hoc* decision; the community, both legislatively and judicially, now provides a set of standards that in some way preempts the earlier and foundational, intersubjective resolution of disputes. In the Isosphere, each case, having a unique set of circumstances, might be thought of as a case of first instance. Admittedly, each individual has garnered his own fund of insights, discovered or inherited, to help him deal with new situations.

The ingredient added in the Koinosphere is the contribution of practical wisdom that the other members of the community have made. This vast accumulation overshadows the narrow experience of the litigants. More is involved than the rule in the individual case; the particular issue can be adequately resolved only in terms of the political context, with its wider comprehension of the pertinent facts and values. Justice, always conforming to a standard, must in the Koinosphere determine the proper standard for a given case by considering community values as well as the values of the parties. Therefore, to appreciate the full dimensions of community, as a prerequisite to an inner experience of law, we must consider the public order, its communal structure, and its subjective infrastructure.

I. THE PUBLIC ORDER

Communities are a response to need; they are the evolving structures of public order: that is, the ever-changing complexus of goods and practices to be participated in by members of the community. Aristotle delineated the commonsense necessity that gives rise to political society. Beginning with the family unit, he indicated the natural progression to village and then to the *polis* or city-state. The family fulfills some purposes: it is made up of "male and female that the race may continue ... and of natural ruler and subject that both may be preserved."[2] Though the essentials are present, the familial-servile relationship is limited to "the supply of men's everyday wants."[3]

When families desire more than that, they unite to form villages.

2. Aristotle, *Politics*, I, 2, 1252 a26–31.
3. Ibid., I, 2, 1252 b12–14.

Village life, too, has its sharp constraints, but "when several villages are united in a single complete community large enough to be nearly or quite self-sufficient, the state comes into existence for the sake of the good life."[4] The state is not, for Aristotle, an artificial imposition from without upon free and happy primitives; it is a communal accommodation intrinsically necessary because of the limited capacities of all human beings.

The proof that the state is a creation of nature and prior to the individual is that the individual, when isolated, is not self-sufficient; and therefore he is like a part in relation to the whole. But he who is unable to live in society or has no need because he is self-sufficient for himself must be either a beast or a god.[5]

Human beings are neither bestial nor divine, nor are they by themselves self-sufficient. Nevertheless, they do seek happiness and thus require adequate means to achieve it. Aristotle gave the philosophic rationale of the state as the machinery of self-sufficiency: "A state is a community of families and villages for the sake of a perfect and self-sufficient life."[6] His basic principle, applicable to the state as well as to all other things, is teleological:

If the early forms of society are natural, so is the state, for it is the end of them, and *the nature of a thing is its end*. For what each thing is when fully developed, we call its nature, whether we are speaking of a man, a horse, or a family. Besides, the final cause and end of a thing is the best, and to be self-sufficient is the end and the best.[7]

People generally recognize the necessity for a political community, if they are to attain the good life. People differ radically, however, about what the good life is, what its goals are, what the best means to attain them are, and what degree of state assistance and control is preferable. To interpret self-sufficiency in specific terms is the task of economics, ethics, political science, practical politics, and law. We are not going to enter here into this arena of competing claims, but will simply look to two major aspects of the goals of political communities: what Prof. Myres S. McDougal has called minimum public order and optimum public order.

4. Ibid., I, 2, 1252 b27–30.
5. Ibid., III, 9, 1253 a25–29.
6. Ibid., I, 2, 1280 b40–41.
7. Ibid., 1252 b30–1253 a1, italics supplied.

The maintenance of public order—when public order is conceived in its minimal sense as community control and prevention of private violence—is commonly and appropriately regarded as the first indispensable function of any system of law. The securing of a public order—understood in a broader sense as embracing the totality of a community's legally protected goal values and implementing institutions—which seeks, beyond an effective community monopolization of force, the richest production and widest sharing of all values, is today also commonly projected as appropriate aspiration by most mature territorial polities.[8]

Self-sufficiency, then, has two aspects: peace and prosperity. Whatever else the state does, it should protect its citizens, but protection by itself cannot adequately foster the good life by guaranteeing the requisite means. Most states act positively by redistributing goods in addition to establishing safeguards against the criminal within and the enemy without. To grasp the implications for subjectivity of this dynamic aspect of the political community, we will look at two theories, from the early 1970's, which take radically contrasting positions on what is the purpose of society.

A. The Minimalist Approach

Robert Nozick's book *Anarchy, State, and Utopia* (1974) presented an apologia for the minimal state.[9] His justification is an up-dated version of the night-watchman theory of classical liberalism: since even a strong man has to sleep, thus rendering his life and property vulnerable, everyone must have recourse to some dominant, protective instrumentality. The activities of the state are justified by its watchman's role and limited to it. The state would have a monopoly on force, which it would use to make sure that the citizens did not violate one another's rights by violence, theft, fraud, or breach of contract. These rights are not created by the state; on the contrary, Nozick said that the citizens already have these rights by nature and that all the state legitimately contributes is protection.

Nozick's limitation on state control is at the heart of his entitlement theory: whatever rights or holdings one has, as long as the original acquisition or subsequent transfer was just, are vested interests to be

---

8. Myres S. McDougal and Florentino P. Feliciano, *Law and Minimum World Public Order* (New Haven: Yale University Press, 1961), pp. 121–22.

9. Robert Nozick, *Anarchy, State, and Utopia* (New York: Basic Books, 1974).

protected by law. If, however, an illicit acquisition or transfer did occur in the past, a "rectification" rather than a technical redistribution would be necessary to correct the earlier injustice. For a state to redistribute property under any other circumstances would be to infringe on a citizen's rights.

For example, Nozick compared taxation of earnings to forced labor on the grounds that, by confiscating the property of one person for the sake of another, the state is asserting ownership of the citizen and his work. If taxation is legal, there is a radical change of principles; instead of a historical principle of distribution concerned with how a citizen happens to possess property, there is an end-result, patterned principle of redistribution that looks to a citizen's degree of participation in a designated objective or condition—merit, need, virtue, production, achievement—an elaboration of *kat'axian* of the Greeks. The entitlement theory will have none of this: one citizen's rights are not to be subject to the merits or demerits of another. Nozick required that the state be blind to everything but the task of protecting what has been lawfully acquired. State actions contravening this entitlement would be ethically and legally *ultra vires*.

The idea of minimum public order is hardly new. Roscoe Pound, writing from a historical perspective, said, "The first and simplest idea is that law exists to keep the peace in a given society"; he labeled this "the stage of primitive law."[10] However sophisticated the development of Nozick's libertarian version may be, it remains primitive, even atavistic. The flaw in his libertarian problematic is its individualism: its disregard for the communal dimension of mankind makes it suitable only for a realm of diminished subjects. The theory and the subjects complement one another. To target his theory, let us scrutinize his subjects.

What kind of subjects has Nozick created to people his minimal state? Since the political community is an ordering of citizens, the parts and the whole rise and fall together. Before answering the question, I note that, although his minimal state would obviously permit altruism, in theory at least he must justify it on its own minimalist principles without counting on a *deus ex machina,* private sector charity. Four observations are pertinent. First, the subject as citizen may be for

---

10. Roscoe Pound, *Introduction to the Philosophy of Law* (New Haven: Yale University Press, 1959), p. 33.

4 results of Nozick's minimal state

Nozick clearly individualistic, moved only by rational self-interest and politically unfettered by a social conscience.[11] Second, each subject may take an absolutist attitude to his main political values, property and liberty; that means that he is the absolute owner of his property without stewardship obligations and that he is free to use his property as he sees fit, observing only the minimal prohibitions already mentioned. Third, as a consequence, his relationship to others remains on the arm's-length level of commutative justice, without further commitment to what Aristotle called political friendship, what Aquinas called charity, what Del Vecchio called the bond of intersubjectivity. Fourth, the logical consistency of the idea of the minimal state depends essentially on dealing with the subject and his rights abstractly rather than concretely; at its core is the deductive formalism characteristic of seventeenth- and eighteenth-century rationalism, concealing persons by conceptualizing them. It is at least in theory a diminished state for a diminished citizenry.

B. The Distributist Approach

John Rawls did not begin with a set of basic rights in trying to foster self-sufficiency through his nuanced but egalitarian sharing of primary goods. But, as the title *The Theory of Justice* (1971), indicates, Rawls, like Nozick, was working on the theoretical level, dealing not with consciousness but with concepts. He belabored this point: "My aim is to present a *conception* of justice which *generalizes* and carries to a higher level of *abstraction* the familiar *theory* of the social contract."[12]

It is noteworthy how he ingeniously rediscovered the abstract man *qua* man of rationalist natural law—but only a limited version. Rawls did not expatiate on the legal subjects who are to choose his system, but he clearly indicated their character: they are rational, self-inter-

11. In a section entitled "The Invisible Hand Explanation of the State," Nozick wrote, in *Anarchy, State and Utopia*, p. 118: "We have explained how, without anyone having this in mind, *the self-interested and rational actions* of persons in the Lockean state of nature will lead to single protective agencies dominant over geographical territories" (italics supplied). Then he moved to the sole dominant monopoly of force, his "minimal state." Lest his reference to Locke seem to water down his above assertion, note on p. 9: "Only when some divergence between our conception and Locke's is relevant to political philosophy, to our argument about the state, will it be mentioned." He mentioned no divergence.

12. John Rawls, *A Theory of Justice* (Cambridge: Harvard University Press, 1971), p. 11. Italics supplied.

ested, and similarly situated. He wrote: "The procedure whereby the principles are proposed and acknowledged represents constraints, analogous to those of having a morality, whereby *rational and mutually self-interested persons* are bound to act reasonably."[13] Again, phrasing it differently, he wrote that by "rationally and mutually disinterested," he meant that "they are conceived as not taking an interest in one another's interests."[14] He explicitly ruled out altruism as structurally necessary to his theory.

Of course, the persons who are to establish the principles of justice are not actually similarly situated; through a pedagogic device, the "veil of ignorance," it is assumed that they will act as if they were, closing their minds to their own personal qualities and particular circumstances, no longer adverting to whether or not they are rich or poor, intelligent or stupid, healthy or handicapped, beautiful or ugly, male or female, or even virtuous or vicious, and so on through life's dualities and diversities. By this hypothetical *tour de force*, they try to overlook their concrete existential state and to grasp their commonalities.

To reach his two major principles, Rawls, in using the "veil of ignorance," also had to postulate for his "deprivileged" subjects a "thin theory" of primary goods ("which it is supposed a rational man wants, whatever else he wants"), namely, "rights and liberties, opportunities and powers, income and wealth."[15]

From this "thin theory" of good, Rawls derived his two principles. By asserting that they depend on a thin rather than a strong theory of good, he tried to stay within the letter of the Kantian priority of right over good, so that he could argue that the principles transcend existing desires or present social conditions. The principles are in tension: the first, a thoroughly libertarian one, is drastically limited by the egalitarian and redistributist second principle. Here they are:

[*The Principle of Liberty*] Each person is to have an equal right to the most extensive total system of equal basic liberties compatible with a similar system of liberty for all.[16]

[*The Difference Principle*] Social and economic inequalities are to be ar-

---

13. Idem, "Justice as Fairness," *The Philosophical Review* 67 (1958): 164–94. Italics supplied.

14. Idem, *Theory*, p. 13.

15. Ibid., pp. 92, 395–99.

16. Ibid., p. 250.

ranged so that they are both (a) to the greatest benefit of the least advantaged and (b) attached to offices and positions open to all under conditions of fair equality of opportunity.[17]

Rawls then explained how to develop a "full theory" of good from the "thin theory" and the two principles. He relied on rational and self-interested citizens who, since they would still be under the veil of ignorance, would logically follow a heuristic device for choice in uncertainty—the "maximin rule" (from *maximum minorum:* the most of the least, here the most of the least undesirable): "The maximin rule tells us to rank alternatives by their worst possible outcomes: we are to adopt the alternative the worst outcome of which is superior to the worst outcome of the others."[18] Rawls argued that when the two principles are applied concretely in accordance with the "maximin rule," a full theory of goods should result.

An intrinsic difficulty with Rawls's whole approach is that to choose wisely, one ought to be free of biases, but he postulated self-interested subjects. As such they are essentially and radically biased; they do not take an interest in one another's interests. Both their judgments and their decisions are thus susceptible to distortion. Their "hunch producers" are not attuned to the communal nature of man, so their theoretical insights and judgments are skewed and thus unreliable.

Furthermore, as one moves from the abstract to the concrete level, practical wisdom proves even more vulnerable to the actual demands of self-interested subjects inevitably aware of the status quo and their actual circumstances. Since they are by definition biased, what they accept in principle they may also reject in practice, for, logically, self-interest would establish the goals, which rationality would implement. This priority is significant since moral decisions are concrete and if wisely made take all circumstances into consideration. In Rawls's system, an original and indispensable circumstance is self-interest. This fact raises a crucial issue: How can even a rational subject, by definition flawed through self-interest, establish in the concrete just norms for all mankind—an apparently altruistic goal? A sound political philosophy must provide for the realities of the human condition or it becomes merely an exercise in game theory.

Rawls, too, seemed to manifest uneasiness about the adequacy of his major principles and the "original position." The principles were sup-

17. Ibid., p. 83.   18. Ibid., pp. 152–53. See also 108–14.

posed to mark out the dimensions of institutional justice, which seemed to be his exclusive focus. But he realized that they are not self-executing or self-motivating. He saw that to make them work, logically and psychologically, more principles were required, principles not for institutions alone but for individuals. He mentioned three categories: a principle of fairness, some principles of natural duty, and the principle of reflective equilibrium. With them his conformity to the Kantian priority of right over good is further eroded as is the institutional character of his theory of justice. Let us examine his supplemental principles, which are rooted in intersubjectivity.

(1) The "principle of fairness" is essential to Rawls's theory of social justice, as a kind of "basic norm" for imposing the primary "ought." It states simply that if one enjoys the benefits, one ought to bear the burdens, or more fully, that "a person is under an obligation to do his part as specified by the rules of an institution whenever he has voluntarily accepted the benefits of the scheme or has taken advantage of the opportunities it offers to advance his interests, provided that this institution is fair or just, that is, satisfies the two principles of justice."[19] So even self-interested people cannot be totally self-interested. Does he thus give rationality precedence over self-interest? If so, according to what principle? At any rate, to make the institution just, he admittedly depends on the virtue of personal justice.

(2) The "principles of natural duty" are also independent of institutional justice but are necessary complements: "The conception of justice as fairness is incomplete until these principles have been accounted for."[20] They would also be chosen in the original position, but only after the choice of the principles dealing with the basic structure of society (the principle of liberty and the difference principle), which would also guide their choice of content. They direct one to establish and support just institutions. If not natural law, then at least natural duty becomes necessary to the state.

Practical problem solving, however, was not Rawls's purpose. He wanted to remain in the realm of abstract theory. Indeed, he generally disregarded what he called "partial compliance theory," which deals with injustice, by presuming that everyone will act fairly and uphold institutions. He does this not naively but in order to work out fully his

19. Ibid., pp. 342–43. See also 108–14.
20. Ibid., p. 333. See also 333–42, 114–17.

conception of the perfect state. Nevertheless, this limitation on the coverage of justice—this disregard of injustice—is a striking illustration of the incompleteness of his views on personal justice and, especially from a lawyer's perspective, the unrealistic character of his system.

(3) Finally, the "principle of reflective equilibrium" reveals another concession to individual justice, as it reaches beyond the veil of ignorance and indeed rends that veil. The equilibrium reflected upon balances personal principles of justice with the major principles and their progeny. Rawls wrote candidly: "Justice as fairness is the hypothesis that the principles which would be chosen in the original position are identical with those that match our considered judgment and so these principles describe our sense of justice."[21] So there is light in the darkness under the veil. The validity of the principles of the original position must themselves be tested by "commonly shared presumptions" about justice.[22] "This is to see if the principles which would be chosen match our considered convictions of justice or extend them in an acceptable way."[23] Nevertheless, the moral principles cannot be strong ones, for they would then dominate the investigation. Their strength would suggest the alien thought that his conception of justice needed necessary or self-evident or derived truths; "instead, its justification is a matter of the mutual support of many considerations, everything fitting together into one coherent view."[24] That is why Rawls concluded that mutual disinterest and the veil of ignorance is best: "And if it is asked why one should not postulate benevolence with the veil of ignorance, the answer is that there is no need for so strong a condition."[25]

As a final point, what fundamentally does Rawls think of the legal subject for whom apparently this theory of justice is being constructed? Of greatest concern, one would think, in every moral philosophy, would be the moral worth of the subject. Rawls's position is startling. Although the end-patterned result of his political theory is egalitarian, it is not because all persons are equally worthwhile, but because no person is intrinsically worthwhile. "The concept of moral worth does not provide a first principle of distributive justice. . . . The concept of moral worth is secondary to those of right and justice and plays no

21. Ibid., p. 48.
22. Ibid., p. 18.
23. Ibid., p. 19.
24. Ibid., p. 21.
25. Ibid., pp. 148–149.

[handwritten marginal note: Rawls' Theory of egalitarianism is not based on all persons being worthwhile but rather that no one is intrinsically worthwhile.]

role in the substantive definition of distributive shares."[26] Rawls acknowledged the role of moral or natural duty, but subordinated it to his major concern, institutional justice, thus reversing the order of Isosphere and Koinosphere, as might be expected from a Social Good theorist, but this subordination does have the unfortunate result of thereby making personal justice an institutional byproduct.

We shall conclude this analysis by noting that, despite radical divergencies, Rawls shared with Nozick the same realm of discourse: they both conceived of the human subject in an abstract and deductive way and never moved out of conceptualistic theory into interiority. As a consequence, both of them envisaged an existentially diminished subject. Together, however, they have presented clearly contrasting formulations of the twofold purpose of the political community, protecting and fostering. But they have done so at the expense of the legal subject, who ends up an abstract and diminished person.

II. THE COMMUNAL STRUCTURE

Purposes alone do not make a state; people do when they structure a community of shared principles to realize their purposes. In Aristotle's words, "the constitution is the government."[27] He meant that the ordering or arrangement of citizens for the common good forms the state. The constitution is what is constituted; it is not the statement about something, but the something about which a statement can be made. To speak of a written or unwritten constitution is secondary; fundamentally, every constitution is a relationship between people civilly united. Of course, the articulation and documentation of that event may well be called the constitution, but only derivatively.

What, then, is the constituting event? First of all, it is a result of power or principle. Aristotle wrote: "A constitution is an organization of offices, which all the citizens distribute among themselves, according the power which different classes possess, for example, the rich or the poor, or according to some principle of equality which includes both."[28] The constitution establishes the roles and the goals for the community; that is, it determines who shall have power and for what purposes: "A constitution is the organization of offices in a state and determines what

26. Ibid., p. 312.
27. Aristotle, *Politics*, III, 6, 1278 b11.
28. Ibid., IV, 3, 1290 a7–11.

is to be the ruling body, and what is the end of each community."[29] Aristotle then distinguished the laws from the principles of the constitution; the proper function of the laws is clear: "Although in most cities the laws may be said generally to be in a chaotic state, still, if they aim at anything, they aim at the maintenance of power."[30] Power, then, is the operative term: the constitution by a new allocation of power (executive, legislative, and judicial), whether imposed or created, establishes public order; the laws as subordinate instruments maintain and implement this power allocation and public order.

Aristotle's basic political insights, often reformulated and elaborated, have generally perdured. On learning that H. L. A. Hart distinguished two sets of rules in the legal community and adopted for himself Austin's phrase in calling them "the key to the science of jurisprudence,"[31] we might ask whether they resemble Aristotle's twofold division. Indeed, there are fundamental similarities.

Hart's "primary rules" (obligation-imposing rules) correspond easily to the Aristotelian notion of laws as commanding or forbidding certain actions. Primary rules, however, can be defective owing to: the uncertainties concerning their existence and scope; their static character amid varying social conditions; their inefficiency in policing violations or resolving conflicts. The primary rules therefore must, according to Hart, be supplemented by "secondary rules" (power-conferring rules), which correspond significantly to Aristotle's tripartite constitution. The secondary rules are: (1) the rule of recognition to enable the citizen to know who has the power and how it can be legally used: (2) the rules of change to provide for the creation of new primary rules and the termination of old ones; and (3) the rules of adjudication, to resolve disputes over whether primary rules have been broken or applied properly. Secondary rules facilitate the use of primary rules in a flexible and ongoing system of law.

Though Hart undoubtedly recognized his debt to Aristotle, he was not simply using new terms for old concepts; he refined and developed these concepts, reshaping them into a new theoretical framework. With that change of context there is a change of meaning. Aristotle and Hart experienced law differently, but they still remain bound together by

29. Ibid., IV, 1, 1289 a15–18.
30. Ibid., VII, 2, 1324 b5–7.
31. H. L. A. Hart, *The Concept of Law* (Oxford: The Clarendon Press, 1961), p. 6. He discussed these rules in Chapter V, pp. 77–96.

the insights they shared. This is not surprising since both sought to understand working legal institutions. Indeed, when it comes to justifying the constitution that validates the law—a fundamental concern of modern analytic jurists—Hart's method is more consonant with Aristotle than with Kelsen, although Kelsen is Hart's more immediate and stronger influence.

The practical context of the jurisprudential problem can be illustrated simply: a man is locked up in a state prison; the legality of that action depends on the legality of a chain of other actions—the warden's authorization, the judge's sentence, the legislature's statute, and the community's constitution, but there remains a further question: why is the constitution binding? Kelsen's answer is to presuppose a basic norm, the *Grundnorm:* one ought to behave as the constitution provides.[32] He added a condition *sine qua non* that the constitution ought to be by and large effective (in that the norms are actually applied and obeyed).[33] Kelsen's recourse to a presupposition has been criticized, even by other positivists, as incompatible with a pure theory, for after explicitly excluding ethics and natural law, he unwittingly admitted them in presuppositional form.[34]

Hart bypassed the theoretical contradiction by moving into the realm of common sense and suggesting that the issue of legality or validity be dealt with, not philosophically but empirically. For him, the rule of recognition—the counterpart of the basic norm—is simply taken as an empirical fact, generally acknowledged. This empirical position comports well with Aristotle's pragmatic approach to the constitution as an arrangement of citizens usually formed after a power struggle but conceivably after a peaceful agreement. For Hart, the crucial point is that the community of officials and ordinary citizens does accept, for whatever reason, the constitution as a political norm legalizing the acts done in harmony with it.

Lasswell and McDougal took a consonant approach. Deeply com-

32. Hans Kelsen, *General Theory of Law and State,* trans. A. Wedburg (New York: Russell & Russell, 1961), pp. 115–16.

33. Ibid., p. 120.

34. For a critical analysis of Kelsen see "A Tribute to Hans Kelsen," *California Law Review* 59 (1971), pp. 609–819, with articles by W. Ebenstein, E. Bodenheimer, T. A. Cowan, G. Hughes, S. I. Shuman, R. S. Summers, J. Hall, F. F. Stone, D. Daube, and J. Raz, and a bibliography. See also George Christie, *Jurisprudence* (St. Paul, Minn.: West Publishing Co., 1973), pp. 631–34.

mitted to the notion of human dignity, they used an empirical approach to describe effectively the legal process.[35] For them, validity depends on the expectations of the people, which, as in Hart's rule of recognition, can be factually verified: citizens do expect that certain persons in certain official positions will be able to do certain things according to certain procedures. This jurisprudential approach comprises three processes: the social process, which is human interaction; the power process, which is controlling decision (policy and sanction); and the legal process, which is authoritative and controlling decision (authoritative in proportion to its conformity with the expectations of the people and controlling in proportion to the effectiveness of its power).

The notions of power and authority, which are relevant to the creation and maintenance of the system, will be analyzed more fully in the next chapter. Here, we continue our examination of the legal institution itself as essentially a complex structure of roles and goals. By roles we refer to the activities of the members of the political community; these activities look to goals: proximately to particular goals and ultimately to the overarching goals of the political community. We shall, as an inner experience of law requires, discuss this structure from the perspective of subjectivity.

III. THE SUBJECTIVE INFRASTRUCTURE

To appreciate the subjective basis of civil society, it is helpful to consider two fundamental human activities—knowing and loving. For civil society is essentially both communion in an idea and political friendship. These are not mutually exclusive categories, but overlapping ones. Both involve knowing and loving: communion in an idea emphasizes the first; political friendship emphasizes the second. As complementary insights into meaning and value, they heighten our awareness of the mental operations underlying the creation of that construct which is the Koinosphere.

A. Communion in An Idea

The Institutionalists of the early twentieth century did much to sharpen the political focus on meaning by using a personalist approach

35. See David Granfield, "Towards a Goal-oriented Consensus," *Journal of Legal Education* 19 (1967): 379–402.

that mediated between individualism and collectivism.[36] Georges Renard caught the spirit of the movement and its subjective turn in his memorable definition of an institution as "the communion of men in an idea," an adaptation of the thought of Maurice Hauriou (1856–1929), the chief prophet of Institutionalism.[37]

Hauriou considered the *idée directrice* to be the central and unifying principle of political theory, but a practical not a speculative one. It was the idea of a work to be done in a social group; it was the object of the enterprise. As such the idea was participated in by rulers and subjects, binding them into an institution. Of course, to realize the idea in practice, there has to be an organized power of governance residing in the rulers but subordinate to the shared idea and existing for the sake of the subjects. In the actual working out of the idea through legal means, both the rulers and the citizens are in communion. Moreover, this working out is flexible as well as stable—it can adjust as interests and circumstances change, but it preserves a formal core in its commitment to its essential structure.

Hauriou was neither a naturalist nor a positivist, although he had followers of both persuasions. In France, Georges Renard and Joseph Delos applied his theories in a natural law context; Santi Romano, in Italy, took a positivistic approach, subscribing to no value system either to validate the directive idea or to resolve institutional conflicts but relying solely on the outcome of the power struggle. He made an important contribution to Institutionalism, however, by including empirical facts and providing for institutional pluralism. Today, we may take these enlargements for granted but the resultant cross-fertilization within Institutionalism has helped facilitate the updating of the natural law as it moved from classicist to modern culture.

Still considering the central focus of Institutionalism, the communion of men in an idea, we should emphasize that these legal and political institutions are themselves constituted by common meaning. They are what, directly or indirectly, we mean them to be. We advert to this fact when we speak of forming or amending a constitution as well as of making or abrogating laws. We note, too, how the interpretation that the courts give to these constitutional and legal norms changes the

36. See Albert Broderick, ed. *The French Institutionalists: Maurice Hauriou, Georges Renard, Joseph Delos,* trans. M. Welling, 20th Century Legal Philosophy Series: Vol. VIII (Cambridge: Harvard University Press, 1970).

37. Georges Renard, *La théorie de l'institution* (Paris: Sirey, 1930), p. 95.

meaning of the community and its shared idea. Any change in political power, in social goals and policies, in the perception of economic and social conditions, in the shared sense of human dignity and destiny, shifts the hermeneutic balance and brings about, however subtly, a reconstitution of the community.

The Institutionalists concentrated on the knowing and doing involved in the participation of the subject in the idea of a work to be accomplished. Their focus on personalism fell short of interiority; they recognized that shared meaning is constitutive of community but failed to investigate the underlying implications of that meaning. The reason for this failure was typical of the times—the heritage of conceptualism. The very focus on the "idea" is revealing. Consequently, despite its many insights, Institutionalism has been largely ignored, perhaps because to establish itself fully it would have had to justify itself cognitionally. This it did not do and, given the times, might have not been able to do.

To speak of participation in an idea over the lifespan of the body politic raises hermeneutical questions. The problem is one of historicity and the interpretation of legal norms: a later generation of citizens, living under new circumstances, tries to understand and apply the constitution and laws established by earlier generations. The inevitability of change and the difficulty of textual interpretation need not undermine the political community; continuity with the past, not identity with it, suffices. But it is essential that contemporaries keep participating in an idea, however it may change. Of course, since individuals, like cultures, have differing viewpoints and levels of comprehension and of commitment, a uniform and complete participation at any given moment is highly unlikely.

Nevertheless, some kind of commonsense and practical communion in the idea of a work to be done remains indispensable. What this flexible participation in shared meaning and value signifies theoretically and how it develops over time are secondary to its present vitality. Indeed, the hermeneutical problems of a political community attest to its historical continuity; its existence, however, depends on the actualization of the directive idea; and its flowering requires both sound ideas and authentic praxis.

Subjectively, then, part of the infrastructure of political society is participation in common meaning and value. Whether it is arrived at through a practical or a theoretical development, this commonality is the fruit of mental operations shared by all citizens: experience, insight, judgment, decision. The recognition that they all employ similar powers in creating and conserving their political structure should ideally facilitate the articulation of the meaning of that structure, for the choice remains theirs and is within their competence and responsibility as thinking citizens.

B. Commitment to Friendship

Communion in a political idea is balanced by a commitment to political friendship.[38] Both are a sharing of intersubjectivity; both focus on the common good or public order. The language of the first, however, refers more to meaning; the second, more to value. Both formulations encompass meaning and value but from different perspectives. Together they bring the members fully into the subjective infrastructure of the Koinosphere.

The very word Koinosphere suggests an element found in friendship and political life, a multileveled participation. Through the sharing in what is common (koinon) to the parties, there results an association or community (koinonia). Aristotle wrote: "Friendship is present to the extent that men share something in common, for that is also the extent to which they share a view of what is just. And the proverb, 'Friends hold in common what they have' (koina ta ton philon), is correct, for friendship consists in community."[39]

Note, too, the intimate relationship that exists between friendship and justice: "It is natural that the element of justice increases with [the closeness of] friendship, since friendship and what is just exist in the same relationship and are coextensive in range."[40] This is understandable since justice is the bond of citizens; and philia, a broader term than our friendship, is also a bond uniting persons, but precisely by what they have in common.[41] So political friendship (philia politikē) is a mutual benevolence mutually recognized for the purposes of the common good or communal self-sufficiency.

Fundamental to this benevolence is the equality or intersubjectivity

---

38. Aristotle discussed at length likemindedness, homonoia, frequently translated as concord, in Nicomachean Ethics, IX, 6, 1167 a22–1167 b16, where he said explicitly: "We see that likemindedness is political friendship," 1167 b2–3.

39. Ibid., VIII, 9, 1159 b29–32.

40. Ibid., VIII, 9, 1160 a7–8.

41. See ibid., VIII, 1, 1155 a22–28.

from which justice derives. Justice, as we have seen, is characterized by proportionate reciprocity and conscious intersubjectivity. As persons interact in terms of a shared human dignity and destiny, to that extent they can be united in political friendship. Moreover, since the ideal focus in conflict resolution is on what can be reasonably and responsibly chosen by both parties, namely, the just thing, *to dikaion*, the choice of what is just for both parties enables them to remain friends, because reason, not superior power, determines the decision. They are not adversaries fighting with one another, but friends, temporarily at odds, seeking an equitable resolution of their conflicting claims.

Already committed to the idea of a community with a constitution and laws, to what Hart called the idea of rules, the members resolve prospectively through legislation possible conflicts, and they hand over the problems that they cannot settle amicably to an antecedently agreed-upon machinery of adjudication so that they can accept with honor and good reason a valid disposition of the case. And they can remain political friends.

CONCLUSION

Political society is a construct. In part it is the result of an accumulation of commonsense insights that have developed over the years as persons have worked out their disputes in a manner satisfactory enough to justify imitation, thus giving rise to standard practices. And in part it is the result of planning and design, that is, of self-conscious legislative or judicial decisions implemented by sanctions. The result is a legal community constituted and operated according to the expectations of the people. It achieves self-sufficiency and social happiness to the extent that it is grounded in reason.

This normative structure rests on a complexus of mental operations, collectively described as likemindedness (*homonoia*) and political friendship (*philia*). For these operations to bind persons together into a community, there is need of communication for the shaping and sharing of meaning and value.

Fundamentally, the focus is on conscious intentionality. Indeed, the various weaknesses in the creation and operation of the state can be traced back to failures in rational consciousness (experience, insight, and judgment) and in rational self-consciousness (deliberation, evaluation, decision, and action). Similarly, the excellence of the state ultimately rests on the authenticity of conscious intentionality. Since jurisprudence usually focuses on the Koinosphere, it must, if it hopes to answer the profound questions that inevitably arise, delve beneath the commonsense and even theoretical surface to confront the underlying mental operations that have structured the political society with its twin pillars of meaning and value.

CHAPTER 7

THE DYNAMICS OF GOVERNANCE

If I have just styled the so-called authorities as ministers of the law, it is because I am persuaded that the preservation or ruin of a society depends on this more than on anything else.—Plato*

"Power, unqualified and unspecified, is one of the vaguest notions in the history of human thought."[1] But power, elusive though it may be, is clearly operative in law. The word may mean simply what H.L.A. Hart intended when he called the Austinian imperative theory, "the gunman situation writ large."[2] Or it may mean what Coke suggested when he answered James I and his claim to rule by divine right, with Bracton's words: "For the king himself ought not to be under man but under God and law, because the law makes the king."[3] Whether power is on the physical level of force or on the moral level of authority, whether it is on both levels or whether both levels are equivalent, power is of utmost juridical importance.[4]

Arrest, which puts a person in the control and custody of the law, is a crucial instance of power in action. The one who arrests must be authorized by a special warrant or by the general law permitting an officer or private person to arrest without a warrant under certain circumstances. When the arrest is made, the authority and the intention of the one arresting must be communicated to the suspect. But authority and intention are not enough; physical force, actual or constructive, is

---

* Plato, *Laws*, 715 d.

1. Jerome Hall, *Studies in Jurisprudence and Criminal Theory* (New York: Oceana Publications, 1958), p. 85.

2. H.L.A. Hart, "Positivism and the Separation of Law and Morals," *Harvard Law Review* 74 (1958): 603.

3. Sir Edward Coke, *Prohibitions Del Roy,* 12 Co. Rep. 63 (K.B. 1612).

4. See David Granfield, "Force, Power, and Law," *The Catholic University of America Law Review* 12 (1963): 79–91. I have adapted this article for this section and the next.

required. A true arrest is always a privileged imprisonment and may involve a privileged touching or battery.[5] The battery is at least token force, the submission is the acknowledgment of superior power. The battery is sufficient without submission; the submission is sufficient without a battery. Some situations, however, require more than a symbolic use of coercion. Under the common law, the police had the right to use all the force that was reasonably necessary, meeting force with force, if the suspect, having been given notice of authority and purpose, resisted lawful arrest or fled lawful arrest. In 1985, the Supreme Court decided that the use of lethal force to prevent escape is limited to situations where the officer has probable cause to believe that the suspect poses a threat of death or serious physical injury to the officer or others.[6]

The problem of arrest with its complexus of authority and coercion, of rights and duties, shows vividly the strong arm of the law. A person may follow his own will for years without any explicit concern for the law or its power. So long as he does not happen to violate a law or to be apprehended doing so, the law for him may subjectively be non-existent. But once he is arrested, the law painfully impinges on his life. Legal phenomena become existential realities to be coped with at his peril. No longer fully free, he becomes subject to the machinery of justice, depersonalized compulsion, and the indignities of police administration. He faces up to the fact of power.

I. THE ANATOMY OF POWER

Power is a familiar phenomenon; it is Eros at work with protean ubiquity. Power dwells at the core of every law; the criminal process simply affords a dramatic manifestation of something operative, less violently perhaps but no less decisively, on all levels of human existence. To try to have a complete experience of law without a profound understanding of power would be futile. To understand power, however, requires that we differentiate its major forms.

---

5. *Kelly v. United States*, 111 U.S. App. D.C. 398; 298 F.2d 312 (1961), discusses the coercive element in arrest: "In order for there to be an arrest it is not necessary for there to be an application of actual force or manual touching of the body or physical restraint which may be visible to the eye. It is sufficient if the person arrested understand that he is in the power of the one arresting and submits in consequence."

6. *Tennessee v. Garner*, 471 U.S. 1 (1985).

First and most generally, since it includes both persons and things, power is an ability to act. Corresponding to this active power is a passive power, the capacity to receive, to be acted upon by something outside oneself, by the environment. This insight into power is hardly new. According to the Aristotelian categories, both active and passive powers are a species of quality, an accident consequent on form. When this ability and capacity are actualized, they are reclassified in the categories of action and passion, respectively.

(1) an ability to act. and to be acted upon

Despite its ancient lineage, this same twofold understanding of power is recognized by empirical science. Most explicitly, it underlies cybernetics, the modern theory of communication and control. The active powers give "messages"; passive powers receive "messages." The feedback loop (input, conversion process, output) coordinates the function of these powers, whose permutations compose all existential interaction. This duality establishes the parameters of the most sublime of man's intersubjective relationships as well as the most monstrous of his depersonalizations. Power, then, in this first and widest genus, is the ability to act and the capacity to be acted upon. Without power, the universe is static.

Second, some powers are exclusively human. Man shares with other beings many of his powers—chemical and physical, vegetative, and animal—but he has abilities and capacities that transcend them and constitute his human nature. Bertrand Russell's definition of power as "the production of intended effects"[7] indicates by the use of the word "intended" that power which is a function of intelligence. Indeed, Paul Tillich has suggested that power, like law, is most properly an anthropological term that is transferred metaphorically to the nonhuman.[8] The implications of the human dimension of power are elaborated by Romano Guardini: "We may speak of power in the true sense of the word only when two elements are present: real energies capable of changing the reality of things, of determining their conditions and interrelations; and awareness of those energies, the will to establish specific goals."[9]

(2) some are exclusively human

(Russell)

Conscious intentionality gives power its truly human character. The

7. Bertrand Russell, *Power* (London: Unwin Books, 1938), p. 25.
8. See Paul Tillich, *Love, Power, and Justice* (New York: Oxford University Press, 1954; Galaxy Books, 1960), p. 7.
9. Romano Guardini, *Power and Responsibility* (Chicago: Henry Regnery, 1961), p. 2.

goal, which is first in the order of intention, is finally achieved through the actualization of those powers which change reality. Freely intended action, neither determined nor accidental, can be predicated of the agent as his own, as something that he experiences. Power of this type ideally is the rational and responsible production of intended effects, although obviously the use of power often falls short of that ideal.

Power can be directed towards persons or things. Our main concern is power over human beings, without forgetting that "the chief cause of change in the modern world is the increased power over matter that we owe to science."[10] Since Russell wrote those words, the "Second Industrial Revolution," based on cybernetics and the "intelligent machines" of automation, have extended not only the frontiers of man's mastery over nature but also the areas of human communication and control. Machines will not, as Samuel Butler envisaged in Erewhon, enslave mankind all by themselves; but *machines à gouverner* may well augment, in a way not hitherto experienced, the power of the state's influence in politics, economics, and public opinion, creating thereby a growing threat to future liberty.

Third, sociologists, political scientists, and jurists use the word "power" more restrictively to refer to that production of intended effects called, by Kant, heteronomous decision—the ability to decide for others. The one who can make himself a law unto others is a person of power. By means of a threatened sanction he imposes his value judgments about what is or what is not to be done. The net result is two parallel choices: the one has chosen to obey what the other has chosen to command. To take a familiar example, a robber makes a successful heteronomous decision when his victim hands over his wallet upon hearing the words, "Your money or your life."[11] The power components are obvious: the policy and the sanction. If the victim, on hearing the threat, refuses to comply, the criminal may well use force to achieve his goal. This use of force might seem logically to reduce the act from the third to the second genus of power, as merely the production of an intended effect and so not in the strict sense a heteronomous decision; but, since the possible objectification of the non-cooperative victim or subject is part of the process, the decision remains a heteronomous one.

10. B. Russell, *Power*, p. 25.

11. For a linguistic analysis of the gunman situation, see H. L. A. Hart, *The Concept of Law* (Oxford: Clarendon Press, 1961), p. 8of.

The distinction between power and force is important, although often overlooked. The sanction implicit in power has a twofold operation: it is force threatened or force applied; as a threat it coerces the will, as an application it compels the body. The application of force is necessary only when the threat does not work. Clearly, if a threat works, it is far more efficient than the use of force, and there is a heteronomous decision in the full sense. The ideal form is an authoritative decision carried out in responsible obedience.

Underlying power on all levels is a common purpose, for power is essentially a power to be oneself, to realize one's potentialities. This purpose indicates power's subjective basis and affords the standard for its proper use. To be oneself requires self-preservation, self-fulfillment, and self-transcendence; that is, the perfecting, through doing and receiving, of one's dignity and destiny. Once again, we see the interplay of Eros and Nemesis. For Eros needs power to achieve his desires, but reaches happiness only by acting properly; Nemesis is ever alert to sanction any abuse of power.

Paul Tillich described power's existential function: "The power of a being is its possibility to affirm itself against the non-being within it and against it. The power of a being is the greater the more non-being is taken into its self-affirmation."[12] Whether or not, in the face of hostility, environmental scarcity, or the ultimate threat of entropy, one is able to perform other actions, there remains this residual power of self-affirmation. Sparked by what Tillich called "the courage to be," a person takes an existential stand.

Since heteronomous decision necessarily involves a plurality of persons, a serious question arises concerning the adequacy of defining power as an ability to be oneself. It seems to connote selfishness and, if not moral solipsism, at least a Hobbesian or Sartrean zero-sum game plan with each person seeking to be himself at the expense of others. The basis for reconciling the principle of self-affirmation and the fact of personal plurality is intersubjectivity. We affirm ourselves as social beings, whose fulfillment requires us to treat others as ourselves. We extend our power to be ourselves by using it to help others be themselves. To do so we must affirm ourselves as part of that higher synthesis constituted by justice: "Self-affirmation, if it is done in spite of the threat of nonbeing, is the courage to be. But it is not the courage to be

12. Tillich, *Love, Power, and Justice*, p. 48.

as oneself, it is 'the courage to be as a part.' "[13] Thus, power has two subjective norms: the ethical consistency between knowing and doing and the just rendering to each his own. Together, they ensure that the ability to be oneself flourishes through personal and social authenticity.

People conform to the dictates of political power either through coercion or consent. Russell's terms, naked, traditional and revolutionary power, highlight the relationship between these two activities.[14] "Naked power" gains obedience only because of its coercive strength. "Traditional power" has the habitual or customary assent of the governed. "Revolutionary power," though newly acquired and lacking a tradition of respect and habit of obedience, relies on assent to a new creed or program or sentiment; it replaces traditional authority and in its turn tends to become traditional, though in the face of opposition it may have the qualities of naked power. Naked power acts without assent or tradition and rests on sheer force, but it, too, tends to become traditional or to be replaced.

If in society some coercion is always necessary, it is even truer that some element of consent is necessary too, or there can be no society to coerce. Only through perduring consent does society stay in existence; on this consensual foundation coercion plays its limited role. Consent is much easier to come by than one might think. Berdyaev writes of a great anomaly: "Man seeks freedom. There is within him an immense drive towards freedom, and yet not only does he easily fall into slavery, but he even loves slavery."[15] If man is not truly free, if he is exteriorized, objectivized, or alienated, he must become one or other of the two correlatives: master or slave.

If the consciousness of a master is consciousness of the existence of some other for him, then the consciousness of the slave is the existence of himself for the other. The consciousness of the free man, on the other hand, is consciousness of the existence of each one for himself, but with a free outgoing from himself to the other and to all. The boundary of a state of slavery is the absence of awareness of it.[16]

The full consent and cooperation of all is a societal ideal, but the law cannot be held hostage by every disgruntled or unruly citizen.

---

13. Idem, *The Courage to Be* (New Haven: Yale University Press, 1952), p. 89. For an underlying reason, see also on p. 89: "The self-affirmation of the self as an individual self always includes the affirmation of the power of being in which the self participates."

14. Russell, *Power*, p. 27.

15. Nikolai Berdyaev, *Slavery and Freedom* (New York: Scribner's, 1944), p. 59.

16. Ibid., p. 60.

"Law is essentially coercible; that is, in case of non-observance, it is possible to make it prevail by force."[17] Law, then, entails more than mere advice, more than a recommended course of action; it is a command. The law establishes relationships between persons in terms of right and duties. For example, the ancient right to torture was based on the legal duty of the suspect to tell the truth; later, when the issue was reformulated as the defendant's right to silence or right against self-incrimination, "third-degree" techniques were held to be no longer justifiable: the state was to refrain from coercing confessions.[18] In both instances, sanctions made the norm obligatory.

A hasty analysis of the coercive aspect of power might seem to limit it to criminal law. Force is most obviously present in this area of public law, yet it is fundamental to all law.[19] When the plaintiff gets an award in a tort case because of the harm that resulted from the defendant's negligence, the state deprives the defendant of his property as truly as if it had imposed a fine on him for reckless driving. The damages may be called compensatory rather than punitive; nevertheless, the subsequent deprivation is mandated by the coercive power of the state, without which laws and judgments would be no more effective than the opinion of one's next-door neighbor.

Obviously, sanctions need not all be negative. They encompass both the carrot and the stick, indulgences as well as deprivations. The criminal law, for example, considers a confession to be coerced and therefore inadmissible in court if it is the fruit of either threats or promises. Pressure to conform to another's will may wear the smile of a reward or the snarl of punishment. Indeed, B. F. Skinner suggests that a system of indulgences rather than of deprivations is usually the more effective way to manipulate others.[20] Nor is it necessary to subscribe to the principle that every man has his price in order to appreciate the power of economic or social indulgences. The incentive approach, the honey rather than vinegar technique, is standard political practice: for ex-

17. Giorgio Del Vecchio, *Philosophy of Law,* trans. T. O. Martin from 8th ed. (Washington: Catholic University of America Press, 1953), p. 260.

18. See Patrick Granfield, "The Theological Development of the Defendant's Obligation to Reply in a Civil Court," *Theological Studies* 26 (1965): 280–98 and 27 (1966): 401–20.

19. See Richard Arens and Harold D. Lasswell, *In Defense of Public Order: The Emerging Field of Sanction Law* (New York: Columbia University Press, 1961).

20. See B. F. Skinner, *Beyond Freedom and Dignity* (New York: Alfred A. Knopf, 1971), chap. 5, "Alternatives to Punishment," pp. 83–100.

ample, the granting of patronage to loyal party members, the granting of federal funds to states carrying out administration policies, the granting of foreign aid to the countries that align themselves with the West.

People are moved by both fear of evil things and the desire for good things. To have power is to be the master of the good and evil that motivate the actions of human beings. Heteronomous decision is the ability to use this dual sanctioning to control others. But, in the last analysis, however desirable control by indulgences appears, force remains the ultimate sanction, always in reserve if indulgences fail.

But sanctions alone, persuasive though they may be, are not enough for political society; consent has an indispensable role to play. The tension between coercion and consent is formulated precisely in H.L.A. Hart's distinction between "being obliged" and "having an obligation."[21] Hart was reacting against Austin's oversimplification of law as the command of a sovereign enforced by a sanction. But law must be more than that, for power alone does not adequately explain political life. From an external perspective, the command and the sanction seem to suffice: to be obliged is to act in response to a sanction; the habit of obedience to commands forms the basis of social continuity and cohesiveness.

The internal perspective, on the other hand, gives a very different insight into political life; it alone can account for one's having an obligation. Hart related obligation to the idea of rules; to recognize the need for a system of rules and to accept this system of rules is to create an obligation to obey the rules. The reason for obedience is not the avoidance of punishment but the furtherance of the common good. A social pressure builds up, partly but not exclusively peer pressure; it is a pressure within the group to preserve and fulfill itself. Reasonable citizens transcend their own individual desires for the sake of public order. Having established community standards, they personally and socially criticize non-conformity and demand conformity. This obligation, Hart said, is not a feeling, not even a feeling of being bound; it is an attitude toward a normative pattern based on the empirical fact of this social pressure.

Tension within the community results from these two different ways of responding to a system of rules; some feel obliged to obey; some

21. See Hart, *Concept of Law*, pp. 79–88.

acknowledge having an obligation. An individual may experience this tension in himself, obeying at times out of fear of punishment and at other times out of a sense of duty; most often he acts habitually, not adverting to the reason for his compliance; but he acts most humanly when he acts with a sense of obligation rooted in rational self-consciousness.

II. THE ROLE OF PUNISHMENT

Punishment brings a jarring note to the ideal harmony that is political friendship. Luther, however, described it as "the strange work of love," a reference that makes Aquinas's term, "the virtue of vengeance," sound less paradoxical. Perhaps we have seen too much of organized sadism to feel easy about ever calling vengeance virtuous. Actually, the *vindicatio* that Aquinas praised did not have the pejorative connotations of revenge or vindictiveness that it may have today. The word refers to punishment for a wrong done, even when its purpose is rehabilitative and medicinal.

VINDICATION

virtuous use of power

In the Middle Ages, *vindicatio* was a virtue concerned with the moderate use of authorized coercion, with the proper function of punishment. The virtue stands revealed when we remove the dark vices related to it, "one by way of excess, namely the sin of cruelty or brutality, which exceeds the measure in punishing; while the other is a vice by way of deficiency and consists in being remiss in punishing."[22] The former leads to tyranny, the latter to anarchy, but true *vindicatio* to peace and order. "For the virtue of *vindicatio* consists in observing the due measure of *vindicatio* with regard to all the circumstances."[23] Certainly, wardens and guards should be able to grow in this virtue through the responsible fulfillment of their prison duties. The virtue of *vindicatio* is also proper for police, prosecutors, juries, judges, and legislators—all part of the criminal process.

The criminal process is society's last bastion of defense. Every law comprises a policy and a sanction; criminal law, however, controls the ultimate sanctions, the deprivations of life, liberty, and property. Here the state's legal monopoly on force, threatened or applied, becomes fully visible. Thus, Johannes Andenaes succinctly defined "the criminal

22. Thomas Aquinas, *Summa theologiae*, II–II, q. 108, a. 2, ad 3.
23. Ibid.

law in the traditional meaning as a body of law regulating the conditions of punishment and the choice of penalty."[24] Correction officials, criminologists, prosecutors, defense lawyers, even criminal law professors are specialists in one or other aspect of punishment. Perhaps the starkness of the title "specialist in punishment" serves to enhance the personal appeal of the notion of rehabilitation, which suggests the kindly physician rather than the cruel turnkey.

People are often emotionally prompted to say: "We ought not to punish criminals; we should help them." It is surprising, however, to find as celebrated a writer as Karl Menninger, M.D., similarly failing to distinguish between the idea of punishment and its purposes. In his popular book *The Crime of Punishment,* he permitted the use of sanctions and penalties, but not punishment; he explained: "Those are not punishments in the sense of long continued torture—pain inflicted over years for the sake of inflicting pain."[25] His characterization of punishment, however, is like a definition of legal insanity in terms of just one or other symptom. Menninger took issue with "the absurdity of the M'Naghten criteria,"[26] but followed the very same method by identifying the essence of punishment with one of its purposes. On the other hand, legal experts such as Johannes Andenaes, H.L.A. Hart, Norval Morris, Herbert L. Packer, and Andrew Von Hirsch always distinguished the essence and its purposes.

We properly define punishment as extrinsically imposed deprivations consequent on fault, and list its four recognized but not universally accepted purposes: retribution, incapacitation, deterrence, and rehabilitation. All four purposes of punishment focus on the subject. (1) Retribution tries to restore the societal balance upset by the convict, who is to compensate for the harm caused to society, if only by becoming a public symbol that flawed actions have negative results. (2) Incapacitation requires the least cooperation from the convict who, treated as an object to be locked up or executed, is prevented from committing further harm. (3) Deterrence appeals to the subject as a responsible decision maker by threatening him with harm if he dis-

24. Johannes Andenaes, *Punishment and Deterrence* (Ann Arbor: The University of Michigan Press, 1974), p. 153.

25. Karl Menninger, *The Crime of Punishment* (New York: Viking Press, 1966), p. 202.

26. Ibid., p. 114. The famous *Daniel M'Naghten's Case,* House of Lords 1843, 8 Eng. Reprints 718, still generally followed in the majority of American jurisdictions, is known primarily for the "right and wrong" test for legal insanity.

obeys. Fear is not the highest motive for obedience, but deterrence is desirable and clearly cost-effective; unfortunately it does not always work. (4) Rehabilitation indirectly involves special deterrence—the fear of going back to prison, of being punished again—but its proper focus is a subjective conversion, whereby, in colloquial terms, the convict learns his lesson and resolves to go straight.

Since the traditional goal of rehabilitation brings into sharp focus the subjective side of punishment, we shall discuss this aspect of punishment at much greater length. Especially significant is the fact that today rehabilitation is an ideal in transition. The failure of the rehabilitative ideal became obvious in the 1970's. The remark in 1974 of a former Attorney General of the United States, William B. Saxbe, that rehabilitation, once "an ingrained belief," is now only "a myth," reveals the radical change that had been taking place in current thinking about criminal punishment.[27] Nor was he alone in that assessment. In 1977, the Director of the Federal Bureau of Prisons, Norman A. Carlson, wrote: "More and more people—criminal justice officials and the public alike—are questioning the validity of rehabilitation as the major goal of incarceration."[28] Acknowledging the high percentage of recidivists in our prisons, he added, "People understandably want to know why we have been unsuccessful in changing the behavior of these offenders. The truth of the matter is, we don't know."[29] By the 1980's Francis A. Allen could write without hesitation a book entitled, *The Decline of the Rehabilitative Ideal.*[30] The 1987 official *Sentencing Guidelines and Policy Statements for the Federal Courts,* although constitutionally challenged in 1988, reflect this emerging consensus, with deterrence and retribution in the ascendancy.

The new emphasis is on making the punishment fit the crime, not the criminal. In some respect, we are going back to Cesare Beccaria— not to the way things were in 1794, when he published his classic, *On Crimes and Punishment,* but to the ideas he so effectively preached. The "grand theorem," with which he concluded his own great work,

[margin note: emphasis today is on making punishment fit the crime]

27. William B. Saxbe, *Washington Post,* 1 October 1974, p. A9.

28. Norman A. Carlson, "A More Balanced Correction Philosophy, *FBI Law Enforcement Bulletin* (Jan. 1977), pp. 22–23.

29. Ibid., p. 23.

30. Francis A. Allen, *The Decline of the Rehabilitative Ideal* (New Haven: Yale University Press, 1981). See an earlier article, David Granfield, "Rehabilitation: An Ideal in Transition," *Social Thought* 3 (1977): 5–14, which I have adapted for this section of the chapter.

seems once more to be giving the impetus to penal reform: "In order for punishment not to be, in every instance, an act of violence of one or of many against a private citizen, it must be essentially public, prompt, necessary, the least possible in the given circumstances, proportionate to the crime, and dictated by the laws."[31]

Our major concern here is not why a restrained and humanized principle of retribution seems to be moving back into popularity, but rather why rehabilitation seems to be falling swiftly and, I would suggest properly, into a subordinate position. Perhaps the real reason is that only if rehabilitation is so regulated and controlled can a true change of heart be justly and successfully achieved. To take a good look at rehabilitation tells us much about a jurisprudence of subjectivity.

Punitive rehabilitation, at first glance, appears to be self-contradictory: it attempts to make people better by first making them worse. In comparison, the other purposes of punishment seem straightforward— if a rapist is hanged or imprisoned for life, there is no question about incapacitation, no ambiguity about deterrence, and no doubt about his paying for his crime. Our immediate question is, however: Do deprivations work with equal effectiveness when their purpose is the reform of the criminal? The crux of the difficulty is suggested by Aquinas's definition of punishment as "the deprivation in an intellectual creature of form, habit, or anything which could be necessary for acting well, whether it pertains to the soul or the body or exterior things."[32] To reform by punishment means to make a person act better by taking away things necessary for acting well.

This less-is-more paradox can work, but it usually requires a favorable context. Norval Morris pointed out the ideal standard: "A prison should be . . . the very paradigm of law and order,"[33] an eminently sensible remark about a still unrealized ideal. To the extent that the punishments or the conditions of punishment are themselves unjust, they impede reform.

Typical obstacles to reform have been detailed by G. M. Sykes in his

31. Cesare Beccaria, *On Crimes and Punishments*, trans. H. Paolucci (Indianapolis: Bobbs-Merrill, 1963), p. 99. Compare with *Sentencing Guidelines and Policy Statements for the Federal Courts* (Washington: Government Printing Office, 1987).

32. Thomas Aquinas, *De malo*, Q.1, ad 4.

33. Norval Morris, *The Future of Imprisonment* (Chicago: University of Chicago Press, 1974), p. 221.

study *The Society of Captives*. In the many years since he wrote the book, we have discovered again and again how widespread are these blindly inhumane prison systems; we wonder, not that so few persons have been reformed, but that any have. Sykes spoke of the "pains of punishment—deprivations of liberty, goods and services, heterosexual relationship, autonomy, and security. Listed abstractly, they do not reveal their concrete harmfulness; and yet these deprivations and frustrations pose profound threats to the inmate's personality or sense of worth."[34] They steadily undermine the very basis of reform and, as Sykes concluded, they leave the inmate feeling enslaved and rejected, materially despoiled, virtually castrated, childishly controlled, and constantly and hopelessly vulnerable.

Why have these conditions perdured, when, for the last hundred years, criminologists have prided themselves on being motivated by the rehabilitative ideal? The answer is complex and problematic. Traditionally, two principles have been at work: the principle of lesser eligibility, which was described thus by Jeremy Bentham: "The ordinary condition of a convict . . . ought not to be made more eligible than that of the poorest class of subjects in a state of innocence and liberty."[35] The second is the principle of retribution, or rather a distortion of it, holding that a convict's life ought deliberately to be made unpleasant, painful, frustrating, as if the prison sentence were not primarily a loss of liberty but rather a systematic thwarting of all human instincts and needs.

Another reason why rehabilitation, though an acknowledged goal of imprisonment, was never given the commonsense context that it required was that it always fitted awkwardly into the overall philosophy of the criminal law; that is, the rehabilitative ideal seemed to run counter to the traditional reluctance to penalize persons for what they think, and the rehabilitative ideal tends to confuse the distinction between law and morals. Let us look at these two points separately.

First, the Roman law principle *Cogitationis poenam nemo meretur* ("No one deserves punishment for his thoughts").[36] has long prevailed in English and American law. Bad intentions, evil desires, wicked schemes are not as such criminally actionable. Even so-called inchoate

---

34. G. M. Sykes, *The Society of Captives* (New York: Atheneum, 1965), p. 58.
35. Jeremy Bentham, *Works*, ed. J. Bowring, 11 vols. (Edinburgh, 1838–1843); *The Panopticon* (1839), Vol. 4, pp. 122–23.
36. *Institutiones juris civilis*, II, 658.

or incomplete crimes, such as conspiracy, require more than the specific intention to violate the law. They need something to get them out of the realm of the mind; thus, for a conspiracy, there must be in addition to the specific intent of each party, an agreement between them, and frequently an "overt act" in furtherance of the agreement.

One's motive for committing a crime, however, although it may be relevant as evidence, is not an element of the crime itself. Whether or not the motive is good or bad or can be proved at all is not determinative. If the defendant had the requisite criminal state of mind, the *mens rea,* and perpetrated the forbidden action, the *actus reus,* he is guilty. Sometimes the question of motivation arises in cases involving mercy killing and civil disobedience, but even here intention, not motive, is the critical factor. Of course, once a defendant is convicted, his motivation and his attitude are influential in setting the terms and conditions of imprisonment. Again, we must make a distinction: the older retributive position made motive and attitude relevant in fixing the sentence once and for all; the newer rehabilitative position uses them both, first in establishing the broad range of an indeterminate sentence and later in judging the appropriateness of its termination.

The second factor reflecting the inconsistent position of the rehabilitative ideal in the criminal process is its reactionary blending of law and morals, strangely out of place in this era of ethical pluralism and First Amendment rights. The rehabilitative ideal requires for its operation a constant intrusion into the privacy of the convict's mind. The courts in the past have not viewed this as unconstitutional, for traditionally prisons were thought literally to be penitentiaries, reformatories, houses of correction. Moreover, the convict himself, as the Virginia Court of Appeals phrased it, was "a slave of the state."[37] Courts, during the last decade, have recognized more and more rights of convicts, but as yet have not eliminated coercive rehabilitative procedures.

Outside prison, the law is concerned principally and directly with external conduct; it leaves morals to the conscience and to God. In prison, the officials or parole boards try to read the conscience and, some say, to play God. Judging another's conscience, apart from ex-

---

37. *Ruffin* v. *Comm.,* 62 Va. (21 Gratt.) 790 (1871). Despite many liberating changes in Virginia law, a Virginia case was decided in 1984 by the Supreme Court, holding that an inmate does not have any reasonable expectation of privacy in his prison cell entitling him to the protection of the Fourth Amendment against unreasonable searches and seizures. *Hudson* v. *Palmer,* 468 U.S. 517 (1984).

ternal conduct, is a rash and uncertain undertaking. St. Paul asked: "Who, for example, knows a man's innermost self, but the man's own spirit within him?" (I Cor. 2:12). Prison adds to the difficulty, for it is hard to be a good prisoner in a bad prison, harder to be a good person in a bad prison. On the other hand, a "good" prisoner might easily remain a bad person—a bank robber with no banks to rob, a child molester in a world of adults, or a confidence man playing the game that leads to release.

One proposed justification of these intrusions into freedom and privacy is the medical model of penal reform. Nevertheless, for all its humane motivation, it tends to dehumanize. In fact, the medical model has been the major source of dissatisfaction with the rehabilitative ideal. Let us see why this is so. Its major premise is that crime is a sickness; its two corollaries are: the convict is not responsible for his crime, no more than for having appendicitis; and the convict can be forcibly treated, as if given an appendectomy.

medical model: crime is sickness

Not all criminologists hold such extreme views; some clearly oppose them. Yet, in practice, many retain the benevolent image of a firm but understanding doctor treating a sick child for whom he must often make unpleasant decisions; the fact that the patient is an anti-social adult legitimates the prescription of harsher methods. As a result, the situation, at best paternalistic and at worst tyrannic, is essentially coercive. Release depends on the prisoner's cooperation with rehabilitative programs and conformity to rehabilitative standards, often neither clearly enunciated, coherently followed, or psychologically sound.

The medical model rests on a strongly coercive base, but what it gains in power it loses in vision. It is ill-equipped for diagnosis or prognosis, since it operates on a misconception that falsifies both the problem and the solution. What is crucial is to recognize in principle and practice that crime and punishment are not, except indirectly, medical problems but legal ones, and that the criminal, though wrong, is a responsible being with human dignity and inner freedom. Indeed, his conviction, as contrasted with an acquittal by reason of insanity, assumes his legal sanity and responsibility. For his keepers to treat him as if he were sick and to require his cooperation in this medico-legal fiction as a price of his release is clearly coercive.

What, then, is rehabilitation supposed to do? Andrew Von Hirsch wrote: "We define 'rehabilitation' as any measure taken to change an offender's character, habits, or behavior patterns so as to diminish his criminal propensities."[38] Though broad, this definition is what criminologists generally mean. If taken literally, of course, it would extend to special deterrence (the intimidation resulting from punishment actually received) and incapacitation (the limiting effects of aging and institutional wear and tear on future wrongdoing).

Looking to the heart of rehabilitation, we find that it is a recommitment to justice, a positive response of persons who are authentically experiencing intersubjectivity. Convicts at the Attica prison uprising in 1971 cried out, "We are human beings." They were keenly aware of their own subjectivity, though in the past by acting criminally they had denied the subjectivity of others and the claims of intersubjectivity.

Del Vecchio, as we have seen, explained the bilaterality of justice in Kantian terms: each person exists as an end in himself and not simply as a means or instrument to be used by others. For a person to be truly just or truly reformed he must be convinced that others are subjects like himself and that he should not treat them as things or slaves, and he must be resolved to act accordingly. Criminals have, at least implicitly, denied human equality and the rights that it implies. Moreover, in violating the rights of others, the criminal justifies his own punishment. With inexorable logic, Del Vecchio reasoned: "The idea of requital is thus revealed as implicit in that of justice; not indeed in the sense of producing a material duplication of the same acts, but rather in the sense that every act performed by anyone with regard to the other implies the virtual authorization of a similar act between the same subjects supposing their parts to reversed."[39] Lifting this notion to the societal level and bypassing the primitive "eye for an eye" formulation, we see punishment as a reciprocal and proportionate deprivation.

When the convict becomes aware of his crime as an injustice against an equal, one who is an existential subject like himself, and recognizes that his own punishment is an act of justice that he himself has virtually authorized, only then does he begin to appreciate what he had done and what he must do. When, finally, he makes the commitment of fidelity to the implications of intersubjectivity, he has then been radi-

38. Andrew Von Hirsch, *Doing Justice: The Choice of Punishments,* Report of the Committee for the Study of Incarceration (New York: Hill and Wang, 1976), p. 11, n. 2.

39. Giorgio Del Vecchio, *Justice* (Edinburgh: The University Press, 1952), pp. 84–85.

cally rehabilitated. Or, to put it in simpler words, when he commits himself to the rule of justice and resolves to give to each his own, or to the Golden Rule and resolves to do unto others as he would have them do unto him, only then has his conversion begun. He may still need help and training, still need to develop the social virtues necessary to strengthen this resolve, but he has made the biggest step—a true change of heart.

Should we, as a practical matter, provide for deterrence, incapacitation, and retribution and let rehabilitation take care of itself? Of course not. To do so would be an ill service to the community, a callous disregard of the convict as a person, and a betrayal of the religious and cultural values of our civilization. But we should keep rehabilitation in its place—not to reject it but to liberate it.

The solution can be found only in the harmonizing of two principles: punishment must be coercive; rehabilitation must be free. Hart gives us the structural insight: "Reform can only have a place within the system of punishment as an exploitation of the opportunities presented by conviction or compulsory detention of criminals."[40] Morris gives us the operating standard: "Power over a criminal's life should not be taken in excess of that which would be taken were his reform not considered one of our purposes."[41]

Voluntariness is the crucial element. We can imprison a man without his consent, but we cannot reform him without his consent. To try to force his conversion casts a chill over his nascent impulses to justice. That means that joining rehabilitative programs (and they should be plentiful and professional) and continuing in such programs or successfully completing them should in no way change the terms or conditions of punishment; for here, even a little coercion is a dangerous thing.

Consequently, we must again speak of rehabilitation as an ideal in transition—a transition that is twofold. There is the general shift toward fitting the punishment to the crime rather than to the criminal. But, even within this framework, there is another shift, which is of the essence and which is, in Morris's words, "the substitution of facilitated change for coerced cure."[42] This approach is not to impede reform,

40. H.L.A. Hart, *Punishment and Responsibility* (New York: Oxford University Press, 1968; reprint, 1975), p. 26.
41. Norval Morris, *The Future of Imprisonment*, p. 18.
42. Ibid., p. 27.

but to remove a prime impediment to reform, so that the convict, while being justly punished, may be able to prepare himself willingly for a just life in a free world.

The psychological potential for conversion is that everyone acts for what appears to him to be good. Rehabilitation comes from both knowing and choosing, on a habitual basis, what is actually good; it is an enlightened commitment to the good of intersubjectivity as legally formulated. But citizens cannot be coerced to virtue, which must remain essentially free. This is true of everyone, even the convict, who, though deprived of many good things, must use his personal power to be himself as fully as possible under all the circumstances of his flawed and constrained life.

The power to punish can mandate some degree of retribution, incapacitation, and deterrence; but it can only facilitate rehabilitation. In other words, by the very nature of the task, the political community is limited to fostering rational self-consciousness, which manifests itself socially as likemindedness and political friendship. Punishment, "the strange work of love," is necessary to protect the likeminded friends who constitute the body politic. Punishment is necessary to vindicate justice scorned as well as to prevent and deter future crimes, but it must also, without undercutting its other purposes, show effective love for the criminal by affording him the opportunity for personal rehabilitation. This requires both wisdom and power, but power is used wisely only by taking into account the basic freedom and dignity of all. To repeat the cry of the Attica prisoners, "We are human beings."

III. THE EXPECTATIONS OF THE PEOPLE

Authority partially resolves the tension between coercion and consent, because it stems from the consent to coerce. Formulated empirically, in the terms used by Lasswell and McDougal, authority is power in conformity with the expectations of the people.[43] I would add to this: and in harmony with the dictates of reason. This qualification is not alien to their thought, though they did not make it explicit or develop it philosophically.

Internal expectation distinguishes authoritative power from naked

43. See Myres S. McDougal and Harold D. Lasswell, "The Identification and Appraisal of Diverse Systems of Public Order," in M. S. McDougal and Associates, *Studies in World Public Order* (New Haven: Yale University Press, 1960), pp. 13–14.

power. Expectation is not an exact synonym of consent; in the political arena, however, it includes both wholehearted agreement as well as reluctant acceptance. At the minimum, people go along with the existing structure and praxis of goverance, recognizing that certain persons have certain power to act in accord with certain procedures, standards, and values. Subjectively, this participation in a political structure consists in a decision by the many to permit the few to make binding decisions in matters of the common good.

Alternatives to authority are unanimity (everyone must consent) and anarchy (consent is irrelevant). Both forms have proved to be unworkable in large social units, because neither can provide for an effective and efficient relationship between means and ends, between unified activity and the common good. Pure anarchy would reject political decision making; absolute unanimity would make it unattainable. Interestingly, anarchy puts its hopes at the mercy of an invisible-hand type of unanimity, believing that if, without law, all do their jobs, the common good will flourish. The underlying flaw in both alternatives is the failure to appreciate the fact that the more members, the more disagreements, for not all persons are good and reasonable and well-informed, and even if they all were they would differ widely in their decisions on practical matters.

Why have authority? Basically because of the plurality of available means and because of the limitations of human beings. Since in all areas of community activity there are many possible ways of handling concrete problems (for example, intestacy, pollution, taxation, corporate proxies, foreign trade, grounds for divorce), political decision making is necessary to ensure unified activity. But even when the goal (child support, freedom to worship, the prohibition of murder and rape) is clearly necessary, authority is still required because many members fail to act authentically owing to subjective defects—in experience, intelligence, reasonableness, or responsibility.

Yves Simon called these two functions of authority the essential (to unify activity when there is a plurality of means) and the substitutional (to enforce activity even though the means are uniquely determined). What he considered to be the most essential function of authority was its overall direction toward the good of the community.[44] The interests

44. Yves Simon, *Philosophy of Democratic Government* (Chicago: University of Chicago Press, 1951), chap. I, "General Theory of Government," pp. 1–71, especially n. 23, pp. 59–62. See also his book *Authority* (Notre Dame, Ind.: Notre Dame University Press, 1962).

of most citizens are predominantly private and frequently selfish, as can be expected; but there must also be a limited subordination of private interests to the common welfare. Authority gives this guidance as gently or as forcefully as the circumstances require.

Authority is the dynamism that springs from consensus and directs cooperation. It harmonizes the efforts of the members of the community toward the realization of their shared goals. Society sets up a policy program with step-by-step correlations to a sanctioning apparatus. But the primary function of authority is direction, not sanction: the directive role is indispensable to unified effort; the sanctioning is ancillary. A political community of well-informed and saintly geniuses would still need directions; but, since no community can so characterize its citizens, all communities need both directions and sanctions.

To understand authority properly, we must keep uppermost in our minds its service function. Authority and the government it constitutes are not sovereign entities, supreme and transcendent, lording it over citizens and unaccountable to them, as Bodin thought. All the legitimate power that the government has comes from the people civilly united, who always have the right to repossess what they have delegated. The government does not have a life of its own; it is an organ of the body politic. In non-metaphorical terms, the government consists of citizens who, through a division of labor, have been given ministerial roles— activities to be performed for the common good in conformity with the expectations of the body politic. The fact that their decisions are enforcible does not make these governmental agents essentially superior to the rest of the citizens, only more powerful and thus more accountable. Let us then examine three basic limitations on political authority.

The first limitation on authority is power itself. Even when a government arrogates to itself the mantle of sovereignty as a "mortal god," it cannot conceal the finiteness of its strength. Whatever appeal authority may make to feelings, reason, and conscience, it must also be able to exercise effective control through its decisions—policies implemented by sanctions—the core of political power. Rudolf Von Jhering made this point vividly: "Powerlessness, impotence of the State force, is the capital sin of the State, from which there is no absolution; a sin which society neither forgives nor tolerates. It is an inner contradiction: State force without force."[45] This kind of weakness does not mean that

45. Rudolf von Jhering, *Laws as a Means to an End*, Modern Legal Philosophy Series, Vol. V, trans. I. Husik (Boston: The Boston Book Co., 1914), p. 234.

the citizen is freer in his quest for meaning and value through society, but rather that without the direction and protection of the state he may find himself "subject to seven other devils worse than the first" (Lk. 17:26). If the state is not in control, other factions will fill up the vacuum and wield power ever more ruthlessly.

The second limitation on authority is its mandate. The political community entrusts the government with a task to be accomplished within prescribed boundaries. Actions that exceed the mandate are *ultra vires,* a usurpation of power by the government, which should confine itself within the scope of the authority granted to it by the people. The Bill of Rights is an explicit protection against governmental intrusion, but the whole Constitution contains many such fundamental limitations, such as the tripartite structure of checks and balances, states rights, and the freedom of contract. At the same time, there remains the hermeneutical problem in applying any general norm— the scope is broad or narrow depending on the complexion of the court that interprets it. Nevertheless, the basic principle of the political consensus is clear: authority without constitutional limitations is tyranny.

The third limitation on authority is the nature of man and society. Although many positivists, such as Comte and Kelsen, would disagree—requiring only force and validity—there is a broad recognition, even among some positivists, that for an ongoing operation, for a functional society, the exigencies of human beings and human society must be taken into the calculations. Thus H.L.A. Hart insists on "the minimum content of natural law" for societal survival.[46]

This third limitation is more difficult to clarify than the other two, because it depends theoretically on fundamental presuppositions concerning man himself. But it also depends on the accumulated wisdom of commonsense judgments about the needs of human beings and the implications of intersubjectivity. Unless force is held to be the sole determinant or unless an absolute majority is held to justify everything, the question remains: whether, beyond the strength of authority and the mandate accorded it, there is a more fundamental limitation, the nature of human society and the political subject. To affirm this limitation on the operations of authority is to bring the rule of ethics to bear on community interactions and international relations.

Sir Winston Churchill made this point in speaking before the British

46. Hart, *Concept of Law,* pp. 189–95.

Parliament in January 1945. Harold Nicholson recounted Churchill's attempt to reassure the members about his demand for the "unconditional surrender" of the Third Reich: "He rebuffed all assertions that it was our intention to exterminate or trample on the German people. 'Not at all,' he said—and then he took off his glasses and turned to face the Speaker. He struck his breast like an orangutang. 'We remain bound,' he shouted, 'by our customs and our own nature.' "[47]

Let us examine the ethical question more fully. Assuming that authority remains faithful to its threefold limitation, do the laws that it establishes bind in conscience? As we have seen in discussing coercion and consent, Hart asserted that the idea of rules from an internal perspective implies "having an obligation," which he distinguished from "being obliged."[48] He did not mention conscience, but he distinguished legal obligations from moral ones. Certainly such a distinction can be properly made; the question remains, however, whether or not a legal obligation is morally binding. From a positivistic approach, this question may be deemed irrelevant to the sphere of positive law. Nevertheless, those subject to the law have an exigency toward responsible action. In any concrete legal event, the fiction of an essentially nonmoral decision breaks down, for whether the subject's action is responsible or irresponsible, the very question itself is a question about moral judgment. This is so, as we shall see, even from Hart's positivist perspective.

Austin's imperative theory, with its command-sanction oversimplification, although it is unworkable in practice, is a more logically coherent explanation of the legal system than one which speaks of a legal obligation without a moral dimension. Unless the legal subject is being forced, is "being obliged," he acts from an internal principle, which involves his own ethical integrity. Hart had two concerns that made him reluctant to equate obligation and moral judgment: he wanted the law to be independent of other disciplines, especially ethics, religion, and "obscure metaphysics"; and he wanted to ground obligation on empirical facts. In attempting to do so, he tried to postulate an obligation based on neither conscience nor force. The source of this obligation Hart attributed to "pressure," with its criticism of nonconformity and its demand for conformity. This pressure springs from an

47. Harold Nicholson, *Diaries and Letters,* Vol. II: *The War Years,* ed. N. Nicholson (New York: Atheneum, 1967), p. 429.
48. Hart, *Concept of Law,* pp. 79–88.

awareness that rules are indispensable for the community and that individual interests must sometimes be sacrificed for the common good.

From this internal perspective, Hart noted, criticism includes self-criticism; an obligation may be present even when no one else is aware of the nonconformity. The existence of legal obligation is clear; Hart's explanation of it, however, seems adequate only if one refrains from asking further relevant questions. A crucial question is: Why should this legal obligation convince us that we are duty-bound, if we are not obliged by force to obey and if no outside social pressure can be applied since no one knows?

The weakness of Hart's position is not his empiricism but its narrowness. He grounded his theory on empirical data, but, despite his insistence on the internal aspect of rules, he did not investigate sufficiently the empirical data of consciousness. As a result, Hart did not present a complete and coherent theory of legal obligation. Yet, in effect though not by name, he did have recourse to some kind of responsible, decision-making process that accounts for obligation.

One can explain the obligatory character of legal norms no less empirically than Hart, but with more subjective penetration through the perspective of conscious intentionality. First, as we have noted in the Monosphere, the moral basis of all action is the exigency for harmony between knowing and doing, which is rooted in the unity and integrity of the mind. Second, as we noted in the Isosphere, all members of the community, all human beings, are linked together by intersubjectivity. Consistent with that factual knowledge, all are morally bound to treat one another reasonably as other selves. This obligation is formulated as the virtue of justice. Third, as we noted in the Koinosphere, factually political society is a human necessity, for it alone can guarantee the self-sufficiency—the protecting and fostering of the common good—that individuals and even groups cannot achieve at all or cannot do well enough.

Knowing all this, we are bound morally to act consistently and obey the just laws of the duly constituted political society, for without by and large conformity to its authoritative directives, this necessary means of human fulfillment could not function. Although moral obligation stands theoretically firm on the abovementioned, three-layered, consensual foundation, it is, of course, strengthened by the social pressure from one's fellow citizens and the coercive power of the state, thereby ensuring, through a blend of consent and coercion, a higher performance rating for the body politic than exclusive reliance on individual consciences might hope to achieve.

The reluctance to commit oneself to content is not exclusively a characteristic of positivists. Lon Fuller, a proponent, once removed, of the natural law, was concerned "not with the substantive aims of legal rules, but with the ways in which a system of rules for governing human conduct must be constructed and administered if it is to be efficacious and at the same time remain what it purports to be."[49] The meaning of "procedural" is explained in his thematic sentence: "What I have called the internal morality of law is in this sense a procedural version of natural law. . . ."[50] As a practical matter, this procedural morality warns against the eight ways that legal rules may miscarry: no rules; only *ad hoc* rules; no promulgation of rules; retroactive rules; contradictory rules; impossible rules; frequently changed rules; no congruence between rules as announced and as administered.[51]

In responding to Hart's view that "on the tacit assumption that the proper end of human activity is survival," one must assert the need of a "minimum content of natural law,"[52] Fuller gave his own substantive minimum. Challenging as hardly sufficient Hart's exclusive emphasis on survival, he opted for communication: "If I were asked, then, to discern one central indisputable principle of what may be called substantive natural law—Natural Law with capital letters—I would find it in the injunction: 'Open up, maintain, and preserve the integrity of the channels of communication by which men convey to one another what they perceive, feel, and desire.' "[53]

Together, Hart and Fuller have suggested the bare substantive minimum: survival and communication or, in more philosophic terms, human existence and human intersubjectivity, the foundational aspects of life to be protected and fostered by law. Incidentally, Fuller's central principle, although too limited in itself and unnecessarily confined by him to a theoretical level, accords well with a jurisprudence of subjectivity, for the perfection of communication requires interiority: we must be aware of our own mental operations in order to grasp meaning and

49. Lon L. Fuller, *The Morality of the Law* (New Haven: Yale University Press, 1964), p. 97.
50. Ibid., p. 96.
51. Ibid., p. 38.
52. Hart, *Concept of Law*, chap. IX, sect. 2, pp. 189–95.
53. Fuller, *The Morality of the Law*, p. 186.

value fully, to share them with others, and to achieve a binding consensus—the communion of men and women in the political idea as
worked out through political friendship.

CONCLUSION

The dynamics of governance centers on authority or authoritative
power—authoritative because it conforms to the expectations of the
people and is grounded in the dictates of reason; power because it
involves heteronomous decision, policies implemented by sanctions.
The blend of consent and coercion helps the members of the political
community to become more fully themselves by ensuring the self-
sufficiency that is a prerequisite of the good life. Punishment, the
deprivation of good things consequent on fault, is the unfortunate but
indispensable safeguard of this self-sufficiency.

Inevitably, as the political process functions, the moral dimension of
authority—whether just laws bind in conscience—surfaces in the questioning mind, because authority concerns itself with the very stuff of
morality, authentic decision making about human values. Authority
supplements the moral life of man as it emerges from the Monosphere,
the realm of personal integrity, and from the Isosphere, the realm of
conscious intersubjectivity, sublating but not replacing these more fundamental moral positions.

The etymology of the word "authority" reveals its supportive function; it derives from *auctus,* the past participle of *augere,* to make
something increase, to cause it to grow. Authority is a kind of love—
the mutual benevolence that constitutes political friendship and becomes operative as legitimate power. For there to be a genuine experience of authority in the regulator or the regulated, and most conspic-
uously in members of a participatory democracy, all citizens must share
in an ordered response to value. Ultimately, the dynamics of governance
are rooted in an enlightened and shared love. Political life should be a
progressive unfolding of that inner reality.

PART FOUR

THE THEOSPHERE
THE SACRAL EXPERIENCE OF LAW

The Theosphere is the realm of the transcendent where we study the legal subject in relation to a divine ground. Starting again with the data of sense and consciousness and focusing on the mental operations that occur when one participates in legal events, the legal subject asks the question: What is the ultimate standard for the meaning and value of law?

There are two avenues of investigation. The first looks to the connection between positive law and divine law that is called natural law—a human construct to enable us to assess the rationality and worthwhileness of behavior. But, as a human construct, it manifests hermeneutic problems, especially those occasioned by the transition from classicist to modern culture. Consequently, after taking a new look at the traditional formulation of natural law, we then consider a current and revised understanding of natural law.

The second avenue of investigation in quest of standards reaches beyond natural law and beyond human nature itself. The world of our experience prompts us to ask whether or not there is an ultimate ground of meaning and value. This is the "God question," and it springs from the operations of our mind. It is a question that authenticity demands that we ask. Whatever answer we reach will definitively characterize our inner experience of law and form the core of a jurisprudence of subjectivity.

CHAPTER 8

THE NATURAL LAW IN TRANSITION

Nature loves to hide.—Heraclitus*

For over two thousand years the idea of natural law, through periods of triumph and decline, has survived in one form or other. Currently, as it moves from a classicist to an empirical culture, it faces one of its most probing challenges. A key question arises: Has this traditional idea outlived its usefulness, or has it still an effective and even necessary function in a radically different intellectual and social milieu?

Any reassessment or reformulation of natural law involves the critical issue of change: Can it admit to change? Can it adjust to change? Is the natural law a platform of immutable principles discovered once and for all by ancient thinkers and handed down as a juridical heritage for subsequent generations? Or is the natural law a process of decision, with a problematic link to human nature, subject to constant and relativistic tinkering? Or is the natural law a process of decision, so rooted in the invariant structures of the mind that in fostering the demands of singularity it provides for continuity and change?

To answer these questions, we must first clarify what traditionally has been meant by natural law. As a law, it is a rule and measure of actions; as natural, it has human nature as its source and its object. There are, of course, many notions about what human nature is, for nature is the term that we give to what we are trying to understand, in this instance, mankind. The issue is whether we can find in nature any rights and laws of a universal and permanent character. Lonergan distinguished the classicist and the empirical bases of our knowledge of natural right: "It may be placed in universal propositions, self-evident truths, naturally known certitudes. On the other hand, it may

---

* Heraclitus, Hermann Diels, *Die Fragmente der Vorsocratiker*, ed. Walther Kranz (Berlin: Weidmann, 1968), 22 B 123.

natural: human nature as source & object

law: rule & measure of actions

177

be placed in nature itself, in nature not as abstractly conceived but as concretely operating."[1]

We learn about nature and the guidelines to its proper functioning through reason, which is the human ability to ask and answer questions. Natural law is a set of answers to fundamental questions about human action, ultimately answers to one encompassing question: What values should all men and women share? Norms are a function of values; through norms, values are translated into directives for right action. Natural law comprehends the basic values of human existence. A set of overarching principles to govern the conduct of human beings is not a mere phantasy; the Constitution of the United States (1789) and the Declaration of Human Rights of the United Nations (1948) enunciated normatively many of the values found in the naturalist tradition. This is not surprising for, as A. P. d'Entrèves rightly concluded: "Perhaps the best description of natural law is that it provides a name for the point of intersection between law and morals."[2]

Moreover, leading representatives from other jurisprudential schools share a consensus about these same values. Two examples will suffice. Judge Jerome Frank, an American Realist, wrote: "I do not understand how any decent man today can refuse to adopt, as the basis of modern civilization, the fundamental principles of Natural Law, relative to human conduct, as stated by Thomas Aquinas."[3] An English positivist, H.L.A. Hart, asserted, as we have seen, that if survival is our goal and if rules are to be obeyed voluntarily, they must have a "minimum content of natural law," and he justified this assertion on the empirical basis of human vulnerability, approximate equality, limited altruism, limited resources, and limited understanding and strength of will.[4]

In an attempt to take a fresh look at natural law, it is not enough to review a variety of theories, even contemporary ones. What is necessary is to re-experience the seminal insights of the past, lest we remain on the abstract level of symbols without being able to appreciate their meaning. Through these foundational insights we regain the immediacy

---

1. Bernard Lonergan, "Natural Right and Historical Mindedness," *A Third Collection,* ed. F. E. Crowe (New York: Paulist Press, 1985), p. 172.

2. A. P. d'Entrèves, *Natural Law* (London: Hutchinson & Co., 1951), p. 116.

3. Jerome Frank, *Law and the Modern Mind* (Garden City, N.Y.: Doubleday, Anchor Books, 1963), p. xx.

4. H.L.A. Hart, *The Concept of Law* (Oxford: Clarendon Press, 1961), pp. 189–95.

of the natural law, which, freed from the paralysis of formalism, discloses a process of decision underlying its value system. Thinking over the process, we look anew at the inner grounding of natural law. To do so, we first revisit medieval natural law as abstractly formulated; and next compare modern natural law as subjectively revised. In that way, we may well discover an overlooked empirical similarity and harmony.

I. THE NATURAL LAW REVISITED   — *Medieval Period*

Classical thinkers would be grossly misrepresented by any suggestion that they lacked an awareness of change. In fact, the idea of natural law was in part an answer to problems occasioned by an existence seemingly ever in flux. As we noted, philosophers such as Plato and Aristotle, in their struggle to bring stability to human affairs, identified reason, the *nous,* as the principle of order, the means of countering the pervasive disorder in man and society. In a similar vein, the Sophists contrasted *nomos* and *physis,* law and nature, hoping by an appeal to the latter to order society more in harmony with reason.

Over the last century, however, the very order enjoined by natural law has been radically criticized as hopelessly outdated, inflexible, unrealistic, unreasonable. Of course, the traditional emphasis on abstract nature and deductive logic partly explains this rejection, especially since the Stoics had infected natural law with an abiding formalism, which emphasized being rather than becoming and moved from the Aristotelian equity model to a rigid rules model.

Aquinas clearly shared the classical perspective, but he was too great a thinker to be locked into any formal structure that would overlook the fact that the subject matter of the law (persons, actions, and things) are all concrete and singular. Aquinas was more Aristotelian than Stoic in his provision for change. After beginning his relatively short "treatise," *De lege,* by showing that law pertains to reason, by which we order our actions,[5] he went on to discuss the problem of change in three of six articles on natural law[6] and in five out of fourteen articles on positive law.[7]

5. Thomas Aquinas, *Summa theologiae,* I–II, q. 90, a. 1.
6. Ibid., q. 94, aa. 4–6.
7. Ibid., q. 96, a. 6, and q. 97, aa. 1–4.

In his analysis of prudence and in his commentary on the *Nicoma-chean Ethics,* Aquinas paid great attention to change and reason's ordering role. Indeed, there is also an explicit statement by Aquinas, discomforting to some traditional disciples, that human nature upon which natural law is grounded is itself in some way changeable: "It is necessary that what is natural, having an immutable nature, be every-where the same. But the nature of man is mutable (*natura humana mutabilis est*). And therefore, what is natural to man is sometimes able to fail."[8] Crucial questions inevitably arise: What are the limitations on this mutability? Do these failings affect the application or coverage of natural law? Do these failings justify exceptions to natural law?

[margin handwriting: human nature is mutable for Aquinas]

It may be helpful to keep in mind that, since it is natural, everyone experiences natural law at least compactly; it is not a new discovery but an emerging consciousness of what we already take for granted. Aquinas was so convinced of this that he stated that natural law cannot be erased from our minds. Our analysis, therefore, is more than a look at time-honored theories; the major part of our task remains a subjec-tive one—an *anamnesis,* a recollection, a mnemonic retrieval of our own first intimations of these key juridical insights. Our pondering of Eros and Nemesis has already struck a familiar chord in our compact consciousness; now we consider those insights already partially the-matized.

In this section, we examine: first, Aquinas's formulation of natural law in order to discover the characteristics of his platform of abstract principles—their empirical basis and their changeability; second, with the additional help of Aristotle, the subjective aspects of the decision-making process in order to appropriate more perfectly those mental operations.

A. *The Abstract Principles*

An image of natural law as a set of abstract principles formulated during the pre-modern period of Western culture is accurate, but it is incomplete on at least two counts: it overlooks both the experiential underpinning as well as the built-in provision for adjusting to changed circumstances.

8. Ibid., II–II, q. 57, a. 2, ad. 1; see also *ibid.,* Supp. III, q. 41, ad 3 and *De malo.* q. 2, a. 4, ad 13. For an analysis of these texts, see R. A. Armstrong, *Primary and Secondary Precepts in Thomistic Natural Law Teaching* (The Hague: Martinus Nijhoff, 1966), pp. 174–77.

The empirical ground of natural law has been effectively disguised by a hierarchic formulation, yet it is certainly present. It is true that Aquinas, writing from a theological perspective, discussed the eternal law first and then analyzed the natural law as a participation in the eternal law. But despite this descent from above, he understood that natural law as a human construct does not begin with God but with Eros; natural law rests on human inclinations: "To the natural law belong those things to which a man is inclined naturally."[9]

Determining the existence and meaning of these inclinations requires experience, insight, and verification—all works of the mind. And decision follows judgment. The inclinations are not postulated; they are empirically observed; they are the specific subject matter of natural law, the dynamic core of the agent-action-end complexus. The general ordinances of reason, ruling and measuring the actions to which these inclinations give rise, constitute natural law.

The precise role of inclinations in structuring natural law has occasioned much discussion. M. B. Crowe stated the decisive issue: "Is an inclination natural because reasonable or reasonable because natural?"[10] This question might seem academic, but its answer has far-reaching results. The second alternative has found greater acceptance, at least in the past, although it may seem to be narrow and restrictive and to have reversed the order of priorities. For to say that an inclination is reasonable because it is natural seems to make biological structure normative (biologism) or, equivalently, to make physical nature constitutive of the moral act (physicalism).

Indeed, to understand inclination in that Ulpianist way seems to imply that the human person is in effect a conglomeration of faculties and powers, each with a finality and law of its own but without being integrated into the whole and without any subordination to the specifically human.[11] On the other hand, to call an inclination natural because it is reasonable seems to establish priorities from the top down, begin-

---

9. Ibid., I–II, q. 94, a. 4.

10. M. B. Crowe, *The Changing Profile of the Natural Law* (The Hague: Martinus Nijhoff, 1977), p. 265.

11. Ulpianus (170–228) wrote: "Natural law is what nature has taught all animals. For this law is not proper to man but is common to all animals whether born on land or in the sea, and birds also." *Dig.* I, 1,1,3. That first sentence, *Jus naturale est quod natura omnia animalia docuit,* has done much to keep alive the spirit of physicalism that has animated much natural law thinking even to the present time.

ning with the *nous,* which judges all things in terms of the person and
is guided but not determined by biological and physiological facts.

Aquinas stated very clearly the determining factor in natural law,
not nature simply but human nature or, more precisely, human nature
as rational:

Man is specified by his rational soul, and therefore anything contrary to the
order of reason is contrary to the nature of man as such. . . . Accordingly,
human virtue, which makes both man himself and his work good, is in accord
with human nature only to the extent that it is accord with reason; and vice is
contrary to human nature to the extent that it is contrary to the order of
reason.[12]

Inclinations, however, lead to norms. For whether natural because
reasonable or vice versa, they point to concrete goods. "All those things
to which man has a natural inclination are naturally apprehended by
reason as being good, and consequently as objects of pursuit and their
contraries as evil and objects of avoidance." Thus Aquinas concluded:
"According to the order of the natural inclinations is the order of the
precepts of the natural law."[13]

How these norms are characterized is important. Are they universal
and absolute, admitting no exceptions? Are they general, allowing
occasional recourse to some higher principle? Are they heuristic rather
than determinate or specific?

Neither Aquinas nor his commentators were clear and consistent as
to the precise classification of the principles of natural law; all were in
agreement, however, on the first principle of natural law, which is:
Good is to be done and pursued and evil is to be avoided, *Bonum est
faciendum et prosequendum, et malum vitandum.*[14]

Aquinas declared that, in addition, there were many first principles,
all of them self-evident. These principles were held in the mind through
synderesis, which he defined thus: "Synderesis is called the law of our
understanding inasmuch as it is a habit containing the precepts of the
natural law which are the first principles of human activity."[15] The
principles are not innate, but are the fruit of reason working on the
data of sense and consciousness; reason then grasps them as self-
evident. Incidentally, we earlier included these basic exigencies under
the term "eros," the first human experience of law.

12. Aquinas, *Summa theologiae,* I–II, q. 71, a. 2.
13. Ibid., q. 94, a. 2.   14. Ibid.
15. Ibid., a. 1, ad 2.

The primary principle has no specific content. Despite the fact that all good is concrete, the principle does not aim even at classes of good, such as knowledge, religion, or friendship. There is not even a necessary tendency or natural desire for God as God. The principle consists in our desire for happiness, for *bonum in communi*.[16] Nevertheless, the principle does have an indispensable function, that of making action intentional; we act only for the *bonum apprehensum*. As Germain Grisez phrased it: "The first principle of the practical reason does provide a basic requirement for action merely by prescribing that it be intentional, and it is in the light of this requirement that the objects of all the inclinations are understood as human goods and established as objectives for rational pursuit."[17]

The primary principle operates only if provided with content; it must be fleshed out if it is to serve as a guide to action; this process of particularization is the work of practical reason. The other first (self-evident) principles do this for the major kinds of human good; secondary principles, though not self-evident, extend the normative scope: "All other precepts of the natural law are based upon this, so that whatever the practical reason naturally apprehends as human good [or evil] belongs to the precepts of the natural law as something to be done or avoided."[18]

This statement seems like a straightforward invitation to work out more specific norms as reasonably as one can, in view of the limits of human intelligence and the exigencies of changing circumstances. Given the confidence that medieval thinkers had in their grasp of abstract nature as well as the constraints on their historical and scientific knowledge, the result, with few exceptions, turned out to be a fairly tight, normative structure.

Aquinas, however, was not always clear or consistent in naming and distinguishing the various principles and precepts of natural law or the process of applying them concretely. Nor were his followers. It is not necessary, however, to resolve all ambiguities before one can appreciate a critical distinction between universal and general norms; on such a distinction depends the flexibility of natural law, as Aquinas well knew.

16. William R. O'Connor, *The Eternal Quest* (Longmans, Green, 1947), pp. 156–57.
17. Germain G. Grisez, "The First Principle of Practical Reason," *Natural Law Forum* 10 (1965): 199.
18. Aquinas, *Summa theologiae*, I–II, q. 94, a. 2.

Let us then take a look at his three major statements about the hierarchy of natural law norms (one in the *Sentences*, two in the *Summa*).

First, in his *Commentary on the Sentences*, Aquinas wrote: "Everything that renders an action disproportionate to the end which nature intends from some work is said to be against the law of nature."[19] Primary precepts forbid actions that exclude the primary end; secondary precepts forbid those actions that hinder the primary end or exclude secondary ends. There still remains the question of what ends are primary and what are secondary, as well as the question of exceptions.

Later, in the *Summa theologiae*, without referring to this ends-of-nature distinction, Aquinas used two, more complicated distinctions. The first, in Question 94, distinguished, in terms of immutability, between universal "first principles" and the general but mutable "particular conclusions."

The first principles of *natural law* are altogether immutable. But *in its secondary precepts*, which we have described as being like particular conclusions close to the first principles, the natural law is not changed so that what it prescribes be not right in most cases. But it *may be changed in some particular case of rare occurrence because of some special causes hindering the observance of such precepts.*[20]

In the final distinction, in Question 100 of the *Summa*, Aquinas spoke of three kinds of precepts: first, "primary and common ones which, being inscribed in natural reason as self-evident, need no further promulgation, such as one should do evil to no one."[21] Second, others are clearly derived from primary principles "for the moral character of some actions is so evident that they can be assessed as good or bad in the light of these common first principles straight away with a minimum of reflection."[22] Third, "others, however, need a great deal of consideration of all the various circumstances, of which not everyone is capable, but only those endowed with wisdom,"[23] or, phrased differently, "those which are found, on careful examination on the part of wise men, to be in accord with reason—these are received by the people from God by instruction from the wise."[24]

In this threefold distinction, there is no specific indication of changeability. Nevertheless, it would seem reasonable to classify the first two

---

19. Idem, *In 4 Sententia,* d. 33, a. 1, a. 1.
20. Idem, *Summa theologiae,* I–II, q. 94, a. 5. Italics supplied.
21. Ibid., q. 100, a. 3.   22. Ibid., a. 1.
23. Ibid.   24. Ibid., a. 3.

types in Question 100, which we have just described, with the self-evident primary principle in Question 94, quoted above, and class the third type in Question 100 with the secondary and mutable precepts in Question 94. Note, too, the recurring theme, a touchstone to common sense, found also in Question 100: "Now since human conduct is such by its relation to reason, whatever conforms with reason is good, and whatever is in discord with reason is bad."[25]

Without trying further to harmonize Aquinas's three statements about natural law principles, we shall comment on the two types of principles underlying practical reasoning: the primary, self-evident, or analytic principles; and the secondary, derivative, or synthetic ones. Let us consider them separately.

(1) By calling norms self-evident, Aquinas did not mean that they are innate or that they are independent of facts or that everyone grasps all of them, but merely that the predicate is of the essence of the subject or belongs to the intelligibility of the subject. Such principles are not demonstrable but comprehensible; that is, they are not derived or inferred from another principle, but are perceived in comprehending the subject matter. They are tautological, but explicative.

Thus, to grasp the nature of human action is to grasp the principle: do good and avoid evil. To understand more about human nature is to understand, for example, that human beings should act reasonably, that they should exercise their sexual powers within limits, that they should not harm one another. Whether or not the norm or principle is self-evident depends on the extent of one's comprehension of human nature.

Those modern thinkers, taking the traditional Thomistic approach to natural law, work out their set of first principles in terms of major values. For example, Finnis suggested seven basic forms of good, which lead to self-evident principles: life, knowledge, play, aesthetic experience, sociability, practical reasonableness, and religion.[26] The resultant norms, though self-evident, are not transcendental but categorical, in that they deal with special aspects of human life (for example, bodily integrity, property, sexual matters), but they are nonetheless universal and unchangeable.

---

25. Ibid., a. 1.
26. John Finnis, *Natural Law and Natural Rights* (Oxford: Clarendon Press, 1980), pp. 85–90.

An important aspect of this collection of first principles is their incommensurability; that is, each basic value is equally fundamental; it is not merely a means to another value, but is an end in itself; and even, in certain circumstances, it may be considered the most important.[27] The moral implications of this position are tremendous; Finnis uses it in his attack on utilitarianism, consequentialism, and proportionalism.[28] The heart of his argument is that each first principle is self-evident.

(2) The second type of principle, the synthetic, is a more familiar one. Here the predicate does not belong to the essence or the intelligibility of the subject; rather, the principle, depending on experience rather than on an analysis of the subject, affirms or denies a predicate of the subject. The connection between subject and predicate consists in a judgment based on a verified understanding of data. In short, synthetic principles are not self-evident; moreover, since they are factually specific they are vulnerable to error, as Aquinas said: "The more you descend into details, the more it appears how the general rule admits of exceptions"; incidentally, his next sentence relates to the notion of judgment as a virtually unconditioned insight: "The greater the number of conditions accumulated the greater number of ways in which the principle is seen to fall short."[29]

Since synthetic principles or norms depend on empirical data to forge the link between subject and predicate, we cannot by reason alone attribute to them the immutability of primary norms, in which the predicate belongs to the essence of the subject. When we deal with sexual, medical, commercial, political, or similar matters, which involve factual determinations, we find an element that is not easily assessed; we must have empirical verification before we can make a judgment. This point is critical, for we may achieve only an emergent probability, which, though it reaches the point of moral certainty, is still not self-evident, still not metaphysically absolute. Secondary norms are mixed: they have an *a priori* element (the obligation to act reasonably) and an *a posteriori* element (the concrete determination of practical reasonableness), so they are not of themselves declarative of immutability. This observation will prove significant in the modern

27. Ibid., pp. 92–97.
28. Idem, *Fundamentals of Ethics* (Washington: Georgetown University Press, 1983), pp. 86–90.
29. Aquinas, *Summa theologiae*, I–II, q. 94, a. 4.

revisionist view of the changeability of natural law, especially on the question of intrinsically evil acts.

Unfortunately, Aquinas did not make a complete list of analytic and synthetic moral principles, in his terms, primary and secondary precepts. He gave but few examples, and even these he liked to repeat. Perhaps he wisely restrained himself, lest he seem to make cut and dried what should actually be an ongoing process. Many of his followers, however, have worked out a systematic and ironclad code with even the secondary precepts taking on the mantle of immutability. The result often appears rigid and unthomistic, especially to those who believe that there is strong scientific evidence establishing the problematic character of some of our convictions about human nature.

At this point, it will be helpful to consider some of the examples of essentially mutable secondary precepts that Aquinas actually does give. We examine them briefly, not for their moral content as much as for the light they shed on natural law. Aquinas, as we have seen earlier, stated very clearly that natural law "in its secondary precepts . . . may be changed in some particular case of rare occurrence owing to some special causes hindering the observance of such precepts."[30]

Consequently, the inevitable question is: What kinds of cases permit exceptions? Aquinas, in the same article, had already phrased the question as an objection: "The killing of the innocent is against natural law, and so are adultery and theft. Yet you find God altering these rules, as when he commanded Abraham to put his son to death (Genesis 22:2), the people of Israel to spoil the Egyptians (Exodus 12:35), and Hosea to take a wife of harlotry (Hosea 1:2). Natural law, then, can be altered."[31] He answered: "It is not only in human affairs that whatever God commands is just, but also in the world of nature, whatever is done by God is in some way natural."[32] Is it not in some way natural because it is reasonable?

This statement of Aquinas gives rise to a question of great practical importance: Is it possible to say that what is natural, in the sense of being in accord with reason, is somehow also a command of God? In other words, prophecies and visions aside, can the command of God be known through reason, thereby justifying an exception to a secondary precept?

30. Ibid., q. 94, a. 5.
31. Ibid., obj. 2.
32. Ibid., ad 2.

Josef Fuchs gave this answer: "The natural law becomes historically, in the concrete situation of man's life, a concrete demand by God here and now."[33] He is at pains to point out the natural basis: "This does not necessarily imply a pure, interior inspiration but rather a knowledge of God's will through the concrete reality of the given situation."[34] This accords with Aquinas's words: "The natural law is nothing else than the rational creature's participation in the eternal law."[35] How, then, is the divine will to be determined in cases involving an exception to the secondary precepts? There is no need of a mystical or direct communication in order to discern the command of God. Intelligent and responsible decisions should suffice. Later in this chapter, I shall discuss the components and stages of the process of such critically important, concrete decision making.

To follow up on this answer, let us consider a non-controversial example of how the command of God, using the term broadly as just indicated, may justify the contravening of a secondary precept, namely, theft by one in extreme need. For Aquinas, theft is always a sin: "Those actions belonging to the very nature of justice cannot be changed in any way, for example, theft must not be committed because it is an injustice. But those actions that follow [from the nature of justice] are changeable in a few cases."[36] His conclusion is: "It is not theft, properly speaking, to take secretly and use another's property in case of extreme need, because that which he takes for the support of this life becomes his own property by reason of that need."[37]

Exponents of natural law share a consensus on the exceptional justification of "theft" in such a case of extreme need. No more is required to make the point about the mutability of secondary precepts. Obviously, matters of life and death or matters of sexual relationships would require cogent reasons before exceptions to secondary precepts could even be considered. But the operative principle is the same. It must be emphasized, however, that just because secondary precepts are not self-evident, it does not mean that exceptions may actually be permitted.

Although Aquinas spoke of "crimes against nature" (masturbation,

33. Josef Fuchs, *Natural Law* (New York: Sheed and Ward, 1965), p. 130.
34. Ibid.
35. Aquinas, *Summa theologiae*, I–II, q. 91, a. 2.
36. Ibid., II–II, q. 66, a. 7.
37. Ibid., ad 2.

sodomy, bestiality) as prohibited merely by secondary precepts,[38] he nowhere justified such actions; never did he indicate the rare occurrence that might permit an exception to these norms. Regarding secondary precepts in general, what must be insisted on is that, since they are not self-evident, they enjoy no *a priori* immutability; there are, however, compelling reasons for not generally allowing an exception to be made; and *de facto,* there may never be adequate reasons for an exception.

Since exceptions to natural law are countenanced within the system, it will be helpful to examine more carefully the techniques of justification. Basically, there are three ways to accommodate natural law to new circumstances: interpretation, dispensation, and *epikeia.*

The first of these, interpretation, is a subtle technique: the law does not change, only our understanding of it. Hermeneutics provides a method of legal change, and the result is that the same words have a different meaning—in effect a new law without repealing the old law.

Although one's individual conscience remains the proximate norm of morality, one must, in good conscience, look to community traditions and the insights of the wise. But even these sources need to be interpreted; the fact that natural law precepts have long ago been discovered, formulated, and redacted—and further developments repeat the cycle—makes interpreting them a complex and demanding task, even though there exists a living tradition. For a tradition easily becomes legalistic and impersonal. This power of indirect legislation through interpretation, however, is so great even in terms of positive law, civil or ecclesiastical, that organized communities may confine such decisions to courts or commissions, which alone may make an authentic interpretation.[39] Indeed, the Roman Catholic Church reserves to itself this right even over natural law.[40]

Going beyond the bounds of interpretation, which reveals preexistent exceptions to general laws, the methods of dispensation and *epikeia* actually create exceptions. These two are polar cognates: dispensation takes the imperial perspective; *epikeia* takes the consumer perspective. Both methods rest on the perceived unsuitability of the general law as

---

38. Ibid., I–II, q. 94, a. 6.

39. See *Code of Canon Law,* Can. 16, sec. 1: "Laws are authentically interpreted by the legislator and by the one to whom the legislator has granted the power to interpret them authentically."

40. See John Boyle, "The Natural Law and the Magisterium," *The Proceedings of the Catholic Theological Society of America,* 34 (1979): 189–210.

applied under the given circumstances of a concrete situation: in dispensation the unsuitability is perceived by the ruler; in *epikeia*, it is perceived by the subject, judging as he thinks the ruler would.

Dispensation was more congenial than *epikeia* to the medieval mind, for it preserved order from the top down. The reasoning was simple: the ruler made the law; he can, when expedient, dispense from the law. Aquinas explained: "It happens at times that some precept, that is for people's benefit in most cases, is not helpful for this particular person or in this particular case, either because it stops something better from happening or because it brings in some evil."[41]

A dispensation in such cases promotes the common good, for it makes up what is wanting in the law and is in accord with the authority of the ruler. But our concern here is not positive law but natural law, an area in which human rulers are not omnicompetent.

Aquinas wisely wrote: "In so far as natural law contains common precepts which never fail, it does not allow of dispensation. In other precepts, which are like conclusions from these, it is sometimes dispensed by men, for example when a loan is not repaid to a traitor, or some such case."[42] Moreover, Aquinas even allowed a presumed-permission type of dispensation when there is an emergency with no time for recourse to higher authority: "The very necessity carries a dispensation with it, for necessity knows no law."[43]

This talk about dispensation and presumed permission leads smoothly into *epikeia*, which assesses one's personal obligation under a law that has failed in a particular case because of its generality. The justifying reason is the same as in the presumed-permission type of emergency dispensation: one can follow what one reasonably understands would be the will of the ruler had he considered this case in making the law.

Here Aquinas followed Aristotle; he saw *epikeia* as a corrective of law and thus perfective of it.[44] *Epikeia* is not an escape from virtue but

[handwritten marginal note: not an escape from virtue but a move towards greater virtue]

41. Aquinas, *Summa theologiae*, I–II, q. 97, a. 4.
42. Ibid., ad 3.
43. Ibid., q. 96, a. 6.
44. The term in Greek is *epieikeia*, shortened in Latin to *epikeia* and translated in English as equity. For an exhaustive analysis of the notion, see Lawrence J. Riley, *The History, Nature and Use of Epikeia in Moral Theology* (Washington: The Catholic University of America Press, 1948); for a more recent work, see Josef Fuchs, "Epikeia Applied to Natural Law," *Personal Responsibility and Christian Morality*, trans. W. Cleves (Washington: Georgetown University Press, 1983), pp. 185–99; it was first published in *Periodica* 69 (1980): 251–70.

a move toward greater virtue. Aquinas did not treat *epikeia* at much length, but found it operative in both natural law[45] and human law.[46] In fact, he used the same example in both contexts, namely, that goods deposited should be returned on request, but not a sword to a madman or to a traitor who would use it against his country.[47] By means of *epikeia,* recourse was made in this situation to a more fundamental rule—the obligation to avoid harm to others. In the past, the equity exception looked to the will of the ruler; more recently, the emphasis has been on the reasonableness of the exception—a shift from will to reason. This makes sense if only because of the difficulty, if not impossibility, of knowing what the ruler would think or what the legislative body or the winning majority of a democratic government would have done had they envisaged the unique equities of a later situation. Moreover, who is the relevant ruler for natural law? Whether it is God or one's conscience or both, certainly reasonableness prevails. "For God is not offended by us, unless we act against our own good."[48]

Epikeia, in short, brings out the spirit of the law. As Aristotle said: "The equitable is just and better than one kind of justice—not better than absolute justice but better than the error that arises from the absoluteness of the statement."[49] So the move is not beyond natural law, but beyond one general principle to a higher principle. Though the general law may fail, the natural law does not fail. Thus, *epikeia* forms an indispensable part of the legal process. "The reason is," Aristotle noted, "that all law is general but about some things it is not possible to make a general statement which shall be correct."[50] Aquinas commented on this point: "Because the material of human acts is indeterminate, it follows that their norm, which is the law, must be indeterminate in the sense that it is not absolutely rigid."[51]

In assessing the need of *epikeia,* we should note that the process of generalization, which is natural law, is a protracted and cooperative effort. Rightly do we envisage natural law as an ordinance of our own reason, establishing our own personal moral foundation and directives.

45. Ibid., q. 94, a. 4.
46. *Ibid.,* II–II, q. 120, a. 2.
47. The example is frequent. See Plato, *Republic,* 4331 C and Cicero, *De officiis.,* III, c. 26.
48. Aquinas, *Contra Gentiles,* III, 122.
49. Aristotle, *Nicomachean Ethics,* V, 10, 1137 b24–5.
50. Ibid., b13–14.
51. Aquinas, *Commentary on Nicomachean Ethics,* V, 16, 1089.

Yet we must be aware of the social dimension as well—the discussions and controversies that have forged the communal commitment to the principles of human dignity. Whether the issue be war, suicide, slavery, or contraception, the generalizations mature only with difficulty. We should never forget that the emergence of the idea of natural law itself came only after a long and involved cultural striving to articulate the full meaning of law for the good life.

Historically, the articulating of the notion of law in Rome was from the *ius civile,* to the *ius gentium,* and then to the *ius naturale.*[52] This last stage of generality, at first tentative and provisional, finally emerged through the dialectic of history. Natural law, because it is a human, communal, cultural, and historical generalization, may well fail in a few of the many singular situations that it covers; hence, the indispensable need for *epikeia,* so that when understanding deepens and circumstances change, natural law can still prevail—and do so reasonably.

In brief, the abstract principles that set up natural law are of two kinds: universal (self-evident) and general (synthetic). If the general precepts fail in some instances, either dispensation or *epikeia* may be able to justify an exception. Moreover, independently of these two methods, there remains a third interpretation, the hermeneutic need to re-experience and rethink the precepts of natural law, since moralists and jurists gradually worked out, articulated, and handed down these secondary norms over many centuries.

In the face of a multiplicity of complex and changing circumstances, there may be a concern over the enduring wisdom of some of these generalizations and also over the linguistic and cultural accuracy of the formulations. Moreover, the very abstractness of the concepts and propositions tends to leave the original insights behind. As a result, we are ever under the obligation of making sure that our consciences are informed by a clear grasp of reality, not because we want to avoid the laws of nature but because we want to find in them truer guidance and fulfillment.

B. *The Practical Decision Making*

The *ad hoc* remedies of interpretation, dispensation, and *epikeia* can never by themselves provide adequately for singularity and change.

52. See Rudolph Sohm, *The Institutes,* 3d ed., trans. J. Ledlie (Oxford: Clarendon Press, 1907), pp. 70–71.

Unless it were attuned to the concrete, natural law, however interpreted, would be an abstract superstructure out of touch with personal
and social life. The task of ethics and law is complicated by more than
just the few non-standard cases over which *epikeia* takes jurisdiction
and dispensation deems to act. General rules, even with pertinent
exceptions, must be applied to individual situations, and this application regularly requires a special skill.

Looking again at the typical example used by Socrates and Aquinas—
the refusal to give back an entrusted weapon to one enraged by marital
or political strife—we see that the right to refuse may be permissible
in theory according to the principles of *epikeia,* but be imprudent under
the attendant circumstances: the refusal may increase the anger, extend
its coverage, precipitate a worse calamity. Moreover, the facts may be
insufficient or ambiguous, the context confused, the time for decision
short, the costs of a mistake personally hazardous. Clearly more than
a grasp of abstract principles and deductive logic is in order; what is
also needed is practical wisdom, called *phronesis* by Aristotle and
prudentia by Aquinas. The latter, abridging a wordier Greek explanation,[53] neatly defines it as *recta ratio agibilium,* the right notion
about how to do things.[54]

For Aquinas, prudence was indispensable to law. Not only must
natural and positive law make use of prudence in their practical appli-
cations, but positive law itself is a prudential determination of natural
law. Moreover, since human nature is changeable, as Aquinas acknowledged, and since actions are singular and concrete, flexibility is clearly
necessary for sound decision making. Aquinas had a very modern
appreciation of the difficulties of praxis.

The teaching on matters of morals even in their general aspects is uncertain
and variable. But still more uncertainty is found when we come down to the
solution of particular cases. This study does not fall under either art or tradition
because the causes of individual actions are infinitely diversified. Hence judgment of particular cases is left to the prudence of each one. He who acts
prudently must attentively consider the things to be done at the present time
after all the particular circumstances have been taken into consideration.[55]

---

53. Aristotle, *Nicomachean Ethics,* VI, 5, 1140 b20–21: "*Phronesis* is a truthful
rational habit concerned with action in relation to human goods. *Phronesis* then must
be a reasoned and true state of capacity to act with regard to human goods."

54. Aquinas, *Summa theologiae,* II–II, q. 59, a. 1.

55. Idem, *Commentary on Nicomachean Ethics,* II, ii, 258–59.

Throughout his discussion of practical reason, Aquinas stayed very close to the thinking of Aristotle. Both distinguished three acts of practical wisdom; traditionally, they have been called counsel, judgment, and command. Today, we more accurately call them (1) deliberation, (2) evaluation, and (3) decision. We shall consider each stage separately, the better to appreciate the mental operations that constitute this decision-making skill.

A preliminary clarification is in order. We must distinguish rational consciousness (which aims at knowing) from rational self-consciousness (which aims at doing). Decision making does not merely repeat the three levels of rational consciousness (experiencing, understanding, and judging); it sublates them and goes beyond them. There may be, however, a temporal parallel in that the mind not only moves toward the true but concurrently responds to the good. Feelings follow insights. In a later corollary, we shall examine this relationship more fully. Suffice it here to point out this factor in the three stages of decision making. Relying on what is understood and known through rational consciousness—known, incidentally, as a degree of emergent probability or as a certainty—deliberation gives an insight into what may be the right choice of a good; evaluation verifies this insight through a value judgment, and command actuates the judgment, bringing the sequence of rational self-consciousness to its fulfillment.[56] Let us consider these stages at greater length.

(1) *Deliberation* or counsel does not mean simply thinking about things or talking things over with someone, taking counsel with a good friend or smart lawyer, although that is often so. Nor is it merely observation, as it is sometimes called, for though it requires and seeks out data, it goes beyond the initial operation of experiencing reality. A look at two related skills described by Aristotle will indicate the function of deliberation.[57] He spoke of *euboulia,* an extended inquiry of reason, and *eustochia,* an instantaneous conjecture. They differ in speed

---

56. See Bernard Lonergan, *Method in Theology,* 2nd ed. (New York: Herder and Herder, 1973), where he stated the components of a judgment of value: "First there is the knowledge of reality and especially of human reality. Secondly, there are intentional responses to values. Thirdly, there is the initial thrust towards moral self-transcendence constituted by the judgment of value itself" (p. 38). On an earlier page, he mentioned the next step: "True judgments of value go beyond merely intentional self-transcendence without reaching the fulness of moral self-transcendence. That fulness is not merely knowing but also doing, and man can know what is right without doing it" (p. 37).

57. See Aristotle, *Nicomachean Ethics,* V, 9, 1142 a31–1142 b33.

of operation, but not in the desired result—the formation of an insight based on relevant data about what to do.

For example, the policeman on the street must often be able to make sense out of his observations very rapidly; the judge at a preliminary hearing can listen to witnesses for both sides before deciding whether to hold the defendant for the grand jury. Both officials must form an insight to enable them to understand the data: the policeman certainly needs the skill of instant conjecture, *eustochia;* the judge, proceeding more leisurely, seems to need only *eubolia,* the skill for an extended inquiry, and yet, in the give and take of courtroom proceedings, he too must often quickly form insights involving action.

In fact, everyone needs both skills; some tasks rely more heavily on one than the other; some people are better at one than the other. But all our responsible actions, regardless of the speed of understanding, require the gathering of data and the gaining of an insight about what ought to be done in a concrete situation. Deliberation, however, is only the first step; other mental operations must follow.

(2) *Evaluation* or judgment is the second operation in practical decision making. What is involved in an evaluative judgment? The words "evaluation" and "judgment," however, signify too many things, especially to lawyers, to convey the precise meaning of the mental operation involved. Once again, Aristotle made a helpful distinction: *synesis* is right judgment about things as they occur most often, about the usual or typical situation;[58] *gnome,* on the other hand, is right judgment about the unusual, the abnormal, the exceptional.[59] The two skills differ as do law and equity: law looks to what happens in most cases (*ut in pluribus*) and formulates its norm as a generalization: equity looks to what happens in only a few cases (*ut in paucioribus*) and formulates its norm as an exception.

58. See ibid., VI, 10, 1142 b34–1143 a18, where Aristotle said that *synesis* deals with matters about which there can be doubt and deliberation (1143 a6–7), but he stated its function clearly: *synesis* merely makes judgments; *phronesis* commands (1143 a8–10).

59. See ibid., VI, 11, 1143 a19–35, where Aristotle described *gnome.* One might have thought *synesis* sufficed for practical reasoning, but both "*synesis* and *gnome* deal with matters of conduct" (1143 a34–35). And both are judgments, but he defined *gnome* as "right judgment about the equitable [*tou epieikous*]" (1143 a19). It is significant that, in the next to last chapter of the preceding book, he spoke at length of *epieikeia* as a corrective of laws that fail owing to their generality. Practical reasoning too may face situations that need a judgment for which general norms do not provide; *gnome* can adjust to these special circumstances.

Aquinas put *gnome* in full context: "To consider the totality of things which are able to happen outside the common course [of events] pertains to Divine Providence alone"; human beings, however, participate in this power: "But among men, the one who is more perspicacious is able to judge with his reason the greater number of these cases. And such is the role of *gnome,* which implies a certain perspicacity of judgment."[60] Traditionally, *synesis,* as setting standards, has been a major concern of moralists; *gnome,* almost overlooked, was treated as a rare possibility. Currently, however, the clearer recognition of the singularity and circumstantial uniqueness of events has enhanced the role of *gnome* and increased the frequency of its application.

In brief, what evaluation does is verify the insight into the worthwhileness of an action arrived at by deliberation. Although the judgment is about action towards a concrete good, it is a value judgment; it concerns a fact in prospect, a future event—not its probabilty or its frequency but its worthwhileness. Hence the word "evaluation" better describes this particular prudential act than does the more traditional word "judgment," which may refer to fact or value. When the evaluation has been made with the help of the virtues of *synesis* and *gnome,* the person says to himself: this should be done, *faciendum hoc.*

So far, in the description of practical wisdom, we have not mentioned conscience, a notion that, though relevant, often proves confusing. Conscience may mean to some the voice of God, to others an emotional reaction. Aristotle does not deal with the notion itself; Aquinas must, however, since it occurs frequently in the New Testament and in the writings of the Church Fathers. To relate it to the Aristotelian structure, we may describe it as a part of evaluation. Conscience differs from evaluation conceptually in that conscience looks back from the act to synderesis, the habit of the first principles of action, whereas evaluation, while including this function, looks primarily to the doing of the singular act. Conscience focuses more on the principles, evaluation more on the action itself. Although we shall not be using the word "conscience," we do include its function in our analysis of responsible action, which is rational self-consciousness achieved through self-transcendence.

(3) *Decision* or command is the next operation, and without it nothing happens. Sometimes a person gains a practical insight into a

60. Aquinas, *Summa theologiae,* II–II, q. 51, a. 4, ad 3.

possible way of acting that could change him or his world, but does nothing further. Sometimes a person judges that a particular action ought to be carried out, but stops there. In each instance, there is a failure in practical wisdom. For the *recta ratio agibilium*, there must be in addition to the judgment, *faciendum hoc*, the command, *fac hoc: do it.* This decision is the principal act of practical wisdom. Aristotle wrote: "*Synesis* is not the same as *phronesis;* for *phronesis* issues commands, since its end is a statement of what we ought to do or not to do, whereas *synesis* merely makes judgments."[61]

Without decision, prudence would be immobile; without deliberation and evaluation, it would be blind. Proper action comprises all three: it takes deliberation to give the practical insight into concrete good; it takes evaluation to determine whether that good is a value to be pursued; and it takes command to make the judgment of value an existential reality, a singular action.

It is important to realize the unique and inalienable role that prudence plays in our lives. So personal is this function that it is ours alone. It cannot even be communicated to others, but remains an individual challenge rooted in a singular dignity, for we alone can know the totality of circumstances that form the matrix of our action and the key to responsible choice.

C. *Four Corollaries*

To appreciate the full sweep of practical wisdom, we must consider four corollaries: the one looking to the reciprocal relationship between means and end; the second defining the peculiar character of prudential truth as conformity with right appetite; the third examining the complementarity of insight and feeling in mediating the world through meaning and regulating it through value; and the fourth showing how natural law in no way involves the fallacious inference of an "ought" from an "is."

(1) The first corollary is that practical wisdom is not strictly limited to the choice of means, as if the end were antecedently fixed or specified. In ethical and legal matters, there is frequently a mutual determination, so the particular end and means emerge together. The basic reason for this is the heuristic character of the major goals of ethics and positive law. Heuristic goals—such as happiness, the good life, justice, due

61. Aristotle, *Nicomachean Ethics*, VI, 10, 1143 a7–10.

process—require prudentially determined specificity to become functional. Also significant is the fact that usually the person immersed in the circumstances can best appreciate the specifics in working out the relationship between a heuristic goal and its proportionate means. By the personal decision of practical wisdom, thus doubly adjusted, the tension between the general norm and the concrete situation is resolved.

The traditional distinction between technical and moral knowledge is important in this context, especially in view of the different ways of formulating the end. In art or technical knowledge, the end is specific— the artifact to be made—and specific means are used to realize it. In ethics and law, on the other hand, the end is often indeterminate and heuristic, and the means to achieve that goal are initially problematic, despite the presence of abstract guidelines. Gadamer wrote: "What is right, for example, cannot be fully determined independently of the situation that requires a right action from me, whereas the *eidos* of what a craftsman desires to make is fully determined by the use for which it is intended."[62] But in the fine arts, artists such as Picasso often fashion artifacts, not as determined antecedently, but as emerging through an ends-means reciprocity.

The two notions of art and prudence run parallel: one is *recta ratio factibilium*, the other *recta ratio agibilium*. But they differ in that the object of the first is an artifact, and the object of the second, an action. Aristotle was clear on the distinction between *techne* and *phronesis;* he was not as clear, however, on the end-means reciprocity. He said explicitly: "Virtue ensures the rightness of the end we aim at; prudence ensures the rightness of the means we adopt to gain that end."[63] Many, more on logical than textual grounds, defend the position that *phronesis* must determine both means and ends; thus, W.F.R. Hardie wrote: "Practical wisdom, if it is to be complete and not headless, must include the intuitive thought of the end as well as the intellectual powers required for the discovery of means."[64] He suggested that Aristotle, though he does not do so, could in this context properly use *nous,* intuitive reason (in Hardie's terms), instead of *phronesis.*

The crux of the textual problem is that Aristotle defined the truth of

62. Hans-Georg Gadamer, *Truth and Method* (New York: The Seabury Press, 1975), p. 37. See also pp. 286–88.

63. Aristotle, *Nicomachean Ethics,* VI, 12, 1144 a7–9.

64. W.F.R. Hardie, *Aristotle's Ethical Theory,* 2d ed. (Oxford: Clarendon Press, 1964), p. 227.

practical reason as conformity with right appetite,[65] and he defined the rectitude of the appetite, the mean, as conformity with right reason. To conform to right appetite is to conform to a proper end, and the end is proper because it conforms to right reason.[66] But, as Thomas Deman pointed out: "Prudence pronounces in each case precisely what is the exigency of right reason."[67] Thus prudence looks to the end as well as to the means. The prudential decision translates into action the emergent balance of means-end reciprocity.

(2) The second corollary takes a further look at the kind of truth that emerges from the process of practical reason; it is not what we generally think of when we speak of truth. Ordinarily truth is conceived of as conformity of the mind to reality. But practical truth is different. Since the goal of practical wisdom is the proper ordering of activity, its truth can be described as the perfection of that order and consists in conformity to the principles of human action, as rooted in the structures of the human mind.

To rephrase this in terms used in the Monosphere, Eros first directs us to goals that practical wisdom tries to realize. This, however, is not enough for practical truth. Plato recognized that Eros, too, had to be directed, that *paideia*—education in the broad sense—was needed if Eros was to attain the good, the beauty, and the happiness desired. Similarly, Aristotle insisted on the formation of character—the habituation for loving the noble and hating the base—as a prerequisite for *phronesis*. This added requirement is understandable, for man is not just a technician whose only goals are efficiency and success; he is a moral being, measured ultimately by virtue, not by mere accomplishment.

The capacity simply to accomplish things, Aristotle called cleverness.[68] He found it present in *phronesis*, but did not identify it with *phronesis;* cleverness is practical skill, not practical wisdom. The word for cleverness, *deinotes,* may mean natural ability or skill; its basic meaning is terribleness. One who can achieve his goals without regard to moral virtue has a fearsome capacity for evil; he is a knave or a rogue. The Greek word conveys a grimmer meaning than do these

65. See Aristotle, *Nicomachean Ethics,* VI, 2, 1139 a29–31.
66. See ibid., VI, 1, 1138 b19–20.
67. T. Deman, *La Prudence* (Paris: Edition de la Revue des Jeunes, Desclée & Cie., 1949), p. 270.
68. See Aristotle, *Nicomachean Ethics,* VI, 12, 1144 a23–29.

English equivalents; a clever person is a *panourgos,* one ready to do anything, one ready for any crime. The more skill he has in choosing apt means, the more dangerous he is. This failure of true affectivity produces a kind of moral psychopath.

Since simply being clever does not suffice, Aristotle concluded with a striking statement: "It is clear that one cannot be prudent without being good."[69] The truth of prudence, then, is not just conformity with appetite, but conformity with right appetite, with the appetite that has been rectified by moral virtues, and ultimately by right reason, which determines the mean of the moral virtues.[70] Thus practical wisdom involves a dual rectitude—it is the conformity with right appetite, which in turn involves a conformity with right reason. There results necessarily a participation in the natural law.

Practical wisdom grasps the truth of deeds. It is not simply knowing, but knowing how to act, so it is not the whole truth about a situation. For example, a lawyer's truly prudential decision to put a defendant on the stand to testify in his own behalf may turn out to be the crucial factor in his conviction. A prosecutor's wisely planned and well-executed search with a valid warrant may well fail to uncover any incriminating evidence. Although a prudent person may have foresight (the word *prudentia* comes from *providere,* to see ahead or beforehand), foresight is not clairvoyance; it only facilitates an emerging probability, a reasonable expectation that, in view of one's necessarily limited knowledge, this singular choice is the proper one.

One can, however, be confident of acting prudently, though not infallibly, if one deliberates, evaluates, and decides properly, with the requisite skill and for proper ends. In the realm of contingent singulars, risk can be minimized; it cannot be eliminated. The truth of practical reason is proved not by the outcome but by the authenticity of the process. Analogously, the constitutionality of an arrest and search for heroin is not determined by the discovery of heroin but by the antecedent presence of probable cause.

The truth of practical wisdom is a tremendous personal achievement: the determination of the right action in view of the manifold singularities of the situation and the exigencies of right reason. Law, as thus experienced in the event, is a nuanced directive, bypassing the blunt

---

69. Ibid., VI, 12, 1144 a36–1144 b1.
70. See ibid., VI, 1, 1138 b20.

opaqueness of generalities. The person of practical wisdom, the *phronimos,* whether or not he theorizes about law, experiences law as something lived, something ever fashioning the structure of his being as he moves, action by action, toward happiness.

(3) The third corollary is that the exigency of the mind toward reality manifests a unitary growth in consciousness of truth and goodness. This relationship underlies not only the reciprocity of means and ends and the conformity to right appetite, mentioned in the two previous corollaries, but also the whole process of practical reasoning. I have already discussed the dynamic character of law in the chapter on Eros; what I intend here is to examine its implications for natural law.

To review the underlying cognitional processes: the exigency of the mind is, as we have seen, directed toward reality; human beings seek to know the truth and to pursue the good. In this quest, the mind takes a unitary approach: its insights are paralleled by feelings. Feelings are the mind's way of responding proportionately to what is good in what it experiences; feelings complement insights, for only with both can the whole person respond to the whole of reality by knowing and loving what is true and good.

Inclinations, which are the subject matter of the natural law, include both insights and feelings. Indeed, human beings experience both the truth and the goodness of their inclinations as well as the truth and goodness of the objects of these inclinations. Men and women do more than know; they have intellects and intellectual appetites; they not only know, they also love.

Feelings can be distinguished from emotions. Although often called feelings, emotions are characterized more by intense bodily reverberations; feelings are subtler, more intellectual responses. Emotions may or may not be proportioned to what is understood; nor are they as nuanced or as necessary as feelings. Without feelings, we would be unaware of good and of value, and be incapable of loving; but "Feelings reveal values to us."[71]

We do not prove the existence of feelings by demonstration; we experience them immediately. Moreover, just as we verify our insights in order to make a judgment of fact, so too, as we have seen, we evaluate our feelings in order to make a judgment of value. The two judgments complement one another and provide for authentic decision

71. Bernard Lonergan, *Third Collection,* p. 173.

making. Lonergan noted: "Intermediate between judgments of fact and judgments of value lies apprehension of value. Such apprehensions are given in feelings."[72] Indeed, ethics depends on consistency between knowing and doing, between judgments of fact and judgments of value. This complementarity plays a role in the ongoing end-means relationship, as consciousness of knowledge and goodness develop apace; it also reveals how prudential truth must be in conformity with right appetite, since there is no action without an end and no proper action without a proper end.

(4) The fourth corollary confronts the is-ought question. The brief analysis above of the eros of the mind does more than indicate that the law has a dynamic component; it also provides the clue to an issue that legal thinkers have hotly debated at least since the eighteenth century, namely, the relation between facts and values or, more specifically, the impossibility of inferring an "ought" from an "is."

Hume also discussed the question in his *Treatise of Human Nature* (1739).[73] Admittedly, some Protestant Rationalists and some Scholastics, like the Stoics before them, did succumb to what G. E. Moore called the "naturalistic fallacy." Major thinkers such as Plato, Aristotle, and Aquinas certainly did not. Yet to this day, the accusation still remains part of the positivist brief in favor of the separation of law and morals and in opposition to the theory of natural law. Actually, the Humean and positivist image of natural law is radically out of sequence and grossly oversimplified, as if natural law were based on a factual analysis of nature, a determination of what is helpful and harmful, and an inferred obligation to act or forbear.

To argue from facts to values is clearly illicit. One need not have waited until the eighteenth century to have been told that by Hume or until the twentieth to hear the positivist legal philosopher, Hans Kelsen, assert that: "The reason for the validity of a norm is always a norm and not a fact."[74]

---

72. Idem, *Method*, p. 37.

73. David Hume, *A Treatise of Human Nature*, ed. L. A. Selby-Bigge (Oxford: Clarendon Press, 1960), Bk III, Part I, sec. 1, pp. 469–70. For an understanding and critique of Hume's position, see John Finnis, *Natural Law and Natural Rights* (Oxford: Clarendon Press, 1980), pp. 33–48.

74. Hans Kelsen, *General Theory of Law and State*, trans. A. Wedberg (New York: Russell & Russell, 1961), p. 399.

But Kelsen was fully aware that natural law did not violate this precept. For him, positive law and natural law functioned similarly as principles of legality; both had a basic norm that validated the subordinate norms. He wrote that natural law, "like morality is deduced from a presumably self-evident basic norm which is considered to be the expression of the 'will of nature' or of 'pure reason.' "[75] His position on self-evidence was clear: "Since the idea of a natural law is one of a 'natural' order, it follows that its rules, directly as they flow from nature, God or reason, are as immediately evident as the rules of logic and thus require no force for their realization."[76] Although convinced that positive law and natural law were ever in conflict, he wrote of "the laws of natural law, derived from nature, God or reason, from a principle of the absolutely good, right or just, from an absolutely supreme value or fundamental norm which itself is clothed with the claim of absolute validity."[77] He may not have subscribed to natural law nor even understood it precisely, but he rightly acknowledged its conceptual coherence and its freedom from the "naturalistic fallacy."

It is clear that here sequence is significant. Natural law decision making does not begin with a factual judgment but with a normative drive, the exigency of the mind toward reality. This direction is a given, a fundamental part of being human; without it there can be no ethical experience or understanding of ethical experience. There is no inference of this ultimate orientation from something else, an outside object to be grasped by the mind; rather, it stems from consciousness of the mental operations of the self, an awareness of one's integral subjectivity. Whether thematized or not, this drive toward reality is a function of unitary consciousness; it precedes judgments of knowledge and judgments of value. Eros precedes duty, but these judgments link them both together. The complementary sequence of value orientation and fact determination results in a specific obligation.

Discussions of the natural law by those who understand it do not involve the is-ought inference, but look rather to how the inference from an "ought" to an "ought" is achieved. There are two basic positions. In the first the major premise is the primary principle: "Good is to be done and pursued and evil is to be avoided," and the minor

75. Ibid., p. 114.   76. Ibid., p. 392.
77. Ibid., p. 394.

premise is a particularized factual statement (knowledge of one's native language is a human good), thus permitting an inference (such knowledge should be sought).[78] The second takes any one of a number of first principles (human knowledge is a good to be pursued) and follows that with a particularized minor premise (the ability to read and write one's native language is such knowledge), thus permitting a prescriptive inference.[79]

The second position differs from the first in holding that the primary principle, being content-free, only establishes the intentionality of action; deduction from it is neither logically proper nor necessary, since there is a set of self-evident principles affording general coverage of all human ends. From one of these principles, as a major premise, a factual minor premise leads to the inference of a concrete duty. The judgment of fact is important. Depending on the circumstances, not all goods, not even all basic goods, are always to be sought after; for example, one may sacrifice the pursuit of knowledge for the preservation of life.

The primary principle links intelligibility and responsibility. The crucial factor is the binding power of the intelligible good; for each person, antecedently directed by this exigency for reality, already has a normative bent. The mind responds to reality as both true and good. Exposed to data, the mind makes the dual response of insight and feeling; through additional operations, it makes judgments of knowledge and value, which parallel one another and interpenetrate.

It is important to recognize that the primary principle is not an abstract proposition; it is a complex mental operation, which functions as a personal and evaluative *Grundnorm*—not presupposed as Kelsen's but self-evident. In calling Eros a daimon, how much difficulty the Greeks avoided. They realized that primarily it was love not logic that animated and directed man, for love could account for the inclinations and the values, whereas logic could at best help verify the insights and inferences. The mind, necessarily tending toward good and away from evil, finds all goods and all evils within its decisional purview. Moreover, this tendency toward good is given content through an awareness of basic human goods, which it finds necessarily implied in human nature. The mind then experiences, in concrete situations, a tendency

78. Mortimer Adler, "Is and Ought," chap. 10 of *Six Major Ideas* (New York: Macmillan, 1981), p. 81.

79. See John Finnis, *Natural Law*, pp. 59–90, on knowledge as a basic good.

to act or forbear owing to its fundamental orientation to be consistent in knowing and doing.

II. THE NATURAL LAW REVISED

A fresh and unbiased look at the insights of natural law in the synthesis of Aquinas reveals a deep sensitivity to the concreteness and singularity of rational decision making. For those who have lost faith in the doctrine of natural law, even these rays of practical wisdom may seem provocative but passé, the fruits of an inquiry that culture has left behind.

Nevertheless, some have used this very cultural change as an inspiration to give natural law a renewed vitality. Is such a juridic rebirth feasible? Whatever the achievements of the ancients may have been, we live in a radically different culture. So we must ask: Can the natural law survive this transition? Can it do so successfully? And, if so, what does it lose, what does it gain?

The standard comparison between the two cultures seems to put them irreconciably at odds with one another. Classicist culture is deemed abstract, deductive, philosophical. It aims at a monolithic rightness, a normative consistency and centrality. Working from the premise of immutable natures, it establishes with logical precision a natural law that is fixed and unchanging—if not in basic theory at least in common acceptation.

Modern culture, on the other hand, is seen as empirical, inductive, scientific, historical. It is skeptical of its ability to grasp the nature of things. It is more comfortable with probabilities than with certainties, more sure of approximating the truth than of having mastered it. Modernity eschews absolutes and the unchanging laws said to derive from them. It does not admit to a definitive knowledge of either nature or the natural law.

A. *The Transcendental Paradigm*

In the natural law tradition, there has been an attempt to adjust to the intellectual demands of a changing culture and to enter into dialogue with other philosophic schools. This development has meant a rejection of Neo-scholastic formalism as it has been understood since the second half of the nineteenth century. This new philosophic perspective has taken shape as a movement sometimes called "transcendental Thomism," which began with Joseph Maréchal (1878–1944) and his reinterpretation of Aquinas in terms of Kant and German Idealism.[80] A leading exponent, Karl Rahner wrote:

The reception of the transcendental method means the end of "neo-scholasticism" in the historical sense of the word. This is not to say that this reception rejects the substance of the heritage of the traditional philosophy of the middle ages (especially that of Thomas of Aquin) as false or insignificant. This, of course, from a variety of points of view, is simply not the case.[81]

Bernard Lonergan, who developed the cognitional theory underlying transcendental Thomism, referred approvingly to Karl Rahner's suggestion that natural law should itself be approached through a transcendental method.[82] Neither one of them actually undertook this task, but their articulated "turn to the subject" did suggest the possibility of a substantial rethinking of natural law as the basis of an ongoing jurisprudential dialogue.

Classicist culture, largely prescinding from circumstances, tended to consider the legal subject as an abstract and rigid nature and to envisage laws as proportionately fixed. Since modern culture looks at the legal subject as a concrete entity in a changing world, it asks that its laws reflect this singularity and mobility.

Lonergan distinguished two components in concrete human reality: a constant, human nature; and a variable, human historicity. Despite the changing circumstances of life, there is this permanent and stabilizing factor, which, however, admits of two interpretations: "It may be placed in universal propositions, self-evident truths, naturally known certitudes. On the other hand, it may be placed in nature itself, in nature not as abstractly conceived, but as concretely operating."[83] In opting for this second alternative, Lonergan, although beginning with Aristotle, went beyond the traditional interpretations of Aristotle.

Aristotle defined a nature as an immanent principle of movement and of rest. In man such a principle is the human spirit as raising and answering questions.

80. See Otto Muck, "Scholasticism," Sacramentum Mundi: An Encylopedia of Theology, 6 vols. (New York: Herder & Herder, 1968), 2:38.

81. Karl Rahner, in the Foreword to Otto Muck's The Transcendental Method (New York: Herder & Herder, 1968), p. 9.

82. Bernard Lonergan, A Second Collection, ed. W. Ryan and B. Tyrrell (Philadelphia: Westminster Press, 1974), p. 6.

83. Bernard Lonergan, "Natural Right," A Third Collection, p. 172.

As raising questions, it is an immanent principle of movement. As answering questions and doing so satisfactorily, it is an immanent principle of rest.[84]

Consequently, in trying to comprehend natural law, we move through a question-and-answer process on the various levels of consciousness. But we should not cherish any illusions of instant certainty; we progress toward the truth about nature and its norms as towards an emergent probability. Subjectively, nature is not a given; it is what is to be grasped. Whatever the insights of classicist culture, they have not made the insights of empirical culture unnecessary. Historicity will always remain a component of human reality. It is through history with its periods of progress and decline that communal authenticity is tested, that proposed human rights are verified or repudiated. The responsibility for authentic choice is above all that of the historical individual in the process of getting to know himself and his world.

Lonergan's fundamental contribution to jurisprudence is his insight into the parallel between metaphysics and ethics and their interpenetration, both of which he grounded on the dynamic structure of the mind: metaphysics is a heuristic structure of rational consciousness; ethics is an obligatory structure of rational self-consciousness. Metaphysics and ethics are the prolongations of the dynamic structures of knowing and doing.[85]

Ethics, for Lonergan, was not deductive but personal: "I base ethics not on logically first propositions but on invariant structures of human knowing and human doing."[86] He explained the process of ethical development thus: "In working out the notion of good, we discovered in the rationally self-conscious subject an exigence for consistency between his knowing and his doing, and we saw how a body of ethical precepts could be derived simply by asking what concretely was implicit in that exigence."[87]

84. Ibid.

85. Idem, *Insight* (London: Longmans, Green, 1957; New York: Philosophical Library, 1958), p. 604.

86. Idem, *A Second Collection*, p. 39. See also on pp. 214–15: "You have also, in intelligent reasonable responsibility, norms, built-in norms, that are yourself. They are not propositions about yourself, but yourself, in your spiritual reality, to guide you in working out what that objective horizon is, the objective pole of the horizon."

87. Idem, *Insight*, p. 618. On the advantages of this method, see p. 604: "It can steer a sane course between the relativism of mere concreteness and the legalism of remote and static generalities; and it can do so not by good luck nor by vaguely postulating prudence, but methodically because it takes its stand on the ever recurrent dynamic generality that is the structure of rational self-consciousness."

In view of the extreme positions of some moralists who claim a Lonerganian influence, it is helpful to note that Lonergan himself did not envisage a necessarily radical departure from traditional positions. Speaking of the parallel between ethics and metaphysics, he said:

In metaphysics I not only assigned a basis in invariant structures but also derived from that basis a metaphysics with a marked family resemblance to traditional views. A similar family resemblance, I believe, would be found to exist between traditional ethics and an ethics that, like the metaphysics, was explicitly aware of itself as a system on the move.[88]

What has been occurring within the natural law tradition—most profoundly exemplified by Lonergan's thought—is what Thomas S. Kuhn called a "paradigm shift."[89] A new model has been proposed and already widely accepted. This empirical paradigm, this new world view, competes with the long-established classicist paradigm. Both are major insights into reality and, as insights, must be verified. But the resolution of the conflict between the two has proved very difficult.

Kuhn's observations about the "incommensurability of paradigms" help explain the dialogic standoff that results when proponents of the classicist and the revisionist natural law theory confront one another; they tend to argue in a vicious circle, each in terms of his own paradigm, each in terms of his own basic insight or understanding. The ascendancy of one paradigm over another rests basically on the degree of verification: how it can account for changes, anomalies, crises; how it can explain data and make reality meaningful. To change one's integrating insight is not easy. Human beings are creatures of habit, virtually intransigent in matters of fundamental perspective. Hence, the discovery of a revolutionary paradigm is usually made, as Kuhn reported, by those who are young or who are new in the field.

Shared paradigms lead to the determination of shared rules. In a fully mature system both may be present, but a paradigm may be creatively operative and widely accepted without the rules having been worked out. Kuhn observed that most will find the "search for rules more difficult and less satisfying that the search for paradigms."[90] Moreover, a new paradigm usually means a pervasive reassessment and redefinition of rules. Again, this is something more congenial to

88. Idem, *A Second Collection,* p. 40.
89. Thomas S. Kuhn, *The Structure of Scientific Revolutions* (Chicago: University of Chicago Press, 1962), p. 103 and passim.
90. Ibid., p. 43.

younger thinkers than to those with intellectual seniority and vested interests; just think, incidentally, of the problems, when a new legal code is promulgated, for established lawyers as contrasted with recent graduates who learned law the new way first.

Eventually, the competition between paradigms is resolved, even if occasionally the paradigms destroy one another, leaving the discipline in a pre-systematic state. But a shift, when it does occur, is probably more communal than we might expect: "As in political revolutions, so in paradigm choice—there is no standard higher than the assent of the relevant community."[91] This does not mean that scientific or philosophic truth is a matter of counting votes, but it does mean in practice that the operative and unifying perspective in a system depends on the intellectual cooperation and assent of its participants. One remains, even as a scientist, part of an intellectual community; the vast amount of data and the need of multifaceted verification require community assent for an ongoing institution.

Currently, a controversy simmers within the natural law tradition over competing paradigms; a proposed shift, though in progress, has not yet proved decisive. Despite overall cultural changes, the classicist paradigm is still solidly entrenched and authoritatively supported, but it is also being stoutly challenged by many thinkers with an empirical perspective.

This new perspective has taken different forms; Lonergan's generalized empirical method, with its transcendental paradigm rooted in conscious intentionality, is an influential one. Although Lonergan was not directly concerned with the specifics of ethical or legal rules, some moralists have found inspiration and guidance in his paradigm for their own rethinking of natural law and the moral teachings associated with it. In addition, as we have seen, his work is also helpful in understanding the various kinds of law from the classicist perspective of Aquinas.

Other moralists, acting independently of Lonergan but taking into consideration the implications of the cultural revolution, have in their own way sought to answer the same questions. So moralists of various backgrounds are trying to revise the natural law so that it can have a more vital and effective role in modern life. For the most part, they are not against natural law, but are rather in dialogue with it. They are working within the natural law tradition, yet they view it from the perspective of a paradigm shift appropriate to an empirical culture.

91. Ibid., p. 93.

B. The Revisionist Rules

Faced with many moral crises—problems of sexuality, contraception, abortion, divorce, poverty, discrimination, mercy killing, capital punishment, torture, terrorism, nuclear arms, war—and disturbed by the presence of radical anomalies in the traditional paradigm, the so-called revisionists have reacted against the deontological approach of the earlier teaching, with its emphasis on law and duty, and they have turned their attention, although not exclusively, to the consequences of actions.[92]

Their position is usually one of moderate teleology or mixed consequentialism; the reason for the qualification is that, although the consequences or outcome of actions are important, other components— the intention and motive of the agent, the character of the action, and the attendant circumstances—are also relevant in determining the morality of a given action.[93]

What the revisionists have tried that is fundamentally different is to liberate themselves from the formalism of an abstract moral code applied mechanically to concrete actions. Their central and most controversial position is the rejection of the notion of intrinsic evil: that is, that certain actions, whatever the circumstances, are absolutely prohibited.

92. The term "revisionist" is used by David Tracy, *Blessed Rage for Order* (New York: Seabury Press, 1975). Although the revisionist model is described briefly, pp. 32– 34, the whole book is "an attempt to clarify the exact meaning and possibilities of just such a revisionist model for our common theological task" (p. 34). I have used the term, however, without attributing to the positions I have described the full freight of Tracy's pluralistic theology. Some ethical revisionists are the Europeans Josef Fuchs, Bernard Häring, Louis Janssens, Peter Knauer, Bruno Schüller, and the Americans Lisa Sowle Cahill, Charles E. Curran, Richard A. McCormick, Daniel C. Maguire. Some traditional or deontolotical advocates are John Connery, John Finnis, Germain Grisez, William E. May, and Paul Ramsey.

93. A creative work in this area is Josef Fuchs, *Natural Law*, trans. H. Reckter and J. A. Dowling (New York: Sheed & Ward, 1965). A collection of revisionist authors can be found in *Readings in Moral Theology*, ed. Charles E. Curran and Richard A. McCormick (New York: Paulist Press, 1979, 1980, 1982, 1984); the first of these four volumes is on moral norms and is especially pertinent to this chapter. The contribution of Richard A. McCormick, in *Notes on Moral Theology 1965 through 1980* (Lanham, Md.: University Press of America, 1981) and *Notes on Moral Theology 1981 through 1984* (Lanham, Md.: University Press of America, 1984) reveals the ongoing dialogue, as does *Doing Evil to Achieve Good*, ed. R. McCormick and P. Ramsey (Chicago: Loyola University Press, 1978). An excellent overall statement on the conflicting positions is "Teleology, Utilitarianism, and Christian Ethics," by Lisa Sowle Cahill, *Theological Studies* 42 (1977): 601–29.

On the contrary, revisionists hold that the circumstances, taken in the broad sense, are also determinative of the moral character of an action. The reason for this rejection of absolutes is twofold: first, the impossibility of learning all the contingencies and circumstances of human actions; and, second, the impossibility of formulating a norm providing for all possible contingencies and circumstances. So revisionists aim at a personalist rather than a mechanical process of decision, realizing full well that simply to apply abstract norms to actions in the abstract makes the existential subject irrelevant.

No longer morally determinative by itself, the action is still the focal point for revisionists. Indeed, the action may even be judged abstractly—for abstraction remains a valid mental operation—and found to be evil. If judged abstractly, however, it cannot yet be judged to be morally evil, for moral evil is in the concrete action, not in the abstract notion. Nevertheless, this abstract evil should be recognized for what it is and clearly distinguished from moral evil. Actually, it is given a variety of labels: premoral evil (Josef Fuchs), ontic evil (Louis Janssens), physical evil (Peter Knauer), and nonmoral evil (Bruno Schüller). Here the term premoral evil will be used. But whatever the term, the distinction between premoral evil and moral evil remains a crucial one in revisionist thought.

To call an action a premoral evil is not to give it a benignly patronizing or mildly naughty label; it is to make a serious charge and to assert that all evil, even premoral evil, should be avoided. To clarify the status of premoral evil, we view it in two positive law categories: it sets up a *prima facie* case of moral evil (W. D. Ross) or a rebuttable presumption of moral evil (Peter Knauer). If the *prima facie* case is not explained away and contradicted or if the presumption is not rebutted by new evidence, the accusation stands, and the action is held to be morally wrong and thus forbidden. The difference between the classicist and the modern approach is that, under the former, the *prima facie* case or presumption is irrebuttable.

The revisionist option is the possibility of rebutting the prohibitive presumption implicit in the premoral evil of the contemplated action. This option is to be exercised in the spirit of Ortega's maxim: "I am myself and my circumstances." The existential subject, in all his concreteness, must satisfy both individual and communal objections, taking into consideration the evolving wisdom evidenced by the status of the abstract prohibition. More precisely, in this rebuttal, the subject must show, as Richard McCormick insisted "a proportionate reason" to justify the decision to sacrifice some values in order to realize others: "Wrongfulness must be attributed to a lack of proportion. By that I mean that the value I am pursuing is being pursued in a way calculated in human judgment (not without prediscursive elements) to undermine it."[94]

It should be carefully noted, since even moralists are apt to overlook it, that a proportionate reason can never make an immoral action moral; what it can do, however, is make a premorally evil action moral—a great difference. Thus it cannot make murder moral, but it may morally justify an act of homicide, for example, a killing in self-defense.

This line of reasoning suggests a way to bypass the traditional Catholic distinction between the direct and indirect intention of evil, as formulated in the so-called principle of double effect, which prohibits every direct intending of evil, whether as an end or means, but does permit an act with unintended though foreseen evil results, if both the means and the end were good and there was a proportionate reason to permit the evil.

An objection to this principle is that it is too abstract and too rigid for the complicated and nuanced moral problems of the present day. With the introduction of the notion of premoral evil, however, a new approach has been proposed. McCormick together with Schüller made the moral notions of approval and disapproval determinative: one may never intend even a premorally evil *end,* for to do so would be to approve it; one may, however, directly intend premoral evil as a *means* on two conditions—if there is no approval of it and if there is a proportionate reason for it.[95]

Despite the rejection by the revisionists of the notion of intrinsic evil and their use of proportionate reason in converting premoral evil to moral good, there remains a significant historical continuity in ethical norms. What has been judged to be evil in the abstract or premoral evil—and there is a substantial consensus on this level throughout the natural law tradition—turns out in many cases even from a teleological perspective to be considered morally wrong. These abstractions or

94. Richard A. McCormick, "A Commentary on Commentaries," *Doing Evil to Achieve Good,* p. 265.
95. See ibid., pp. 263–64.

generalizations are by and large the proper directives for human conduct; the presumption is in their favor and is not easily rebutted—nor should it be.

McCormick touched upon a major reason for this in responding to the charge that so-called "proportionalism" is dangerous. There is, he said, a communal dimension to the assessment of proportionate reason: "In a sense, the very values one desires to achieve in such conduct have been judged disproportionate by the community to the disvalues inhering in it."[96] This community calculus is not infallible or immutable, but it does establish a set of working directives giving moral and social stability.

What is initially surprising is a seemingly inconsistent deontological turn by which the revisionists speak of "practical absolutes" or "virtually exceptionless norms." Thus Fuchs, while insisting that theoretically there are no absolute norms, would admit that practically speaking there are certain actions for which no justifying combination of intention and circumstances can be conceived, so the norms forbidding them would be in effect universal.[97] This admission does not afford an argument against the newer approach; it does, however, highlight the fact that ethical continuity reflects human reasonableness.

What the revisionists are trying to do is not to relax moral restraints but to put moral decision making on a sounder and more nuanced basis. As a practical matter, there is no need to strain after complete certainty in establishing the intrinsic character of the action or the universality of the norm, as if the choice were between certainty or anarchy. Without metaphysical proof, we can appreciate when we are approaching cloture, when sufficient conditions for making a sound judgment are fulfilled, when we have no reasonable doubts about norm or action, presumption or its rebuttal. Natural law is a sensible guide to living well, not an over-protective restraint on making a reasonable mistake. It is a living process of moral growth. Balancing all these considerations, I understand a moderate revisionist, natural-law position to encompass the following principles:

96. Idem, "Notes on Moral Theology 1981," *Theological Studies* 43 (1982): 90 (p. 70 in *Notes on Moral Theology 1981 through 1984*).
97. Josef Fuchs, "The Absoluteness of Moral Norms," *Gregorianum*, 52 (1970): 415–58, reprinted in *Readings in Moral Theology No. 1*, pp. 94–137, esp. pp. 124–26.

(1) There are no intrinsically evil actions, except for the violations of self-evident universal norms, transcendental or categorical.

(2) There are, however, actions that are premorally or ontically evil.

(3) The strong presumption is that premorally evil actions are morally evil and so forbidden.

(4) The presumption that premorally evil actions are morally evil can be rebutted, if, in comparing the values and the disvalues, there emerges a proportionate reason to perform the premoral evil.

(5) One must neither approve the premoral evil nor intend it as an end; one may, however, and this is essential to the revisionist position, intend it as a means.

(6) The proportionate reason encompasses the action itself, together with all its attendant circumstances. Of special weight, in addition to intention and motive, is the social context, both horizontal (being part of a present community) and vertical (being part of a living tradition).

An underlying difference between the older and the newer positions on natural law is that the revisionist approach deals with the subject existentially rather than abstractly. In doing so, it incorporates subjectivity and historicity in its ethical structure. The more traditional natural-law approach does not, in its quest for a rapprochement with modernity, utilize sufficiently the thinking of Aquinas on the mutability of the secondary precepts of natural law or on the necessity of prudence for concrete decision making.

These two points afford the real possibility of an updating within the older position. Of course, the traditionalists put to good use in the pastoral area the findings of psychology and medical science, by applying their absolute norms with a greater understanding and compassion for human weakness in a sinful world. Both positions are internally unified, but from two culturally different perspectives. The task of traditionalists is to complete their move into modern culture without sacrificing the values of their heritage; the revisionists think that they themselves have done so.

The teaching of Aquinas reviewed from the perspective of conscious intentionality may do much to bridge the gap. The resultant open and searching dialogue between two groups that share a common background can thus clarify the meaning and value of natural law, nuancing and facilitating that indispensable human achievement—a moral life.

CONCLUSION

What does the idea of natural law, revisited and revised, contribute to a jurisprudence of subjectivity? Our analysis may seem to have done nothing more than keep us in the realm of theory, formulated according to a classicist and then an empirical perspective. Indeed, that is almost all that an analysis can do, for interiority depends on each individual. Analysis, however, can do something important: it can point out where we ought to look and what we ought to look for. Where do we look? Within at our mental operations. What do we look for? Our inclinations and their meaning and value.

We have prepared for this task from the beginning of the book; the first three chapters have focused on our own subjectivity and on the role of Eros and Nemesis in our lives. Doing that has been an inner experience of natural law, the experience upon which further understanding rests. Unless we are conscious of natural law as something that stems from our mind and not from other people, the idea of natural law stagnates in the realm of theory, abstract and impersonal. We must become conscious of natural law as an inner disposition, not as an outside imposition.

Once we have understood that natural law, as natural law, is rooted in each individual consciousness, we can profitably learn to differentiate and thematize our experiences of it. We find that the principles of natural law are not in a realm of Platonic ideas, but are functions of our own mind, and some of them can be neither rooted out nor erased. The term "self-evident principles," instead of sounding like an appeal to a distant metaphysics, stands manifested as an affirmation of individual, human intelligences.

To speak of natural law in transition is then to refer to two movements of the mind. The obvious one is from classicist to empirical culture. The turn to the subject has characterized that transition, but the transition may be merely a horizontal one, which remains in the realm of theory. Of more crucial importance is the literal turn to the subject—not as subject matter but as self-consciousness—by which the mind moves from theory to interiority, for in that inner realm is natural law most profoundly experienced. Only consciousness of our own subjectivity, by putting us into vital contact with truth and value, can enable us to enunciate that personal dictate of reason which is the natural law.

But natural law, however finely attuned to human nature, will fail to overcome the challenge of absurdity, unless further relevant questions are answered concerning the very ground of natural law. Our next chapter deals with the transcendent realm of legal meaning and value.

CHAPTER 9

THE DIVINE GROUND

Every answer is always just the beginning of a new question. Man experiences himself as infinite possibility because in practice and in theory he necessarily places every sought-after result in question.—Karl Rahner*

[handwritten margin note: many claim: if law is to be meaningful and worthwhile there is need for a divine ground]

Asking questions about law leads to questions about its ultimate ground—logically but not inevitably. Men and women can, at any time, terminate further inquiry. If, however, they continue to experience wonder and curiosity, if they ask relevant questions, they will sooner or later have questions about God. They may not all get the same answers, but they will at least share a common concern.

From the beginning of history, human beings have searched for the ultimate meaning and justification of the laws that govern their conduct. Until the seventeenth century, God or gods had usually played an active role in their cosmos. But beginning with the Age of Rationalism and continuing to the present, there has been a dramatic change. Philosophers and legal theorists have by and large eliminated God from their jurisprudence or have denied God a significant legal role; some have even proclaimed the death of the divine Lawgiver.

Nevertheless, there still remains in this pluralistic culture a sizeable segment of the population, even of the intellectuals, that affirms not only the relevance but also the necessity of a divine ground, if law is to be meaningful and worthwhile.

Two complementary viewpoints are in order here: the historical affirmations of a divine ground and the current questions about its actuality. The first is necessary because the history of law and legal philosophy has been structured over the centuries from this perspective; the second is necessary because many modern thinkers are reassessing, some grudgingly, the divine role in an integral jurisprudence.

---

*Karl Rahner, *Foundations of Christian Faith: An Introduction to the Idea of Christianity,* trans. W. V. Dych (New York: Seabury Press, 1978), p. 32.

In this chapter I first reflect on the persistence of a consensus on the divine grounding of law from ancient times through the Middle Ages. I do not repeat what I noted in the first chapter concerning the changes in legal thinking that have occurred since the 1600's. But I do discuss how the God question, apart from religion and theology, may arise today, and I suggest the basis in conscious intentionality that makes asking the God question a subjective exigency. This psychological grounding is currently important in view of the pervasiveness of the absurdity response and the growing hunger for ultimate meaning that characterizes so many modern thinkers.

I. HISTORICAL AFFIRMATIONS

In examining the past consensus on the existence of a divine ground for law, we note a subjective progression from compact to differentiated consciousness. For the ancients, their world of experience was mediated by meaning, first on a commonsense level and then with an emerging systematic understanding: the poets made the undifferentiated phase eternally memorable; the Pre-Socratics, the first scientists, initiated the second phase. Theoretical thinking, further developed by the Sophists, by Aristotle and Plato, by the Stoics, and by others, earned a permanent place for itself in the Western world. When Greek thought combined with Christian faith in such great minds as Augustine and Aquinas, a new philosophic synthesis and a new theory of law resulted. Subjectivity, however, was not fully differentiated from common sense and theory, yet from Heraclitus in 500 B.C. through Plato and Augustine this realm of consciousness was clearly discernible. As we survey these various periods, observing the mental operations at work, we shall endeavor to differentiate for ourselves the various realms, especially that of subjectivity or interiority.

A. The Mythmakers

The Greek poets played a critical role in a pre-scientific age—they gave convincingly beautiful explanations of the world of their experience and of its social structures. The storms and thunderbolts of Zeus, Poseidon's raging seas, the wars instigated by Aries, the punishments exacted by the Furies, the emotional turmoils of Eros and Aphrodite, the troubles springing from Pandora's box—all these were attempts to

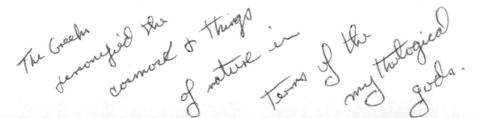

The Greek personified the cosmos of things of nature in terms of the mythological gods.

make sense of a world of conflict and change. An abundance of questions remained, but the answers of the poets were so rich artistically and psychologically that they would survive even demythologizing.

Laws, their sources buried in the darkness of the past, were attributed to the gods. The root of the word for law, *nomos,* as we have seen in the chapter on Nemesis, means "to allot," so laws signified the duties allotted to mankind by the gods. Themis, the daughter of Zeus, was the goddess of law and order. In practice she stood for the legal establishment, the kings or nobles who administered these god-given laws. Mere human beings could not alter such decrees; thus the tradition of sacredness afforded both dignity and stability to the legal structure. At the same time, the hermeneutics of common sense and the felicitous inexactitudes of memory provided some flexibility. But, always, to interpret the law was to discover its divine meaning.

Nevertheless, the concrete operation of this divine heritage left much to be desired. Not even an appeal to the gods could forestall political agitation for reform.[1] From the eighth to the fifth century B.C., Ionia, then part of Greece and now part of Turkey, experienced a spate of civil rights movements. As the economic position of the freemen improved, their expectations increased, and their dissatisfaction with the time-honored but one-sided administration of justice intensified. For them *dike* was a demand for equality through written laws. Although the nobles might still man the courts, the standards for judges and litigants would now be publicly visible.

Perhaps it is difficult for us to realize today what a major victory codification was. For even discretion works more justly when the guidelines are public, with equity correcting the clear deficiencies of general norms. This codification, however, had another effect—it secularized the law, because it actually involved more than simply chronicling established norms: it required legislative drafting. Once men recognized themselves as lawmakers, Themis and the myths surrounding her succumbed to the exigencies of a changing civilization.

We should not, however, underestimate the value of myths. They are not just imaginative stories but rather attempts to explain things and events—not the whole explanation, but intuitive efforts to under-

---

1. See Werner Jaeger, *Paideia: the Ideals of Greek Culture,* 3 vols. (New York: Oxford University Press, 1939), 1:102–03.

stand the cosmos by means of the cosmos, to find the ground of things and events within the cosmos itself.[2] It is significant in terms of the divine ground that the Greeks were not willing to subject themselves to blind forces of nature; rather, they personified these forces as intelligent and free beings—not below them but above them, not natural forces but gods.[3] Eventually the gods were done to death by the questions that human beings asked, dissatisfied with the symbolic answers given by the poets.

B. The Pre-Socratics

Urged on by a sense of wonder, the Pre-Socratics put aside religious and poetic accounts and asked probing questions about the world of their experience. These first scientists, men such as Thales, Anaximander, Empedocles, Parmenides, and Pythagoras, dealt with problems of stability and change, of order and disorder, of justice in the microcosm and the macrocosm. Thus Anaximander (611–548 B.C.) wrote of justice as a principle of order: "Justice is the separating out of the elements from the primal boundless material."[4] Every answer about the material universe threatened at least indirectly the existence of some god: one by one they were unmasked as powers of nature. Thales, whom Aristotle called the first philosopher of nature, phrased this discovery ambiguously in a way that would please traditionalists and theorists alike: "All things are full of gods."[5] But Thales did not mean what the poets meant.

These early scientists, however, concentrated on things external and material; it remained for Heraclitus (c. 500 B.C.) to move the investi-

2. See Eric Voegelin, *Conversations with Eric Voegelin*, ed. R. E. O'Connor (Montreal: Thomas More Institute, 1980), pp. 11f. See generally, Mircea Eliade, *Images and Symbols*, trans. Philip Mairet (New York: Sheed & Ward, 1961).

3. See Etienne Gilson, *God and Philosophy* (New Haven: Yale University Press, 1941), p. 22: "The Greek gods are crude but telling expressions of the conviction that since man is somebody, and not merely something, the ultimate explanation of what happens to him should rest with somebody and not with something."

4. Anaximander, in Simplicius, *Physica*, 24, 18 (Hermann Diels *Die Fragmente der Vorsokratiker*, ed. Walther Kranz (Berlin: Weidmann, 1968), 12 B 1; hereafter cited as *DK*. Philip Wheelwright suggested that *apeiron*, the "primal boundless material," reflected Anaximander's insight into the notion of potentiality, "a boundless reservoir of potential qualities." Wheelwright thus called it the "Qualitatively Unlimited," in *The Presocratics* (New York: The Odyssey Press, 1966), p. 287. If we follow this suggestion, we see how the fragment might contain the radical notion of justice—the giving to each his own—here the bestowing of that system of qualities that is the nature of a thing.

5. Thales, in Aristotle, *De anima*, I, 5, 411 a7.

gation into the inner arena of the soul. He carried the attack on the gods into human consciousness. It was all well and good for the poet Homer to attribute human passions to divine influence, the lust of Paris for Helen of Troy to the machinations of Aphrodite, but Heraclitus would have none of that: "The character of a man is his daimon."[6] Neither the credit nor the blame for our actions belongs to the gods but to ourselves. Our emotions, abilities, and training, our virtues and our vices—all fashion our response to the world. Above all, we are shaped in part by our own free choices, which in turn condition our freedom. With that insight, the last justification for the gods had disappeared in the clear light of reason. But, although the gods were dead, religion was not. Man still sought transcendent reality. Not finding it on Olympus, man looked elsewhere, his questioning mind ever craving ultimate meaning and value.

Heraclitus had dismissed the gods, but he discovered a divine principle. Acutely aware of the ever-changing universe, he also recognized the presence of an abiding order. His subjective awareness of a principle of order in himself suggested a similar principle for the cosmos. It was wisdom, human and divine, that ordered all things. Heraclitus makes a remarkable statement: "Wisdom is common to all. . . . They who would speak with intelligence must hold fast to the [wisdom that is] common to all, as a city holds fast to its laws, and even more strongly for *all human laws are fed by one divine law*."[7] Here is perhaps the first formulation of a divine ground for law that is derived, not from myth or revelation, but from human reason. This insight will reach its full articulation in the thought of Plato, especially his last work, the *Laws*. Belief in the gods had been dealt a fatal blow, but the glimpse into the divine character of the law, now transformed and transcendent, would perdure.

C. The Sophists

The Sophists, in the fifth century, brought to Greek thought an iconoclastic and even revolutionary strain. Inspired in part by Heraclitus, they were not able to preserve the profundity of his insights. For them, law stayed on the level of advocacy. Their skeptical bias marshaled reason, armed with logic, to attack current cultural and political

6. Heraclitus, *DK*, 22 B 119.
7. Heraclitus, *DK*, 22 B 114. Italics supplied.

norms. The cutting edge of the Sophist offensive was a distinction between law and nature, between *nomos* and *physis*.

Laws meant for the Sophists matters of convention, human constructs reflecting conflicts of interests as resolved by the power of the dominant class—a familiar Marxist characterization. Laws were no longer sacred, for the Sophists had seen too many different peoples with different gods and different laws for them to accept ancient tales of divine legislators. Moreover, watching human lawmakers at work and even participating in the legislative process themselves, they came to appreciate more fully the role of power in political decision making.

Nature for the Sophists, with their relativism and opportunism, was not so much a standard as a weapon. Having broken from the natural philosophy of the Pre-Socratics, they needed something to help in the attack against convention—the entrenched parochialism, intellectual and social, of Athens. Speaking in part from the consumer perspective, they focused on *physis*, as earlier generations had focused on *dike*, but in a negative manner. W.K.C. Guthrie called Sophism a profession rather than a philosophy. We might more accurately speak of it as a methodology: the Sophists proposed to teach *arete*, excellence in general, without limiting themselves to specifics, although as a matter of fact rhetoric was their chief commodity, the rhetoric of the courts and assemblies. For example, Gorgias, an eminent Sophist, would challenge anyone in the public theatre: "Propose me a theme," and would then deliver an oration on that subject.[8] What the Sophists professed to teach, and at high prices, was a method of doing things well or, more narrowly, a method of political success.

Despite self-serving and extremist tendencies toward nihilism and anarchy, the Sophists participated obliquely in that resistance to disorder that was to culminate in the discovery by Plato and Aristotle of the *nous* or reason. The Sophists certainly appeared to be purveyors of disorder. Yet in undermining conventional distinctions, which often masked actual discriminations, and in challenging the rigid rules that fostered no social or rational interest, they were helping to break down walls of organized disorder. From the resultant rubble there emerged the possibility of rebuilding society on the basis of sound principles, such as natural equality. Note, for example, the liberationist ring to the words of Hippias of Elis: "I count you all my kinsmen, family, and

8. Quoted by Philostratus, *Laws of the Sophists,* 482.

fellow citizens—by nature not by law (*nomos*). By nature like is kin to like; but law, the tyrant of mankind, does much violence to nature."[9]

The Sophist appeal to nature should not be overestimated. Some, like Protagoras, were convinced that human necessity or exigency required laws and a kind of social contract; others, like Thrasymachus, believed: "Justice is simply the advantage of the stronger."[10] And yet, despite the inner contradictions, to use the idea of nature even to destroy the fabric of society was to give currency to the idea of nature, which others would use to justify and foster political life. The Sophists questioned political institutions in terms of nature, and nature became a key philosophical issue. Plato and Aristotle would try to determine what was right by nature (*physei dikaion*); and the Stoics would construct a natural law out of part of their answer.

The Sophists continued the process of questioning that had begun with Thales and the other Pre-Socratics, but they looked, not at the material universe but at the political society, not at physical nature but at human nature and human interaction. The gods were gone; the laws were in disrepute; philosophy had turned into logic and rhetoric; but the eternal desire for meaning and value burned on—the questioning continued, even among Skeptics.

D. Plato and Aristotle

Long before Plato (428–347 B.C.), and Aristotle (385–322 B.C.), the Greeks were brilliant artists and thinkers. The myths of the Poets, the speculations of the Pre-Socratics, the dialectics of the Sophists—all revealed the mind perceptively and creatively at work. Nevertheless, a pressing problem remained: the mystery of disorder.

Like all other human beings, the Greeks faced the inevitable process of aging, illness, and death; they experienced constant change and insecurity, as well as the apparent senselessness of many events in their lives. So they were hungry, even desperate, for answers to the questions that their precariously disordered lives occasioned.

The desired answers were not to be found in human beings, limited, dependent, vulnerable, lacking a sufficient reason for their own existence. Nor were they to be found in the gods, now revealed as personifications of natural forces. The sobering question gradually emerged:

9. Hippias of Elis, quoted by Plato, *Protagoras*, 337 C–D.
10. Thrasymachus, quoted by Plato, *Republic*, 338 C.

Is meaningless disorder man's destiny?—a question phrased some two thousand years later as: Is absurdity man's destiny? The Greek answer and achievement was the discovery of the *nous,* so well analyzed by Eric Voegelin.

The *nous* (*ratio* or reason) naturally characterizes all mankind. To speak of its discovery is not to imply that prior to that event the Greeks were witless automatons. The discovery consisted in moving from a compact to a differentiated consciousness; thinkers became aware of a power within themselves that could help them order their personal and social existence. The attempt to understand, resist, and overcome disorder heightened their awareness of what was already operative within them—reason. They appreciated order, and they appreciated ordering; what was excitingly new was the insight into a principle of order in the cosmos and in themselves.

This noetic understanding was not a single leap forward to a designated goal. It came rather as a byproduct of the search for the ultimate ground, the principle of order for the whole cosmos. Becoming aware that they could order things within their control, the Greeks attributed the manifest order in the world outside to some proportionately greater principle, which like themselves had to be intelligent and free. Yet only after concluding that the cosmos has an ultimate and intelligent ground and after articulating and symbolizing it as the divine *Nous,* the principle of cosmic order, did men become fully conscious of their own *nous,* their own principle of personal and social order, which—and the thought was breathtaking—made them like God. This dual noetic experience shattered the absurdity barrier, convincing them that existence, human and divine, is fundamentally intelligible, though its full realization would remain an open-ended challenge.

The understanding of law increased tremendously, owing to this profound grasp of the principle of cosmic order. For the Greeks, to speak of order was to think of law. "In man's consciousness, the divine order is present through the mediation of *Dike.*"[11] This *dike* or right, as Heraclitus had suggested, symbolized the grounding in divine wis-

---

11. Eric Voegelin, "Wisdom and the Magic of the Extreme," *The Southern Review* 17 (1981): 272. In addition to *Conversations,* mentioned above, I have found Voegelin's analysis of the emergence of noetic consciousness in ancient Greece very helpful here, especially his series *Order and History,* 5 vols. (Baton Rouge: Louisiana State University Press, 1956–1987) and *Anamnesis,* trans. B. Niemeyer (Notre Dame, Ind.: Notre Dame University Press, 1978).

dom of the laws that guide human existence. These laws are discover-
able through human reason. Thus Plato found the true principles of
law in the order (*taxis*) of the soul. Man, transcending himself by
following reason, becomes as "like unto God as he can and that again
is to become just with the help of wisdom."[12] Through justice one
achieves optimal fulfillment: "Nothing is more like the divine than one
who becomes as just as possible."[13]

In the *Laws,* the largest and last of his works, Plato dealt profoundly
with the relationship between God and law. He began his work with
the word "God"—a literary device signaling the immense importance
of the divine in his mature thought: "God or some man, O strangers—
who is supposed to have originated the institution of your laws"?[14]
The rest of the book comprises Plato's answer to that question. He
introduced his answer by contrasting his own position with that of the
Sophists. He took the famous remark of Protagoras, "Of all things the
measure is man, of the being that they are and of the non-being that
they are not,"[15] and he then opposed to it his own parallel statement,
"God is for us the measure of all things, of a truth; more so than, as
they say, man."[16]

In stating his disagreement with the skeptical humanism of the Sophists, Plato did not forget to nuance his thought. He did not take the
extreme view that all laws are received directly from God, as the Greek
poets might have imagined, although he did posit divine participation
in all lawmaking. To speak broadly: the first three books of the *Laws*
develop the notion of God as the author of the political community;
the remaining nine books focus on man's part in shaping society in
harmony with divine wisdom. In short, the noetic experience forms the
core of lawmaking.

Consciousness of the divine ground, Plato warned, must guide all
one's political activities, or one would suffer the consequences: "God,
who, as the old adage has it, holds in his hands the beginning, end, and
the middle of all that is, moves through the cycle of nature straight to
his end, and ever at his side walks right, the judge of them that forsake
God's law."[17] Clearly, despite the slanted and polemical use made of

---

12. Plato, *Theaetetus,* 176 B.   13. Ibid., 176 B.

14. Plato, *Laws,* I, 624 A.

15. Plato quoted Protagoras in the *Theaetetus,* 152 A; the sentence is found also in
Sextus Empiricus, *Adv. Math.,* VII, 60.

16. Plato, *Laws,* IV, 716 C.   17. Ibid., IV, 715 E–716 A.

the word "nature" by the Sophists, Plato fully integrated it into his thinking. Indeed, throughout the *Laws* and the earlier *Republic,* God always works according to nature. "Plato's thought finds a fixed point of rest in this new concept of nature as implying standards."[18] This is a rich insight for legal development, but to know nature adequately so that the norms derived from it truly lead to righteousness, one must have the noetic experience.

Analysis of the noetic experience reveals the dimensions of one's dependence on the divine ground, which is not only the basis of cosmic intelligibility and the end toward which human nature moves, but is also the reason for the existence and the activity of all things. In his puppet myth, Plato imaginatively symbolized the divine influence. Puppets, made by the gods and moved by cords or strings—that is, "interior states"—represent human beings.[19] The cords are twofold: a gold cord, which is the pull of reason, and some iron cords, which are the counterpulls of the passions. Reason attracts us gently; the passions, violently. The issue is self-conquest or self-defeat. Of course, man is not an inanimate puppet; he ought to respond by cooperating with "the sacred and holy golden cord of reason called by us *the common law of the state*"[20] and by resisting the tension toward the passions, for "therein lies the division between virtue and vice."[21]

Plato made a further distinction between the individual and the community. The individual experiences both pull and counter-pull and should choose to follow the dictates of the *nous,* the pull of the golden cord. The community, however, has laws that have already incorporated the reflective judgments of reason, laws that are needed to help citizens in perceiving and following right reason, even when their own judgments are deficient. Plato concluded: "So the many must always cooperate with the noble drawing of the law, for judgment, though a noble thing, is as gentle and free from violence as noble, whence its drawing needs supporters, if the gold within us is to prevail over the other stuff."[22]

The noetic experience—the discovery of the *nous,* divine and human—gives us the foundational insight for an understanding of law.

18. Werner Jaeger, *Paideia,* 2:241. He also remarked that God's ways in the *Laws* and early *Republic* are *kata physin,* according to nature, ibid., p. 346, n. 216.

19. Plato, *Laws,* I, 644 E.

20. Ibid., 645 A.   21. Ibid., 645 B–C.

22. Ibid., 645 A.

Let us now consider briefly how the noetic experience, which, as we have seen, characterizes the Theosphere and the Monosphere, is also essential for understanding the human subject in the Isosphere and the Koinosphere.

In the Isosphere, the value of intersubjectivity depends on the value of the individual subjects, their fundamental dignity. What noetic consciousness does is lift this relationship between subjects to a higher level. The I-Thou relationship is perceived as occurring between persons who share both similarity to the divine and openness to it. At least potentially, they are moved by the divine, permeated by it, and luminously reflective of it. According to Aristotle, as Voegelin pointed out, the first existential virtue is a kind of self-esteem or self-love; by that he meant "due respect for the cultivation of the noetic self—that is, the divineness, the divine part of man."[23] In the Isosphere, this mutual self-love is the radical intersubjectivity from which justice springs; its source is the noetic experience.

In the Koinosphere, these noetic intersubjectivities are brought to a higher perfection. The Greeks believed that only in the *polis* could man achieve the self-sufficiency necessary for happiness. But the political structure must have content, if it is to realize its goals. Aristotle, as we have seen, used two terms, both of which imply noetic content: he called the basic political virtue *philia politike,* for order depends on noetically grounded friendship or love; and he spoke also of *homonoia,* literally having the same *nous* or a common *nous,* therefore likemindedness or concord. Only a community that shares noetic awareness can achieve the practical order that is a prerequisite for personal fulfillment.

In discussing the insights of Plato, we have referred only briefly to Aristotle, his disciple; this apparent neglect has three reasons: first, what was crucial in discussing the divine ground was the noetic experience best formulated by Plato; second, we have seen in other chapters many of Aristotle's more specific contributions to legal theory; and, third, in the process of further working out the implications of the Platonic insight into the divine ground, Aristotle did not develop as adequate an understanding of the divine ground as one would have hoped; nevertheless, his insights have enabled thinkers through the Middle Ages and beyond to work out a more satisfactory natural theology.

23. Eric Voegelin, *Conversations,* pp. 9–10.

Aristotle was able to reason formally to the existence of a prime mover, even of a plurality of prime movers. His idea of God, however, was substantially different from what Judaeo-Christian thought arrived at, even on the purely philosophic level. Aristotle's God was a *noesis noeseos,* an *intelligentia intelligentiae,* an understanding understanding. This God, however, had no care for men, being more like the Hindu Ishvara than the Hebrew Yahweh, more a model than a father and lord.

Although Aristotle had shed some of the mystery and richness of the Platonic understanding of God, he did believe that he had found the ground for his own being and becoming, as well as the requisite intelligibility for the highest type of life, the contemplative. Constrained by the limitations of his metaphysics, he nevertheless shared the overriding vision of his master. He too gave law a transcendent quality rooted in the noetic experience: "He who commands that law should rule may thus be regarded as commanding that God and Reason alone should rule."[24]

Plato and Aristotle differed in the character of their genius and the implementation of their insights, but they shared a noetic experience, to the understanding and articulating of which they dedicated their lives. Together, they have given Western civilization lasting insight into the sacred character of law.

E. *The Stoics*

After a creative period, there is often an attempt to consolidate gains and to achieve inner coherence. Sometimes this organizational phase deteriorates into formalism. This was the situation in third-century Athens. The Stoics had readily acknowledged the noetic experience, which Plato and Aristotle objectified and symbolized, but they proceeded to diminish it by thinking of it too abstractly. In place of the living experience, there eventually arose a conceptualistic system once removed from the data and the insights that first occasioned it. The resultant Stoic viewpoint perpetuated a flawed legal subjectivity that Western culture would dutifully internalize.

Unfortunately, the law is highly susceptible to such a conceptualist distortion. Since norms must be stable so that they can order society and must be communicated to have any effect, propositional formu-

---

24. Aristotle, *Politics,* III, 16, 1287 a29.

lation is a necessary medium but not an entirely satisfactory one, for it does not provide equally well for the law's other needs. To be fully adequate, the law must be rooted in an ongoing and open-ended noetic experience and must be attuned to the concrete exigencies of the singular situation. Unless the law keeps in touch with both poles, it remains deficient. Conceptualism, in its search for clarity, so narrows the intellectual horizon that the subject no longer experiences his ground or his context. Though he may pay lip service to both, he is in full contact with neither, for he operates in an abstract world, not an existential one. The conceptualist fails to realize that the reality of the ultimate ground and the singularity of the legal event cannot be completely reduced to concepts.

Concepts are general formulations of the intelligibility of insights into data—what is essential to having an insight. Although enriching the mind, this process of abstraction involves literally leaving behind the empirical residue. Thus we experience more than our concepts contain. Abstraction does, however, enable us to grasp and control the systematic, but it does not provide equally well for the non-systematic. Therefore, when we try to apply abstract laws, we should take into consideration the conditions and the circumstances that determine the experienced but non-systematic event.[25]

The Stoics thought that they could bring the divine ground and their experience of it into an abstract system. Even though they did have some experience of tension toward the divine ground and of participation in it, their experience was not as profound or pervasive as that of Plato and Aristotle. In attempting to symbolize their partial grasp, they identified the ground of the cosmos with the cosmos itself. They were led into this conclusion by the very narrowness of their quest—to discover the object of their concepts. In succumbing to the seductive power of conceptualization with its promise of definiteness, they did indeed find a concrete answer—the material universe as God.

Voegelin identified the key point in the transition from the Platonic to the Stoic account of reality: the Stoics recognized man's tension toward the divine, but did not, as did Plato and Aristotle, think of it in concrete terms as an experience of questioning, seeking, loving. Instead, they formulated it in abstract ideas that they took literally.

25. Bernard Lonergan, *Insight* (London: Longmans, Green, 1957; New York: Philosophical Library, 1958), pp. 25–32.

The divine-human encounter, carefully analyzed by Plato as the immaterial in-between of divine and human reality, and by Aristotle as the metaleptic [participative] reality, becomes for the Stoics under the name of tension the property of a material object called the psyche. The materialization of the psyche and its tension is then extended to the divine reality and the cosmos at large.[26]

The deformative principle, Voegelin identified as an overlooking of insight: "Literalism splits the symbol from the experience by hyposta-tizing the symbol as a proposition on objects."[27] No object represented by this tension exists, but the Stoics fashioned one by taking literally the language that they used, a language that lost sight of the experience that initially produced it. Once the psyche, with its wondrous powers, was conceived of as material, there was no difficulty in attributing materiality to God and to everything else. In the words of Marcus Aurelius: "There is one Universe made up of all things, and one God who pervades all things, and one Substance, and one Law, and one common Reason in all intelligent creatures, and one Truth."[28]

The net result of this transition to materialistic monism was a dim-inution of the noetic experience and a sinking back into compact consciousness. The abstractness of the symbols and the materiality of their objects would long prove effective barriers to any rediscovery of the true tension toward the divine. The Stoics would continue to speak of a divine ground, but it was a divine ground conceived of by a truncated subject who thought of it less as a spiritual mystery and more as the material being of the cosmos.[29]

Let us consider Stoicism and its formalistic texture in more detail, as an example of how even sound legal insights can be distorted by an unduly conceptualistic method that overlooks the noetic insight. Natural philosophy was the concern of the Early Stoa (third century B.C.), but in the Middle Stoa (second and first centuries B.C.) the emphasis

26. Eric Voegelin, *Order and History*, vol. 4: *The Ecumenic Age* (Baton Rouge: Louisiana State University Press, 1974), p. 39.

27. Ibid., p. 37. The *pneuma* is material and is the basic component of the Stoic universe, a kind of fire, of which this tension is a physical property, a vibration like the twanging of a taut string; on this point see J. M. Risk, *Stoic Philosophy* (Cambridge: University Press, 1969, paperback edition 1977), p. 86, and S. Sambursky, *Physics of the Stoics* (London: Hutchison, 1959), p. 5.

28. Marcus Aurelius, *Meditations*, VIII, 9.

29. Stoic materialism facilitated a rehabilitation or reaffirmation of the ancient gods. Through a process of *allegoresis*, the gods could now be understood in scientific terms, retaining their names but updating their functions as forces of nature. See Eric Voegelin, *Conversations*, pp. 33–36, 40.

was shifting, and by the Late Stoa (first and second centuries A.D.), the emphasis was primarily ethical with, of course, political implications.

Stoic ethics had become a function of philosophy; its basic maxim was: *Zen kata physin,* more fully formulated as *Homologoumenos te physei zen.* Both mean: "Live according to nature." The word *homologoumenos* adds to the meaning of *kata,* the further implication, especially dear to the Stoics, of a similar *logos* or mind. *Logos* was first used philosophically by Heraclitus, who meant by it the principle of regularity in a changing world, the principle of law and order in a cosmos ever in flux. Men participated in the "common law of nature," as he called it, by thinking and doing. The monistic ideal of the Stoics was that of one God obeying himself. Men achieved fulfillment and happiness by becoming more and more fully identified with the divinity, that is, by recognizing and conforming to the *Logos.*

In their attempt to explicitate as natural law the symbol, *Theos = Cosmos = Logos = Nomos,* Stoics became propositional. One might not have suspected this development at the beginning of their ethical theorizing, when they held all moral actions to be equal and all sins to be equal.[30] Ethics seemed as simple as saying: do good and avoid evil, and forget the specifics. But fundamental difficulties quickly arose and proliferated, and the solutions offered became more and more abstract. First of all, Stoic philosophers tried to distinguish between appropriate moral actions (*kathekonta*) and perfect moral actions (*katorthomata*).[31] The latter looked to the intention and the motive of the moral agent. They did not focus on content but took it for granted; that is, they assumed the matter of the decision would be an appropriate moral action.

But this distinction led to other questions, for the *kathekonta* were based on natural inclinations to things, which things were either naturally good and so preferred (*proegmena*) or naturally bad and so rejected (*apoproegmena*). Already the Stoics were in treacherous waters, even on their own reckoning. They held that Nature and God are one, so it would follow that all things are good, inasmuch as they

30. See J. M. Risk, "All Sins are Equal," *Stoic Philosophy,* pp. 81–96; the author, aware that Stoicism began when Aristotelianism was dominant, notes the emerging differences.

31. See I. G. Kidd, "Moral Actions and Rules in Stoic Ethics," in *The Stoics,* ed. J. M. Risk (Berkeley: University of California Press, 1978), pp. 247–58; this is a short but technically helpful article.

are natural. Thus there would be no naturally bad things, nor would natural inclinations be bad. Incidentally, the Scholastics would wrestle with the same difficulties and in similar fashion. The Stoics did avoid the simplistic answers of physicalism and biologism; they would, for example, argue that the "unnatural" act of suicide could be reasonable. Moreover, they found new questions in the realization that even among good things, one might be better than another. If so, how should a proper choice be made?

To distinguish between actions that are all morally appropriate, so that the ultimate choice be a morally perfect one, the Stoics added a further complication, illustrated by a distinction, which Seneca made in two of his letters, between rules (*praecepta*) and principles (*decreta*).[32] The distinction is familiar enough even today.[33] Rules, for him, indicated the action to be done or the thing to be chosen without any reason or standard being given. Principles, however, imply a basis for acting so that a wise choice can be made between comparable goods; only in the light of a principle can perfect moral acts (*katorthomata*) be accomplished, for such an act presupposes the determination of the appropriate action, which it then lifts to a higher level by the right intention and motive.

In mandating the determination of the appropriate and the perfect, the preferred and the rejected, the rule and the principle, the Stoics laid the foundations for ethical formalism. The objection is not that they tried to analyze precisely and articulate accurately. Indeed, they developed a rich apparatus for ethical investigation. What impeded a fruitful development of ethics was their attempt to do so on an incomplete basis; they shortsightedly limited their scrutiny to the conceptual dimension, overlooking the existential.

Aristotle had insisted that ethics could not be taught, for the agent, the action, and the good sought were all singular and concrete, while the ethical ideas and principles that could be taught were all abstract and general and thus pedagogically helpful but inadequate. The Stoics,

32. Seneca, *Letters,* 94 and 95. See discussion of them in I. G. Kidd, "Moral Actions," pp. 251–54.

33. For instance, see Ronald Dworkin, "Model of Rules I," *University of Chicago Law Review* 35 (1967), where he discussed the notions of a rule as "applicable in an all or nothing fashion" (p. 14) and a principle that "states a reason that argues in one direction but does not necessitate a particular decision" (p. 16). The article is reprinted in his *Taking Rights Seriously* (Cambridge: Harvard University Press, 1978). See pp. 24 and 26. For a full discussion, see pp. 23–28.

nonetheless, presumed to teach a complete ethical system to the world, an ethical system, moreover, out of contact with the noetic experience of the divine ground, which gives ultimate meaning to ethical choice.

Stoicism's most enduring influence was not in natural philosophy, logic, or ethics, but in law. To appreciate that fact, it is necessary to see how Stoicism moved from Greece to Rome. It was able to travel and prosper because it was topical—not primarily an attempt to implement or supplant classical thinking, but rather a reaction to the changes in Greece that were due to the conquests of Alexander the Great.

By extending his empire to the boundaries of the known world, Alexander had demythologized Athens, shattering once and for all its exclusive preeminence. It still remained the intellectual and artistic center, but other dynamic and creative voices were to be heard and listened to; a new day was dawning. The ideal of one world, *he oikoumene ge*, had been briefly realized under Alexander; he died, however, in 323 B.C., at the age of thirty-three, and his empire fell apart shortly after. But the world, united or not, would never be the same. The Stoics tried to make this change philosophically and politically significant; they had a vision of human dignity in a world at peace under God and Law.

The founder of Stoicism, Zeno of Citium (336/5–263/4 B.C.), was not a Greek; perhaps that fact suggests why the cosmopolitan ideas of the Cynics would attract him. Foreign-born intellectuals in Athens and non-Athenians everywhere must have harbored a certain *ressentiment,* to use Scheler's term, toward the Athenian establishment. Stoicism, however, was to be a philosophy for everyone, not just for the Greek elite. In the second century B.C. Panaetius introduced Stoicism to Rome. His pupil Posidonius was the teacher of Cicero (106–43 B.C.), the great lawyer and statesman, philosopher and writer. How fortunate for Stoicism was that move to Rome, for much of what we know of it comes from Romans, especially from Cicero, but also from Plutarch, Sextus Empiricus, and Diogenes Laertius.

Stoicism flourished in Rome; its emphasis on order, unity, reason, and virtue proved to be the perfect vehicle for the emerging Roman Empire that would in its turn rule the world. The Stoics taught that strong and unified political control was essential to the overall divine plan. In fact, Posidonius explicitly linked Roman imperialism with the Stoic mission—a most persuasive idea for Cicero. The Stoics, however, were even-handed: they imposed a duty on the citizen to obey the state as the vicar of God, and they imposed a duty on the state to be ministerial, serving men not lording it over them. As a consequence, both the officials and the citizens felt they had a stake in this new ethical and political philosophy.

By the death of the Emperor Marcus Aurelius (A.D. 121–180), Stoicism was in its decline. The golden age of Roman law was also coming to an end; it had begun in the first century B.C., the time of Cicero, and would last only to the middle of the third century A.D. and the reign of Servus Alexander. The great Roman jurists were imbued with Stoicism, and so it was that even after the Fall of Rome in 476 Justinian was able to salvage much of this legal heritage. His *Codex Juris Civilis*, completed in 534, preserved the Stoic influence on law forever.

The Roman law did not ever regain its full strength, but it did have its slow and partial revivals. Only bits and pieces of Roman law were used during the Dark Ages. Not until the twelfth century did a substantial restoration begin on the Continent, profoundly influencing civil law, canon law, and moral theology. In England, Roman law had an indirect impact; Glanville in the twelfth century and Brackton in the thirteenth century knew some Roman law and made use of it in shaping English common law. The ecclesiastical courts in England, more directly influenced by Roman law, were also indirectly to shape the common law. Legal formalism might be said to be a geographical function: the closer to Rome, the more abstract and conceptual the law. Continental Europe remained largely faithful to the juridic mentality of the Stoics; the British Isles developed a freer and more concrete approach. But Dickens's *Bleak House* (1852–1853) reminds us that formalism is an occupational hazard of all legal systems, of even the English common law.

Getting back to the last days of Stoicism, we can see how its spirit was also to continue in a new but related field, theology. It was possible for Judaeo-Christian thinkers to read the Stoic writers and find words that described precisely their own beliefs. Of course the meanings of the words might be radically different, but the words themselves were perfectly acceptable. No hermeneutic inhibitions prevented these early Christians from agreeing, for example, with Cicero's impassioned statement:

The same law, unchanging and eternal, binds all races of men and all times; and there is one common, as it were, master and ruler—God, the author, promulgator, and mover of this law. Whoever does not obey it departs from [his true] self, condemns the nature of man, and inflicts upon himself the greatest penalties even though he escapes other things which are considered punishments.[34]

F. The Christians

The advent of Christianity brought a new dimension to the idea of a divine lawgiver. Stoic thought, however, would greatly influence its juridic formulation. Indeed, that influence may have been present from the beginning. The *Acts of the Apostles* (17:18) relates how Paul, when he visited Athens, spoke on the Areopagus to a group including Stoics and Epicureans. It is certainly arguable that there was an intellectual relationship deeper than this casual meeting would indicate.[35] Not only is there intrinsic evidence—the ideas, images, and comparisons that Paul used—but there are extrinsic reasons as well. Paul was an educated man at a time when Stoicism was flourishing, and he was from Tarsus, a center of Stoic thought, connected with such names as Chrysippus, Zeno of Tarsus, Antipater of Tarsus, and a contemporary, Athenodorus Calvus. An apocryphal correspondence between Paul and Seneca (a Latin Stoic of the first century A.D.) was at one time widely accepted: it reflected at least the superficial similarity of their legal and moral teaching.

Paul's memorable statement in the *Epistle to the Romans* is a key example of the kind of thinking that led many early Christians to see in him a Stoic strain. He wrote: "When the Gentiles who do not have the law, do by nature those things that are of the law, these having not the law are a law to themselves, who show the work of the law written in their hearts" (2:14–15). Whether or not Paul was so influenced is perhaps not as important to the development of legal theory as the perceived parallels that the early Christian writers noted, men such as Tertullian, Irenaeus of Lyons, Clement of Alexandria, Lactantius, Ambrose of Milan, John Chrysostom, and Jerome. This kind of support made Stoic theory highly respectable, as long as it had been duly christened.

34. Cicero, *De re publica*, III, 33.
35. See Michael Bertram Crowe, *The Changing Profile of the Natural Law* (The Hague: Martinus Nijhoff, 1977), pp. 52–57.

Above all, it was Augustine of Hippo (354–430) who took some major steps in integrating Stoic and Neoplatonic thought into an emerging Christian philosophy of law, steps to be later developed more fully by Aquinas. Augustine's philosophic sources were Heraclitus, Cicero, and Plotinus, all of whom he read in the light of the New Testament, especially John and Paul. Of the three, Heraclitus had the fewest writings to survive; nevertheless, his brief remarks about the *Logos* and his fundamental insight, which we have seen, that "all human laws are fed by the one divine law,"[36] were to have profound effects on Augustine, as they did on the Stoics, although Augustine differed radically from the Stoics in interpreting this point.[37] He made use of verbal similarities, but utterly rejected Stoic materialism and monism; for him, there was a distinct realm of the spiritual and a real distinction between God and his creatures. That much Augustine knew from revelation; he was now to assess it philosophically.

Furthermore, Augustine understood the Platonic Ideas, not as existing independently in a world of their own but as a plurality of ideas in the mind of God.[38] Divine ideas were the basis of God's knowledge of the universe—how his own essence was to be imitated in creatures. Correspondingly, God's knowledge included how these beings should act if they are to fulfill their ends. So there were in God both ideas (*rationes entis*) and laws (*rationes ordinis*), together encompassing all beings and all actions, real or possible.

Augustine then took the Stoic notion of natural law, which was identified with God, wisdom, and the universe, which formed the *theos* = *cosmos* = *logos* = *nomos* complex, and reinterpreted it as God's eternal law, one with God, operative in the universe but distinct from it. Augustine did so, with some help from Plotinus, by adapting the monistic, Stoic notion of providence to the complexities of the Christian, Creator-creature dualism. For Augustine understood God to be both immanent and transcendent. The indwelling God was not to be identified with his creation, although he lovingly directed its workings: "Divine wisdom is the law of the universe."[39] All other laws share in

36. Heraclitus, *DK* 22 B 114.
37. See A. Schubert, *Augustins Lex-Aeterna-Lehre nach Inhalt und Quellen* (Munster: W. Aschendorff, 1924), pp. 3–20.
38. Augustine, *De diversis quaestionibus*, Lib. 83, Q. 46, (Migne, *Patrologia Latina*, 40:30). Hereafter cited as *PL*.
39. Ibid., 83, 1 (*PL,* 40:90).

this divine wisdom: "In the temporal law, there is nothing just or lawful but what man has drawn from the eternal law."[40] Centuries later Aquinas would use this notion of participation through human reason in the eternal law to explain both natural law and positive law.

Thomas Aquinas (1224–1274) brought Greek and Christian philosophy to a new synthesis. Although not a jurist, he worked out a coherent jurisprudence, one that reflected his larger vision of reality. Here we will focus only on the divine role in the experience of law. For Aquinas, God's eternal law is primary; every other law participates in it. Thus he achieved the unity that the Stoics prized, but preserved the dualism between Creator and creature that his faith required.

Aquinas's jurisprudence remained ever in harmony with revelation, but it was not logically derived from revelation. For him, reason may be enlightened by faith, but it stands on its own footing. Some knowledge of God's existence and attributes, he asserted, can be grasped by natural reason. Aquinas did not, however, keep the two categories of reason and faith separate at all times, for his main purpose in writing was a theological exposition, with philosophy serving as an ancillary discipline. This perspective is manifested in the way Aquinas structured his treatise on law; he did not start with the legal subject and eventually arrive at the divine lawgiver, moving from the Monosphere to the Theosphere. Rather, he preferred to look at things as they are in themselves (*quoad se*) rather than as they are in reference to us (*quoad nos*). So he began with God and the eternal law, not with human reason and natural or civil law.

Aquinas's notion of the eternal law was straightforward: "The eternal law is nothing else than the idea (*ratio*) of divine wisdom as directing all actions and movements."[41] In this definition, we hear echoes of the Greek notion of *Nous*, the principle of order in the cosmos. Moreover, he related this to creation, which had been at best implicit in Plato and Aristotle: "All that is in things created by God, whether it be contingent or necessary, is subject to the eternal law."[42] This philosophical inference that the maker of all things should be able to control their activities had been made long ago. Aquinas quoted the remark of Augustine: "Nothing evades the laws of the most high Creator and Governor, for by him the peace of the universe is administered."[43] By peace, Augustine

40. Idem, *De libero arbitrio*, Bk.I, c.6. (*PL*, 32:1230).
41. Aquinas, *Summa theologiae*, I–II, q. 93, a. 1.
42. Ibid., a. 4.   43. Ibid., q. 92, a. 6, *sed contra*.

meant "the tranquillity of order," *Pax omnium rerum tranquillitas ordinis,*[44] a concept that reflected the noetic insight of the Greeks.

Although the Sacred Scriptures laid down the basic elements of the legal structure of the universe for Jews and Christians, Aquinas was interested in understanding these truths philosophically wherever possible. Even on this basis, he was quick to assert that the eternal law could not be known in itself but only in its effects, just as God cannot be known in himself but only in his effects. Nonetheless, the eternal law can be known by reason and not just through revelation: "Every creature knows it [the eternal law] in its reflection, greater or less. For every knowledge of truth is a kind of reflection and participation in the eternal law, which is the unchangeable truth."[45]

The idea of participation, an insight of Plato and Aristotle, characterized the thought of Aquinas, including his legal theory: "All laws, in so far as they partake of right reason, are derived from the eternal law."[46] Natural law participates in the eternal law through the grasp by reason of general principles of behavior common to human nature; positive law participates in natural law by a prudential determination of these general principles. "For human law has the nature of law in so far as it partakes of right reason."[47] Despite his theological perspective, which looks first to God and the eternal law, Aquinas, as we have seen in the preceding chapter, did not fail to find man participating in law as he participates in divine wisdom: that is, through the use of his reason—the power to ask and to answer questions about the data of his experience, here specifically about his inclinations.

Aquinas's listing of the subjects of eternal law is all-inclusive: things necessary and eternal as well as things that are contingent. The existence, activity, and meaning of all things are explained by the divine ground. Nevertheless, a distinction must be made between the irrational beings and the rational subjects of eternal law. Irrational beings are moved by divine providence, which gives to each the principles of its proper actions; rational beings, gifted with knowledge and freedom, are subject to eternal law in an additional way, a way proper to themselves while remaining a function of virtue. On the one hand, a good person is subject to eternal law through an inner inclination as

44. Augustine, *De Civitate Dei,* bk. 19, ch. 13 (*PL,* 41:640).
45. Aquinas, *Summa theologiae,* I–II, q. 93, a. 2.
46. Ibid., q. 93, a. 3.
47. Ibid., q. 93, a. 3, ad 2.

well as through knowledge. In such a one, knowing and doing are consistent, and his whole being is in harmony with eternal law. An evil person, on the other hand, although subject to eternal law, is subject only imperfectly; his knowledge of the good is diminished in proportion to his inordinate emotions and vicious habits; his inner inclination to virtue is corrupted by these same habits.

Does that mean that the wicked are no longer subject to eternal law? Not at all, argued Aquinas: "This imperfection on the part of action is supplied on the part of passion."[48] Pythagoras earlier symbolized this notion by speaking of justice as a square number, so what is lacking to an action because it is unjust will be compensated for by a proportionate penalty so that the squareness be achieved. Aristotle quoted the definition that Pythagoras gave of justice as reciprocity: "The just is simply to suffer with another in turn."[49] We have seen the inexorability of retribution, when we considered Nemesis. Augustine's remark will recall the personal character of that sanction in a Christian perspective: "When God punishes sinners, he does not inflict evil on them, but leaves them to their own evil."[50]

In distinguishing the various components in the jurisprudence of Aquinas, we should note a possible source of confusion between three kinds of divine law. There is the divine *eternal law,* which is in God himself. The other two kinds are human participations in the eternal law: the *divine positive law,* which is given through revelation; and the *divine natural law,* which is arrived at through natural reason. Although a person can experience in the operations of his own mind the existence of a divine natural law, he looks to historical fact to ascertain the existence of a divine positive law.

Such laws were given, Aquinas explained, to ensure man's full perfection and happiness: "By the natural law the eternal law is participated proportionately to the capacity of human nature. But man needs to be directed to his supernatural end in a yet higher way. Hence the additional law given by God, whereby man shares more perfectly in the eternal law."[51] Revealed law is necessary not only because of man's supernatural end, but also and subordinately because of the limits of human judgment, especially on contingent and particular matters, and

48. Aristotle, *Nicomachean Ethics,* V, 5, 1132 b21–23.
49. *Ibid.,* q. 93, a. 6, ad 2.
50. Augustine, *Enarrationes in Psalmos,* V, 10 (PL, 36:87).
51. Aquinas, *Summa theologiae,* I–II, q. 91, a. 4, ad 1.

because of the inability of human law to deal with interior movements and to forbid all evil deeds.

In Aquinas's synthesis, then, God's law is threefold: the eternal law in God himself; the divine natural law, whereby man participates through reason in the eternal law; and the divine positive law, whereby reason is supplemented by a fuller communication of the eternal law.

The blend of Judaeo-Christian revelation and Greek philosophy produced in the Middle Ages an elaborate jurisprudence unified by an idea of the eternal law. Aquinas himself, although his writing was propositional, enjoyed a profound noetic awareness of the divine ground. Using abstractions fruitfully, he preserved a sense of concrete reality, never losing sight of the existential tension between the divine ground and the individual subject.

Unfortunately, the thought of some of Aquinas's contemporaries and followers became so formalized, so definitively articulated, that it was easy for subsequent generations to overlook the noetic experience, which made the earlier, systematic elaborations profoundly meaningful. Taking the answers for granted, some followers lost sight of the questions. Without a living experience of the questioning unrest and keen awareness of the role of divine reason, they found their answers turning into abstract propositions and their philosophy into deductive logic. But each generation faces the same challenge, each must experience afresh the discovery of the *Nous,* each must ask and answer its own questions about the divine ground.

With the philosophic turn to the subject in the sixteenth century, as we noted in Chapter One, there began a conscious attempt to exclude God from legal thought. We traced the development from the so-called "impious hypothesis" of Grotius in the sixteenth century to the "death of God" and the legal positivism of the nineteenth and twentieth centuries. During the latter half of this century, however, there has been a renewed interest in the divine ground and its role in law. In the next section, therefore, we shall examine the dimensions of this current form of questioning unrest.

II. THE CONTEMPORARY REAFFIRMATION

Having surveyed the historical affirmations of the divine ground of law, I shall now consider the same topic from a more modern perspective. My purpose is to retrieve the law from the shadow of absurdity by appealing, not to revelation or history, but to the questions and answers emerging from a contemporary mind touched by ultimate concern.

I shall raise the God question in two ways. The first is by looking at the hermeneutic need to understand law, like all other things, in context. The implication is that the law cannot be adequately known without a grasp of its "divine milieu." The second is by squarely confronting the need to raise the God question from the perspective of subjectivity.

A. The Hermeneutic Milieu

The Greek word to interpret, *hermeneuein*, relates back to Hermes, the messenger of the gods and the inventor of language and writing. Much of what the gods allegedly communicated to human beings involved commands or laws, *nomoi*, which had to be translated into human speech and interpreted. So the idea of legal hermeneutics and its relationship to the divine goes back to the roots of civilization.

Law may well be the first hermeneutic paradigm. The divine character of ancient laws supports that claim. At any rate, hermeneutics has long been a useful legal tool in the task of understanding and applying past norms. The hermeneutic problem actually antedates mythology and even lawmaking; it is as old as intersubjectivity. Every attempt at communication is an exercise in hermeneutics. We are ever reciprocally involved in trying to understand what other persons mean by their words and actions, their looks and silences.

We can even push hermeneutics beyond legal interpretation and intersubjective communication in the direction of the ultimate ground of law. Such an extension does not throw hermeneutics out of alignment, for the task still remains one of understanding.

Traditionally, of course, hermeneutics has been limited to the interpretation of texts, juridical, biblical, and literary. In the nineteenth and twentieth century, the focus turned to history in its attempt to reconstruct the human constructs of the past. More recently, science, too, has become an object of hermeneutics and, according to the same line of reasoning, philosophy as well. Finally, since we do not know God directly, but only through his effects, which must be understood and interpreted, we also move hermeneutically into natural theology and revelation, which, of course, is the way it was in the beginning, as symbolized by the divine messenger, Hermes.

Thus, Hans-Georg Gadamer can speak of "the universality of hermeneutic reflection," which he based on "the universality of human linguisticality as a limitless medium."[52] Hermeneutics is a search for understanding. Our world is mediated through meaning; language is needed for that mediation; by using language, we construct our mental world commensurately with our intelligence and its exercise. Gadamer wrote of this drive to know: "The principle of hermeneutics simply means that we should try to understand everything that can be understood. This is what I meant by the sentence: 'Being that can be understood is language.' "[53] The process is one of inquiry leading to insights, which Gadamer referred to as "the hermeneutical Urphänomen: No assertion is possible that cannot be understood as an answer to a question, and assertions can be understood only in this way."[54]

In this attempt to give an account of reality, whether it be a text or something else, the questioning process involves the context. In the usual process of interpretation, one moves from the text to the context, indeed to expanding spheres of context, so that, by understanding the circumstances and the conditions of a particular text, one better understands the text itself. We move from word to sentence, to book, to author, to society, to culture, to history.

The process is similar whether our subject matter is a text or some other thing or event. We cannot understand it in isolation. We try to comprehend both its nature and its historicity: that is, what it is in itself and in its interaction with a changing environment. Hermeneutics is an adventure in discovering the unknown.

To apply philosophic hermeneutics to our account of legal understanding, we consider law, not only as a commonsense construct to be reconstructed through a recognition of its historicity in a cultural matrix, but also as a trans-temporal part of a larger framework. Law is so pervasive in individual and cosmic arenas that the question of context raises the question of a transcendent being.

Radical historicism is the hermeneutic counterpart of legal positivism; both despair of getting answers to the probing questions about truth and justice. For the legal positivist, all law is convention, power validly systematized; for the radical historicist, all meaning consists in what the past signifies for us now; the original intention is forever lost.

52. Hans-Georg Gadamer, *Philosophical Hermeneutics,* trans. and ed. D. E. Linge (Berkeley: University of California Press, 1976), p. 25.

53. Ibid., p. 31.   54. Ibid., p. 11.

But beyond these narrow categories there exists a richer world of meaning and value, open to the mind that questions honestly. Law is more than power; history is more than reader repsonse. Proper inquiry, reflection, and deliberation can bring us into contact with a larger reality. Transcending the self-imposed limitations of legal positivism and radical historicism, we can ask questions with the reasonable expectation of achieving deeper understanding. This expectation, even in the field of law, raises the God question.

It is possible, of course, to break off questions prematurely and to march into the darkness, refusing the light that questioning alone can give. An example of this refusal to continue relevant questioning is Jean-Paul Sartre, who opted for an atheistic position, without articulating his reasons: "There is no human nature for there is no God to conceive it."[55] His atheism afforded him freedom to choose, but gave him no standard for choice other than to choose freely. He insisted that, for existentialists, subjectivity is the point of departure; but he spoke from the perspective of a deficient subjectivity, the negative implications of which he proceeded to elaborate, almost as if he were reducing his own position to absurdity. The Sartrean subject proved to be contracted within the narrow limits of an impoverished universe; he is the by-product of a philosophy of rejection: "Existentialism is nothing else than an attempt to draw all the consequences of a coherent atheistic position."[56] So Sartre continued to ask questions, but only after an *a priori* cloture on the level of fundamental relevance.

Therefore, it is not surprising that, despite his practical concern for ethics, politics, and philosophy, Sartre failed to construct an ethical or political philosophy. He too seemed keenly aware of the futility of such a task in view of the stark implications of his commitment to absurdity. He wrote:

Dostoievsky said, "If God did not exist, everything would be permissible." That is the very starting point for existentialism. Indeed, everything is permissible if God does not exist, and as a result man is forlorn, because neither within him nor without him does he find anything to cling to. He cannot start making excuses for himself.[57]

We see this utter permissibility in legal positivism, and most clearly in the work of Hans Kelsen (1881–1973). He erected an imposing

55. Jean-Paul Sartre, *L'Existentialisme est un humanisme* (Paris: Les Editions Nagel, 1957), p. 22.
56. Ibid., p. 94.   57. Ibid., p. 36.

jurisprudential structure, a pure theory of positive law, without recourse to nature or God. In such a realm, since God is not a factor, all
things are permissible, and power then becomes the sole arbiter of
legality. Kelsen frankly defined positive law as "a specific order or
organization of power,"[58] and as "a coercive order of human behavior."[59]

The key to Kelsen's theory is the basic norm—obey the constitution
that is by and large efficacious. This norm is to give unity, validity, and
meaning to all legal norms dependent on it. Kelsen explained what
prompted his conclusion: "The basic norm is the answer to the question: how—and that means under what condition—are all these juristic
statements concerning legal norms, legal duties, legal rights, and so on,
possible."[60] He was trying to justify legal validity in a purely formal
way.

The basic norm, it must be made clear, is a hypothesis, a postulate,
a presupposition. "The basic norm is only the necessary presupposition
of any positivistic interpretation of law."[61] It does not rest on a dynamic
principle, but rather introduces such a principle. Ultimately, it is a
condition of validity; that is, if there are to be valid laws and legal
events, some such norm must be present. Nevertheless, Kelsen admitted
that it is possible to go beyond the basic norm, though he did not
choose to do so, calling such a step "religious."

Certainly one may ask why one has to respect the first constitution as a binding
norm. The answer might be that the fathers of the first constitution were
empowered by God. The characteristic of so-called legal positivism is, however,
that it dispenses with any such religious justification of the legal order. The
ultimate hypothesis of positivism is the norm authorizing the historically first
legislator.[62]

Kelsen appealed to a practical presupposition. In attempting a similar
positivistic grounding, H.L.A. Hart, as we have seen, looked to an
empirical fact, substituting a rule of recognition for the basic norm.
Both of them cut off further questioning along that line in accordance
with their understanding of positive law, if not as a fully self-contained

---

58. Hans Kelsen, *General Theory of Law and State*, trans. A. Wedberg (New York:
Russell and Russell, 1945), p. 121.

59. Idem, *The Pure Theory of Law*, trans. M. Knight (Berkeley: University of
California Press, 1967), pp. 31, 33, 57.

60. Idem, *General Theory*, pp. 116f.

61. Ibid., p. 116.   62. Ibid.

unit, at least as one separate from morals. God is not made a part of that understanding, however relevant he may be. For the sake of systematic purity, Kelsen and Hart have abridged the hermeneutic exigency for full context. The result is that their positivism hangs suspended in a commonsense realm of unanswered questions, and to that extent the positive law remains a law without an adequate justification or foundation. Both have failed to include the full hermeneutic context of law; and thus have neglected the reciprocity between the part and the whole, which is prerequisite to a full understanding.

B. The Ultimate Concern

What is the role of God in an integral jurisprudence? Without rehearsing the traditional proofs for the existence of God, I shall discuss, from a subjective viewpoint, whether it makes a significant difference for law that God does or does not exist. I shall show briefly how the God question is raised through three complementary approaches: first, psychological moralism; second, conscious intentionality; and, third, the noetic experience of the Beginning and the Beyond.

First, we look at the accessible, rational, but largely moralistic approach of Hans Küng, found in his book *Does God Exist?* He took his inspiration partly from Kant, following his emphasis on practical reason. Kant postulated God's existence as necessarily following from the categorical imperative; he reasoned that if you ought to do something you can; so, since God's existence plays an indispensable role in moral life, he held it to be "morally certain" that God exists.

Küng stated that Kant had shown that the traditional proofs were not conclusive; and so, with him, resorted to a practical but rational approach: "We are starting out not only from a moral obligation, a stern moral law within us, a rigorous categorical imperative, but, as hitherto, from the whole reality of the world and man as concretely experienced."[63] Moreover, he looked for verification, which he got from experience: "Ours is an *indirect criterion of verification.* This means that God as the supposedly all-determining reality will be verified by *the experienced reality of man and the world.*"[64]

One seeking to prove God's existence might find himself in a quandary here, for, according to Küng, atheism can neither be eliminated

---

63. Hans Küng, *Does God Exist?* trans. E. Quinn (New York: Vintage Books, 1981), p. 547.
64. Ibid., p. 550.

rationally, since it is irrefutable, nor can it be established rationally, since it is indemonstrable. But even verification does not demonstrate God's existence, but rather only "justifies" that affirmation. Küng's thesis is:

Affirmation of God implies an ultimately justified fundamental trust in reality. As radical fundamental trust, belief in God can suggest the condition of the possibility of uncertain reality. If someone affirms God, he knows why he can trust reality.[65]

When one is openly receptive to the divine ground, said Küng, one finds in the very action itself confirmation of one's rightness. "Then I know, *not* indeed *before, nor* yet *only afterward, but by the very fact* of doing this, that I am doing the right thing, and even what is absolutely the most reasonable thing"; Küng concluded with a resounding affirmation of himself: "At the same time, in all the uncertainty, I experience a *radical reasonableness of my own reason.*"[66] This is neither a solipsistic cry nor an assertion that man is the measure of all things, but rather that through "fundamental trust in reality" one affirms God: "The first and last reality, God, is thus seen more or less as the guarantor of the rationality of human reason."[67]

Küng indicated basic inconsistencies in the counter-positions: the agnostic is in doubt about God, but trusts reality anyway; the atheist denies that God exists, but illogically also trusts reality; the nihilist does not believe in God or trust reality, except of course in practical matters where theoretical consistency would prove suicidal. Küng concluded that if one does not believe in God, one cannot rationally justify one's actions or one's life.

Logically, as Küng pointed out, these denials produce adverse personal and social sequelae. His studies of Feuerbach, Marx, Nietzsche, and Freud suggest some of the disvalues of atheism and nihilism. Of course, atheists and nihilists might deny experiencing negative feelings or results and might insist that even positive feedback does not imply justification and rationality for theism, that there is no proof one way or the other. One is not, Küng asserted, compelled by pure reason to affirm or deny God's existence; one must rely on a practical judgment.

This psychological moralism does make effective use of common sense (using the term technically), supporting it with a pragmatic ver-

65. Ibid., p. 572.   66. Ibid., pp. 573–74.
67. Ibid., p. 574.

ification of probability based on feelings and observations. But though he formulated this argument in a theoretical framework, Küng failed to move it properly into interiority, where it really belongs. By not going far enough, the argument seems to appeal to subjectivism rather than to subjectivity. Küng's position is important, but it is limited by the weakness of its underlying cognitional theory and its failure to ask further relevant questions. Nevertheless, by bringing the challenge to the ethical center and its requirement of consistency between knowing and doing, Küng has provokingly revealed the necessity of raising the God question in the realm of interiority, although he himself has not done so sufficiently.

Second, Bernard Lonergan's work on conscious intentionality long antedated this commonsense and moralistic approach. He had located the God question in the fundamental questioning of the human mind.[68] Beginning with the data of sense and consciousness, the mind inquires, reflects, and deliberates. Inquiry results in understanding or intelligibility: we grasp what something is. Reflection results in a judgment of fact: by marshaling and weighing the data, we grasp that something is or is not and the level of affirmation or negation that we can reach. Deliberation results in a decision about value that is consistent with our knowledge or verified understanding; we grasp that something is worthwhile.

If we continue inquiring, reflecting, and deliberating, we eventually arrive at the God question, which, with Lonergan, we formulate thus: (a) Can the persons, things, and events of our experience be intelligible if the universe is not intelligible? and can the universe be intelligible without an intelligent ground? (b) Can a judgment be made about the existence of the persons, things, and events of our experience, contingent beings that can be conceived of as nonexistent, if there is no necessary being as their ultimate ground? (c) Can any objective choice be made about the value or worth of the persons, things, and events of our experience, if the universe, of which we are a part, is amoral and has no moral ground? Since law is concerned with intelligibility, with existence, and with value, one who thinks profoundly about law comes in time to these three questions.

We shall then discuss in more detail how the God question arises

---

68. See Bernard Lonergan, *Method in Theology*, 2nd ed. (New York: Herder and Herder, 1973), pp. 101–03.

The God question arises from 3 basic functions of the mind.

from a consideration of these three basic functions of the mind: inquiry, judgment, and deliberation.

(a) Albert Einstein directs our thoughts to the first question, with his far-reaching observation: "The mystery of the world is its comprehensibility."[69] His professional life was a passionate quest for a unified field theory, an integrated explanation of the universe. Convinced that the universe can be understood, he sought to understand it. Thinkers such as Einstein affirm the intelligibility of the universe or their work becomes absurd. But can one make this affirmation of intelligibility, without assuming that the cosmos has an intelligible ground?

To phrase the issue in another way: What is the sufficient reason to explain the order, coherence, and intelligibility of the universe or any part of it? If it is assumed as a given, how do we account for the gift? Conversely, if the universe does not have an intelligent ground, why is all not sheer disorder, incoherence, chaos? To say with Bertrand Russell that the universe is "just there and that's all" is not responsive to the question of meaning.[70] Without an intelligent ground, the world is not mediated through meaning; it is absurd. That the alternatives are ultimate meaning or pervasive absurdity sharply raises the God question. But even to debate about a *tertium quid* raises the God question, too. If there is any intelligibility anywhere, can it be so without a divine ground? Can laws and the legal institution and the underlying ethical norms ever be understood without an intelligible ground?

(b) Leibnitz formulates the second question: "Why is there something rather than nothing?"[71] Contemporary existentialism may well have sensitized us to this by thematizing our contingency: we can conceive of our non-existence in the past (once we did not exist), in the present (we need never have existed), and in the precarious future (we may cease to exist). Lives so vulnerable and so contingent teach us daily of the possibility of non-existence in all three time phases. But we actually do exist. How can that be?

We accept the empirical fact that something, which need not exist, actually does exist. To make it more personal: we accept that empirical

69. Albert Einstein, quoted in Wilder Penfield, *The Mystery of the Mind* (Princeton: Princeton University Press, 1975), p. xxiii.

70. Bertrand Russell's remark made in a BBC debate was quoted in *Time Magazine*, April 7, 1980, p. 68.

71. G. W. Leibnitz, *Principes de la nature et de la grâce* (Paris, 1714): *Pourquoi il y a plutôt quelque chose que rien?*

fact as referring to ourselves. Lonergan called such a being virtually unconditioned; that is, its existence is conditioned, but all its conditions are fulfilled. A lot of "if's" must be realized, for the "then" to occur. It is in virtue of the fulfilling of the conditions that we actually do exist. So the question presents itself: How do we account for this fulfillment? As Kant wrote: "When the conditional is given to us, the unconditional is posed before us as a problem."[72]

We do not find the reason for our existence in ourselves, for, being able to conceive of ourselves as non-existent, we understand that we do not exist necessarily. To attribute one's existence to parents, as a sufficient cause, simply pushes back the question. To attribute one's existence to an infinite series of contingent beings—beings who by definition do not necessarily exist—is the same question slightly reformulated. The question properly phrased is: How did the one who started this series of finite beings—for there had to be a first—account for its existence?

To account for one contingent being or to account for many, the question remains the same. And the answer is always: a necessary being, a being whose essence it is to exist, a being that is strictly unconditioned—that is, has no conditions to its existence. This ground of existence, which alone can account for the multitude of contingent beings whose existence we constantly affirm, is in part what we mean by God. We may have further questions about contingency and possibility, about the virtually unconditioned and the strictly or absolutely unconditioned, about the real distinction between essence and existence in us and real identity of essence and existence in God. We may have these and other questions, but in asking them we raise the God question.

Since jurists are ever dealing with facts, they have to ask themselves, in trying to achieve a profound understanding of law: How can there be facts at all? How can there be certainties or even probabilities, unless there is somewhere a ground of being, an ultimate reason for existence?

(c) Dostoyevsky suggests the consequences of a negative answer to our third question by his perceptive statement: "If God did not exist, everything would be permissible."[73] This does not mean that atheists have no ethical standards, but that their ethical standards have no ultimate justification. This statement has far-reaching implications.

[Margin note: How can there be certainties or probabilities w/o a ground of being —]

72. Immanuel Kant, quoted by Ortega y Gasset, *What is Philosophy?* trans. M. Adams (New York: Norton & Co., 1960), p. 98.

73. F. Dostoyevsky. See Sartre, *L'Existentialisme*, p. 22.

The commonsense realm, with its accumulated insights and its trial-and-error testing, gives us a pragmatic set of norms based on results. Moving from common sense to theory, we have the problematic hypothesis of Grotius that there would be a natural law "even if God did not exist." Nature, not convention rooted in power, would then set the standards for human conduct. But what do we mean by norms and by good and evil?

How can we say that nature is moral or immoral? How can we say that we who are part of nature are moral or immoral? Are not value, worthwhileness, and ethical standards indifferent or simply preferential in a universe without a divine ground? If without God the universe is amoral, then human morality is an idiosyncratic anomaly: all is permitted, subject of course to the amoral limits imposed by a calculus of power, for to be free is not to be omnipotent.

Since values, especially human dignity, justice, and rights, are at the heart of our laws, a jurisprudence that falls short of ultimate grounding would prove ultimately valueless. To ponder values is ultimately to raise the God question.

Third, to complete our investigation, I shall return briefly to Eric Voegelin, whose words keeps calling to mind the fact that the God question is more a quest than a question. The answer to the God question is not just a proposition that solves a problem but an actuality that accounts for our own actuality, its beginning and its end. Voegelin captured the dimensions of the God symbol: "The consciousness of questing unrest in a state of ignorance becomes luminous to itself as a movement in the *psyche* toward the ground that is present in the *psyche* as its mover."[74] His words reflect those of St. Paul: "For us there is one God, the Father, from whom are all things and toward whom are we" (I Cor. 8:6). The two prepositions of motion, *ex* and *eis,* express the dynamic quality of the divine encounter.

Like Hans Küng, Voegelin recognized need of the existential virtue of trust, which he put in the context of other existential virtues. Far from relying on a psychological moralism, he demanded more: "The virtues make no sense unless they are understood as the trained habits (*hexis*) of the man who consciously forms himself by the erotic tension toward the divine ground of his existence."[75] For Voegelin, knowing

74. Eric Voegelin, *Anamnesis,* trans. G. Niemeyer (Notre Dame, Ind.: Notre Dame University Press, 1978), p. 96.
75. Idem, *The Ecumenic Age,* p. 196.

God's existence precedes trusting him. He went beyond Küng in his conviction of the existence of the divine ground and his noetic appreciation of its pervasiveness in the cosmos and in himself.

Like Bernard Lonergan, Voegelin saw noetic experience as an overcoming of self-contraction: "The nature of man is openness to transcendence."[76] Although he did not articulate a philosophy of conscious intentionality with the exactness and scope of Lonergan's, he too was keenly aware of its paramount importance. His own vision was the mystery of "the Beginning and the Beyond," as it emerges through history toward an eschatological fulfillment. He pointed out the two subjective modes of this developing consciousness: "The Beyond is present in the immediate experience of movements in the psyche; while the presence of the divine Beginning is mediated through the experience of the existence and intelligible structure of things in the cosmos."[77]

If, with Lonergan, we learned that reason is the ability to ask and answer questions; with Voegelin, we learned to formulate the meta-question that subsumes all the others. "The Question capitalized is not a question concerning the nature of this or that object in the external world, but a structure inherent in the experience of reality."[78] Voegelin was referring here to the experience in the In-Between of the tension of the divine encounter, to which through myths, philosophy, or revelation, through fulfillments or derailments, human beings respond. Their lives, individually or communally, reflect the history of the emerging noetic and pneumatic consciousness of the divine ground. "History is not a stream of human beings and their actions in time, but the process of man's participation in a flux of divine presence that has eschatological direction. The enigmatic symbolism of a 'history of mankind' thus expresses man's understanding that these insights, although they arise from concrete events in the consciousness of concrete human beings, are valid for all men."[79]

CONCLUSION

The questions that we have been asking in this chapter are ultimately God questions. They confront the possibility of an ultimate ground for meaning, for existence, for value. Moreover, from our specifically legal

---

76. Idem, *Conversations*, p. 23.   77. Idem, *The Ecumenic Age*, p. 17.
78. Ibid., p. 317.   79. Ibid., p. 6.

perspective, they bring to a focus the inner experience of law. Although we speak of God, these questions intimately concern the existence of law, its own meaning and value.

All roads, if travelled long enough, lead to this question. Obviously not every answer given leads to God or to the same truths about God. Nevertheless, despite the variety of philosophies, religions, and ideologies, there has persisted an historical consensus in favor of a divine Lawgiver and Judge.

We have, however, gone a step beyond the consensus to examine the reasons why the consensus persists. By looking at the invariant structures of the mind operative in all human beings, we have seen the inevitability of the God question in those whose minds and hearts are open to reality.

With this chapter, we complete the analysis of the Theosphere and present the dramatic possibility of bringing knowing and doing together in the most fundamental way: by knowing the divine ground and by acting in accord with the divine law. In this experienced consistency, the thrust toward reality, which we described earlier, realizes its full fruition—self-fulfillment through self-transcendence.

This accomplishment, however, is not a linear, one-time solution to an academic problem; it is only the starting point for an ever-deepening consciousness of law. Absurdity, at least in principle, has been by-passed; the continuing task now is to perfect this achievement, in practice, by fusing the insights of legal subjectivity into a vision of law for authentic living. In the next and final chapter, we shall study the stance that the subject must take and the existential process that he or she must go through, in order to make this vision a reality and their actions a function of their vision.

CONCLUSION

CHAPTER 10

THE VISION OF LAW

A man's vision concerning such things is dullest when he is young and at its sharpest when he is old.—Plato*

Law exists for man, not man for law. This truth sheds a benign light on the sometimes painful conflict between liberty and authority. The inner experience of law is an experience of the tension whereby free actions guided by law can lead to the paradoxical goal of self-fulfillment through self-transcendence.

As responses to this tension, actions bring self-awareness: if they are inconsistent, unreasonable, disorderly, we begin to suspect that we are the same; if they are in harmony with what is right, we experience in ourselves an integrity that endows the enduring tension with personal, social, and religious meaning and value. Through the self-appropriations of conscious intentionality, this inner experience becomes an exercise of harmony between judgment and decision, knowing and doing, norm and action.

"In the beginning was the deed," said Goethe's Faust, *Im Angfang war die Tat*.[1] This sentence is more than a play on words. As between the two major components of the legal event—action and norm—action does have a certain priority: not only do all laws exist for the sake of actions, but positive laws are occasioned by the consequences of action. Human beings did not start off with a code of law but with a capacity to act. The Ten Commandments appeared long after men and women had become concerned over flawed actions. Leibnitz was clear about this central focus: "Jurisprudence is the science of actions."[2]

Indeed, the norms of positive law are themselves actions about ac-

---

* Plato, *Laws*, 715 D–E.
1. Goethe, *Faust*, Part I, lines 1224–37.
2. Leibnitz, *Nova methodus discendi docendaeque jurisprudentiae*, p. ii, 14.

tions. Constitutions, statutes, and judicial decisions are actions taken by human beings to articulate values. They are the continuing actions of the people civilly united, actions to structure community and to achieve the good life. As heteronomous decisions imposing normative actions on others, positive laws are human actions, not things or reified ideas. Moreover, natural laws, too, as dynamic participations in the divine light, are human actions enunciating the ways that human beings actualize the potentialities of their nature. They are ordinances of reason, comprising light and love, by which, from within, all human beings can direct themselves to completion and transcendence. Finally, in the ascending hierarchy of being, although the eternal law is prior to human actions, it is identical with the divine essence, which is pure act.

To ensure an inner experience of the law, we turn to the subject—the subject in action. For we must keep in mind that not only is the action prior to the norm but the subject is prior to the action. Meaning and value, whatever their roots, are experiences of the subject. The fullness of these experiences, however, requires an undiminished subject, one able to function on all levels of legal activity—usually with the support of other subjects and ideally with that of the whole political community.

To achieve this fullness, the subject's consciousness of legal events should be differentiated, not compact, a goal made possible through interiority, with its nuanced awareness of the mental operations that constitute the infrastructure of legal participation. Such profound subjectivity facilitates bringing actions themselves into harmony with the world of concrete reality; objectivity is not expendable in a jurisprudence of subjectivity. For this legal awareness of law to be genuine and complete, the subject must, with full consciousness and adequate self-appropriation, participate in concrete legal events.

In this final chapter, we look first at the requisite characteristics of the subject, the subjective posture, and then at the concrete participation by the subject, the existential process. Bringing them together, we comprehend, through this jurisprudence of subjectivity, an inner vision of law.

I. THE SUBJECTIVE STANCE

For heightened consciousness, the legal subject acts with interiority and authenticity. More concretely, such a one is open, committed, unified, and luminous. I shall consider these four characteristics separately.

First, the integral legal subject is *open* to meaning and value. Openness to meaning seems to be obvious, but in practice it requires that the subject keep alive a sense of wonder and a spirit of inquiry; his questioning mind must not rest until there are no more relevant questions to be asked. We have already seen two of the many instances of cutting off relevant questions: Hans Kelsen's refusal to probe beyond the presupposition of his *Grundnorm;* and Jean-Paul Sartre's unsubstantiated assertion of an atheistic starting point. Often this aversion toward following where reason and relevance beckon is solemnly flouted as a formal postulate brooking no discussion and is cavalierly used to dismiss as intellectually irrelevant any question not consonant with the adopted position. In so doing, the closed mind undercuts its own conclusions, however logically and brilliantly they are derived.

In addition, there must be openness to value; that is, an abiding preference for value over pleasure, an unqualified willingness to respond to whatever is perceived as worthwhile, and an ongoing self-transcendence, which leaps the barriers to the achieving of one's destiny.

To be able to be open implies freedom from biases, a psychological state especially requisite in matters of justice, with its need for proportionate reciprocity; for, as Thomas Hardy observed, "The well-proportioned mind is one which shows no particular bias." Most people do have various predilections and prepossessions, but unless they recognize and counteract their inordinate ones, their biases, they find that their questioning goes astray or is brought to a premature close.

Love, however, heals these biases by directing the mind to perform its intersubjective actions according to the proper hierarchy of ends. Truth in practical matters such as law is found in conformity to right appetite. Rational self-consciousness is based on the exigency of the mind for truth and goodness. But biases skew every operation; distorting one's contact with reality, they impede the authentic subjectivity upon which objectivity is based. Knowledge alone will not cure the distortion, for it is itself distorted by biases. Only love can do so by ensuring that the subject is ready to follow without prejudice wherever, in the realm of meaning and value, relevant questioning leads.[3] Call it intersubjectivity, call it political friendship, or call it noetic participation in the divine, it is love that opens up the mind and heart.

Second, the integral subject is *committed* to meaning and value. This characteristic follows naturally from the loving spirit of inquiry just mentioned. Aristotle's key distinction between the act and the habit of justice illustrates the role of commitment, without which one may perform a just and worthwhile action and yet be unjust.[4] The point of his observation is that if one is not committed to justice, but is ready, given the occasion, to act unjustly, one remains by disposition and habit an unjust person. For the just acts of an unjust person, grounded as they are in expediency, do not afford a true experience of the law. Interiority cannot reveal the beauty of justice even in the good actions of one who is basically unjust. Moreover, the very presence of unjust habits usually impedes any prolonged and clear-sighted attempt at true self-consciousness, by making it too painful or upsetting.

Commitment, naturally, does not require perfection: the just man is said to fall seven times a day. What is required is an abiding disposition to do justice. Of course, since this disposition is developed by just acts and weakened by unjust acts, its effect on our experience of law will vary proportionately. The variation is a function, not of one's theoretical knowledge, but of one's concrete choices.

A person can be a lawyer for a criminal syndicate, facilitating the wholesale commission of antisocial activity, and still be legally effective. Such a one may well have made a career out of Holmes's purely pedagogic suggestion: "If you want to know the law and nothing else, you must look at it as a bad man, who cares only for the material consequences which such knowledge enables him to predict."[5] He may know the law theoretically and functionally, but he cannot, from that perspective alone and without committing himself to justice, have an

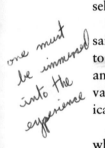
[handwritten marginalia: "committed"; "one must be immersed into the experience"]

3. See Bernard Lonergan, "Healing and Creating in History," *A Third Collection,* ed. F. Crowe (New York: Paulist Press, 1985), pp. 106–08. He distinguished four biases: the egoistic, individual and group; the neurotic; and the general (i.e. "the illusory omnicompetence of common sense"), p. 105. The lecture was originally given at the Thomas More Institute, Montreal, May 13, 1973.

4. See Aristotle, *Nicomachean Ethics,* V, 9, 1137 a5–26.

5. Oliver Wendell Holmes, Jr., "Path of the Law," *Harvard Law Review* 10 (1897): 459.

experiential grasp of the full meaning and value of law. He has deliberately limited the scope of his vision by excluding its ethical dimension.

Third, the legal subject is *unified* through awareness of meaning and value—a necessary state for making a full response as he progresses step by step to a comprehensive legal vision. Four unities constitute this jurisprudence of subjectivity: the unity of mind, the unity of justice, the unity of community, and the unity of transcendence. Unity must not be understood in a simplistic or perfectionistic way; it is an ongoing approximation, flawed perhaps, but functional, the product of a lifetime effort to achieve full legal meaning and value.

The experience results from a process of growth through authentic actions; it is not just the fact of a plurality of decisions. The process is incremental not linear, for it incorporates the whole series of past decisions; it does not just move from one case to another, leaving the subject no better or no worse than before. The inner experience of law should be progressive and cumulative, encompassing the insights of the four Nomospheres, the higher ones sublating the lower.

The basic unity, found in the Monosphere, is the unity of the mind, the personal integrity that results from authentic subjectivity, that is, from the proper performance of each mental operation and, specifically, from the consistency between knowing and doing. If these mental operations are in harmony with one another, rational consciousness and rational self-consciousness unite, enabling the legal subject to experience his own psychic oneness. No longer is he fragmented; for his actions are in accord with his fundamental identity of consciousness, and he has discovered his ethical center, his normative exigency.

When, in the Isosphere, one subject relates to another, the unity of intersubjectivity becomes possible. It consists of the recognition and the implementation of mutual subjectivity, so that one subject treats another as another self. Participated value is the bond uniting the two subjects. To the extent that each one has achieved personal integrity, this new relationship reveals a valuable social dimension with a more complex and more satisfying unity. Moreover, it is a fertile and productive interaction, bringing a new reality into existence, the "we" that is formed by the bonds of justice and perfected through the intimacy of friendship.

By moving from a person-to-person relationship to one organized communally, legal subjects enter the Koinosphere, thereby realizing a wider unity, a bonding that is essentially the practical sharing in a political idea and the personal sharing in a political friendship. The *polis,* the symbol of this relationship for the protecting and fostering of self-sufficiency, enables individuals to do that which, by themselves or in small groups, they cannot do at all or cannot do well enough. The community attempts to achieve unity amid diversity and has as its lofty ideal a body politic formed by people who are personally integrated, intersubjectively just, and societally cooperative. No doubt every concrete community falls short of perfection in many ways and must try to provide for the common good under far less suitable conditions. The ideal gives it direction and motivation.

Finally, the natural perfection of unity comes in the Theosphere through the noetic experience, by which individuals consciously participate in transcendent order itself and, in some way, in the divine Reason or *Nous.* We are also aware of having received from God our own natural reason or *nous,* enabling us to participate with him in conscious decision making. This participation is not the reception of a set of precepts from above, but the use of the ability, given to us by God, to ask and answer questions, and it is employed with the recognition that human reason is a sharing, to the extent that its decisions are reasonable, in the divine Reason.

Although at the core this is a relationship between the legal subject and the divine lawgiver—involving principally the Monosphere and the Theosphere—it unifies noetically the experience of law in the Isosphere and in the Koinosphere. For whether in an intersubjective or politcal context, the parties to these relationships are themselves participants, actually or potentially, in the noetic experience. Meaning and value become fully manifest only in terms of this overall unity, for it is the consciousness of noetic participation that reveals the profound significance of our existence and actions. The inner experience of law at its height is a savoring of this perfect unity of meaning and value.

Though we have been speaking of the Theosphere on the noetic and philosophical level, there is also a pneumatic or spiritual dimension, which involves revelation and grace and which makes possible a sharing in the life of God, whose essence is one with his eternal law. This union with the divine promises to human beings ultimate legal unity.

Fourth, the integral legal subject is *luminous,* if docilely open and truly committed to meaning and value and thus proportionately unified.

Luminosity is the awareness of the self and the world in terms of the noetic experience;[6] it is being conscious of one's participation in the divine through one's being and action. This enlightened participation is an ultimate event, for these experiences so illumine legal subjects and so permeate their minds and hearts that they manifest the harmony of vision and decision that is the goal of the law. Embodying justice, they are truly men and women of the law—lights of the world. Note here Aristotle's observation that a good judge is "animate justice,"[7] a title that also applies to those who have realized in their thoughts and actions an authentic legal subjectivity.

consciousness

one of the points of light.

In a striking passage, Plato pointed out the transcendent character of this luminosity:

> In the divine, there is no shadow of unrighteousness, only the perfections of righteousness, and nothing is more like the divine than anyone of us who becomes as righteous as possible. It is here that a man shows his true spirit and power or the lack of spirit and nothingness.[8]

Some centuries later, in the Gospel of St. John, there was this related insight:

> Everyone who practices wickedness hates the light and does not come near the light for fear his deeds will be exposed. But he who acts in the truth comes into the light so that it may be shown that his deeds are done in God (Jn. 3:20–21).

In short, God is the ultimate ground of our existence, meaning, and value. Moreover, the whole legal order depends on the divine Reason. Through human reason, by experiencing, understanding, judging, and deciding authentically, we are able consciously to participate in this right order and thereby reflect it in our thoughts and in our actions.

EX - IN- JU -DEC

Of course, skill and success in legal matters are not necessarily a sign that one has had the noetic experience. That experience is the realization, practical as well as theoretical, that the principle of order in the

6. To express this profound enlightenment or expanded consciousness, Eric Voegelin made much use of the term "luminous," with its Platonic overtones in connection with noetic experience; see especially his "Reason: the Classic Experience," *Anamnesis,* trans. G. Niemeyer (Notre Dame, Ind.: Notre Dame University Press, 1978), pp. 89–115.

7. Aristotle, *Nic. Eth.,* V, 4, 1132 a21–24: "For the nature of the judge is to be a sort of animate justice; and they seek the judge as an intermediate, and in some states they call judges mediators, on the assumption that if they get what is intermediate they will get what is just."

8. Plato, *Theaetetus,* 176 B–C.

world is the divine *Nous* and that, having received the gift of reason from this source, we participate in it, to a greater or lesser degree, by bringing personal and social order into our lives.

The noetic experience is consciousness of our source and our end; jurisprudence is ultimately the attempt to comprehend and articulate this experience in the legal order. A jurisprudence of subjectivity does so through an interiority ready to be objectified as theory. Ideally, the theory should reflect the luminosity of the community of legal subjects. If that achievement is not fully realized, the theory can light the way so that the legal subjects can strive to be so open, committed, unified, and luminous that they will be able eventually to reach the fulfillment in meaning and value that is the inner experience of law.

The idea of luminosity is not just a high-sounding metaphor. One way or another, everyone shows one's character—not the deeds, necessarily, but something of the complexus of meanings and the hierarchy of values that structure the personality. However, many judgments and decisions are deformative, warping the personality that tries to incorporate them. The result is a diminished subject—exemplified by the typical brutal cop, perjured witness, shyster lawyer, hanging judge, venal politician, and even by many an average person—who tries to do the impossible—that is, to achieve personal order while conforming to a principle of disorder.

This attempt contradicts the very essence of law as an ordinance of reason. Such intrinsic disorder effectively prevents the legal subject from becoming luminous to himself or to others, for he does not see himself or the world around him as manifesting legal coherence and worth. If justice is not obeyed in the microcosm, it is not perceived in the macrocosm. If the legal subjects do not have these qualities in themselves, they cannot manifest them to others. They can teach about them and preach about them; they can hypocritically act as if they were part of them, but they cannot embody them, so their words are empty, their persona opaque. Both justice and injustice are declarative of themselves; they paint their own portraits in the souls and eventually in the bodies of their possessors. The true man or woman of law emerges resplendent in the beauty of that participated order which is the bond of peace.

II. THE EXISTENTIAL PROCESS

Clearly the goal of a jurisprudence of subjectivity is to help us become more and more conscious of meaning and value in legal events. This can be realized only by internalizing the law through a conscious harmony of vision and decision. In some way, we must become the law, but not as Constantius II, who claimed, "My will is canon law,"[9] nor as Louis XIV, who boasted, *"L'Etat c'est moi."*[10] Both attitudes, assertions of egoistic power, deform the law and abort the experience. Yet they do catch something that all of us must have—if we are to experience the law accurately and fully—not an identification with the law, but a participation in it. We must consciously and rationally do so, not necessarily by wielding authority but at least by recognizing and executing the social order that structures our personal life and our relationship with others. Otherwise the subject, alienated from the legal universe, is affected by it only extrinsically.

As a practical matter, however, there remains the crucial question: How is this experience of law to be realized concretely? Let us glance at the process theoretically and then devote the rest of the chapter to its more practical side. To speak of theory brings the specter of an older approach, one moving from the top down, beginning with primary principles and following their deductive and opaque descent to the realm of singular decision making.

By this stage in our study of the inner experience of law, however, we have realized that there is a different and arguably a better way to become aware of law. Instead of propositions, we begin with the invariant structures of our own minds and confront data concerning our natural inclinations. Since traditionalists and revisionists agree that the mind starts out as a *tabula rasa,* initial recourse to experience is hardly a bone of contention. We shall recapitulate, from a subjective perspective, the mental process involved.

Having discussed at great length the levels of consciousness, experience, understanding, judgment, and decision, we here need only to note where this process takes us. Authentic subjectivity leads to objectivity, first through experience-based synthetic judgments and then to

9. Constantius II (337–351) told this to the Gallic bishops at Arles, see Athanasius, *History of the Arians,* 3.

10. Louis XIV said this before the *Parlement de Paris,* April 13, 1655, see Dulaure, *Histoire de Paris.*

corresponding concrete decisions. Generalized norms may emerge from particular decisions; some of these norms, those dealing with basic forms of good, may be seen to be self-evident, the predicate clearly belonging to the essence of the subject. Underlying all these decisions, explicitly or implicitly, is the meta-principle: good is to be done and pursued, and evil is to be avoided.

Good is to be done; evil to be avoided

Subjectively, the process leads to a twofold consciousness: self-appropriation terminates in rational self-consciousness; self-transcendence terminates in God-consciousness. Through conscious intentionality, we are able to achieve participation in the consciousness of God. This enlightened, transcendent consciousness perfects itself through articulation, which makes its meaning more accurate, memorable, and communicable. But it flowers only in concrete decision making, without which the fullness of consciousness ever escapes us. These decisions should manifest consistency between knowing and doing; that consistency is a function of the meta-principle and as well as its crown.

The perfect consistency between knowing and doing reflects the thrust of the eros of the mind as it consciously participates in God, its source and its end. Conscious intentionality enables us to discover the principles of the inner experience of law, because consciousness is intrinsic to all our mental operations and most fully present in authentic decision making. This luminousness becomes a peak experience, when, as with Plato, the juridical and the mystical blend.

Let us now move to some practical considerations involved in seeking fulfillment through an inner experience of law. We ask ourselves again: How is this experience to be realized concretely? Philosophers of law and lawyers may differ on the answer. The philosopher of law, if he moves out of the realm of the abstract, might attempt an in-depth analysis of a singular situation, searching out all its dimensions—its ethical core, its bilateral implications, its political context, its divine directives. The individual case would be thought of as Tennyson did the flower plucked from the crannied wall: "But if I could understand what you are, root and all, and all in all, I should know what God and man is."[11]

The lawyer, on the other hand, might be suspicious of such a legal *tour de force*. He would think of legal experience more in terms of the

11. Alfred Tennyson, "Flower in the Crannied Wall," *Works*, Cambridge Edition (New York: Houghton, Mifflin Co., 1898), p. 274.

image used by Marcus Aurelius: "Time is like a river made up of the events which happen, and a violent stream it is; for as soon as a thing has been seen, it is carried away and another comes in its place and this will be carried away as well."[12]

The solution is a blend: the inner experience of law will be most fruitful and profound if we consider law as a series of events, while trying to be intensely aware of each individual case and its overarching structures. In this river there flows an abundance of legal data, more than sufficient to reveal law's true dimensions. The legal subject has a psychological need for this continuing exposure, for insights must accumulate and be verified, biases must be discerned and, if not eliminated, at least counterbalanced, skills in practical decision making must gradually be perfected, and the memory itself must be kept precise and well-stocked through the steady confrontation with concrete cases. Holmes, speaking of positive laws, wrote: "They present themselves as a finite body of dogma which may be mastered within a reasonable time."[13] Then presaging the current legal proliferation, he added: "It is a great mistake to be frightened by the ever increasing number of reports. The reports of a given jurisdiction in the course of a generation take up pretty much the whole body of the law and restate it from the present point of view."[14]

Holmes may have been naively optimistic, but his observation has a point: we do need a long apprenticeship in law, but we can eventually master our calling and experience it fully. Since our notion of law includes more than what concerns the courts, we must also apprentice ourselves in the other legal spheres if we wish to have a complete and unified experience of law. In this broader project, those who believe in God have an additional encouragement from the doctrine of Providence, rooted in divine wisdom and power, which underlies God's role in all the happenings of life and gives an individualized significance to the river of events in which we must swim to achieve fulfillment.

The process of the concrete realization of a vision of law is still too general, so I shall examine more fully the practical participation in a legal event from four points of view: the participation itself; the participatory roles, the main areas of that participation; the basis in conscious intentionality; and the vision achieved by participation.

12. Marcus Aurelius, *Meditations*, IV, 43.
13. Holmes, *Path of the Law*, p. 458.
14. Ibid.

(1) Participation in decision making is indispensable to an inner experience of law, since law is fundamentally a normative decision. Obtaining data, grasping an insight, forming a judgment—all are indispensable, but it is above all responsible decision making that gives us the requisite experience. We get closest to law in our concrete decisions. So we try to bring into sharper focus the process of realization by centering our attention on choice, a direction suggestive of a Kantian *volo ergo sum*.

The need of the decisional dimension for a full experience of law is found, as we have seen, in the complementarity between knowing and doing. To know transcends the subject; to do involves the subject, that he may transcend himself. The knower can learn and study things that do not involve himself; the doer always involves himself. By deciding, the legal subject changes himself or his world; by deciding authentically, the subject both fulfills and transcends himself. This twofold perfection through action is the key to the inner experience of law.

We may be active or passive participants, but participants we must be if we are to succeed. The eyewitness perspective is not that of the detached third party; it is that of one who is involved in the legal event and who can view the event from the inside, from the vantage point of interiority. Only such a one can be fully conscious of what he or she is actually doing. A person can know about law without participating in decision making, but cannot experience law fully without doing so. It is not enough to be a spectator; one must be a participant.

But this perceptive eyewitness must act authentically in order to avoid distortion and derailment. We have seen what biases and disvalues do to legal experience. But it is clear also that, for a vision of law, one action does not suffice, that not even one good action reveals the whole truth. Historicity gives the lie to any such vain endeavor. Inserted in a temporal matrix, we experience ourselves little by little. Yet even the past and the future can be pulled into the present. We are part of a continuum of choices, and our minds are structured by memories of past decisions and by the prospects and plans for future ones. The past as lived or retrieved authentically and the future as projected authentically impinge upon the present. The full experience of law recapitulates the past and anticipates the future, even as it incorporates the present.

This inner experience of law then is conscious participation in a succession of authentic decisions. The intensity comes from deciding concretely and authentically; the profundity, from the succession of such decisions. The resulting vision is an awareness of being in tune through our choices with right order. The harmony is not a fantasy; it is a confident assessment based on the values one has learned to prize and the disvalues one has rejected or regretted.

The full vision of law does not require an unblemished record, but it does require a rectified conscience. Beyond that it is a sense of doing what is right in the concrete case plus the sense of linking oneself with what is right everywhere—in the past, present, and future. We become conscious of participating through our deeds in the eternal law of God. Why God? Because without a divine ground there is no meaning or value in law or in life. The inner experience of law is a conscious reaffirmation of this ultimate and sacred ground.

(2) Participation in decision making encompasses a diversity of roles. The obvious ones of ruler and the ruled offer no problem when both act reasonably. Both, however, may act unjustly: the ruler may have recourse to force or deception, and the subject may disobey, stealthily or contumaciously. In so doing, they both limit their experience of law, and do so radically if their immorality and illegality become habitual. A less obvious dulling of legal experience comes from mixed motives, where the ruler acts justly but is motivated by power and glory and the prerequisites of office or where the subjects, obeying the letter of the law, do so only out of fear of punishment or some other social sanction.

A more difficult question is how the unwilling victim of a unjust system, ruler, functionary, or fellow citizen can manage to experience the law positively, when he or she has been objectified and treated like a thing. Stripped of political justice and rights, such a person might seem incapacitated for decision making and thus deprived of the fullness of legal experience.

To answer this question, we begin obliquely by looking first at the unjust ruler or person of power who has belatedly realized his faults and has taken up his burden of guilt. Often there is no realistic way of compensating for the injustice, since the appropriate time for decision making may have passed once and for all and the harm may be irreparable, as in the killing of a political rival. Acknowledged guilt, however, sharpens the unjust person's awareness of the deformity of his past choices and partially rehabilitates his damaged conscience. In addition, there remains the obligation to redress as fully as possible the injustice to the victim and to society by a series of prospective decisions.

We can now better understand the victim's position. Unable to affect his external situation by his own decisions, he has a more acute sense of the value of justice and the evil of injustice. He participates legally in his own situation, above all by willing that justice be done him. The concrete legal event then serves as an opportunity for him to participate radically though ineffectually in the concrete legal event.

Significantly, the victim too has inner obstacles to overcome for an integral experience of law: the temptation to hatred, revenge, despair. It is so easy to wish to meet injustice with injustice. How many terrorists and political radicals, reacting against serious wrongs, undercut their moral base by using injustice in their fight for justice? But as Viktor Frankl and Aleksandr Solzhenitsyn have revealed, it is possible for victims even in terminal situations to achieve an attitudinal transcendence by reaffirming the values of justice and love.

(3) Participation in legal events is a concrete occurrence. The basic spheres are clear from the overall structure of the book itself in its focus on individual, bilateral, communal, and sacral activities. Certainly the most visible sphere, the one that is called to mind most readily by the word "law," is civil or positive law. We have already seen the interpenetration of law and morals; nevertheless, it is helpful to focus here on the general types of action involving members of the political community, both because the interactions of positive law are most obvious and tend to characterize our thinking about other spheres of law.

Despite its complexity, positive law can be reduced to three major categories: property (real and personal), liability (torts and crimes), and contract (express and implied). We can best understand these basic categories if we describe them in terms of the relationships that they give rise to and that the law protects and fosters. Thus, property looks to the obligations stemming from the socially protected relationship between persons and things; liability looks to the obligations involuntarily imposed that arise from injury or loss caused by one of the parties; and, finally, contract looks to obligations voluntarily assumed by both parties. Laws, as we have seen, are actions about the actions involving these relationships. All the courses taught in law school, all the cases decided by the courts, can be reduced to these three categories.[15]

Our participation in legal events can be further reduced to the relationship between justice and rights. Formulated according to the defi-

15. Roscoe Pound discussed this division in chapters four, five, and six of his *Introduction to the Philosophy of Law* (New Haven: Yale University Press, 1959).

nition of a right, we see that there is in each category a relationship between the actions of one person and the interests of another, protected by law and based in equality. Descriptively, every element but the last is readily apparent. The basis in equality, as we have seen, depends on a more fundamental understanding of the political community as grounded proximately in intersubjectivity and finally in the human dignity of the individual subject.

Litigants are clearly not spectators, but participants in an existential situation. Beyond their positive law, political involvement, they may have incurred other types of obligation stemming from personal integrity, bilateral reciprocity, or divine sovereignty. Ethical questions abound: May I foreclose this mortgage, knowing that someone who has suffered an unexpected loss will, nevertheless, be able to pay me in a reasonable time? May I refuse to help a child in danger of drowning, since most jurisdictions do not impose on me a positive duty? May I be ungrateful to my parents, breach my promise to marry, commit adultery, have an abortion—when no civil law sanctions these actions? In short, must my concrete decision be made not only in terms of positive law, but also according to my individual conscience, my sense of justice, and my duties toward God?

Ultimately, whether the event is covered by positive law or by other kinds of law, the issue is one of decision making. It is the decision that opens the door to full legal experience. But not every personal and concrete experience of law, though it opens the door, also turns on the light. If we are not acting authentically, we are acting in the dark. Of course, an intelligent person, good or bad, who knows what he is doing may learn from his mistakes. But what is indispensable is to learn to act with integrity and responsibility.

(4) From the perspective of conscious intentionality, we expand our awareness to include not just the objects made present through intentionality but also the self that is present through consciousness. This latter expansion of coverage is not a new act, but one intrinsic to all mental operations; we simply allow our awareness to permeate us fully. Through this self-consciousness, we can appreciate what underlies objective thinking. By appropriating these operations, we are best able to understand and communicate our convictions.

In other words, having moved beyond common sense and theory to interiority with its intensified consciousness of the subject and his mental operations, we return again to theory and to common sense.

Although interiority, as Lonergan pointed out, is a realm distinct from theory and common sense, a realm concerned with the appropriation of one's own mental operations, it also facilitates our return to these other two realms by objectifying the results of this self-appropriation.

In an age of pluralistic controversy, what we have called an interiority pregnant with theory can have tremendous value for jurisprudence in affording the basis for an intellectual exchange otherwise unattainable. In fact, the subjective perspective may lead to a shared recognition of the mental operations employed in the various spheres of legal events, thus laying the foundation for a theoretical dialogue.

The dialogue with its emerging areas of consensus might help, by obviating the perennial need for radical revision, to achieve a new jurisprudential stability. This is a well-grounded expectation. Since interiority involves the appropriation of the mental operations of experience, insight, judgment, and decision, for someone to overturn a theoretical conclusion solidly based on interiority, he would have to resort to further operations of experience, insight, judgment, and decision. To hold otherwise would be to abandon reason's role in the thought process. Admittedly, improvements would always be possible, but they would still be made on the common ground of a shared method, a method based on the invariant structures of the human mind.[16]

The role of these invariant structures in grounding dialogue and fostering a consensus is crucial to a jurisprudence of subjectivity. Invariant structures are patterns of activity, of knowing and doing. They are the common patterns of mental operations found in all human beings. Hence, any revision would necessarily involve the same invariant structures.

To base jurisprudence on conscious intentionality in its fourfold pattern of operations—experiencing, understanding, judging, and deciding—is to explain the very possibility of ethics and law. Although the objectifications of that basic pattern may still be argued and revised, the pattern itself gives not only a firm foundation for facts, principles, and rules, but also an intrinsically sound method for the discovery and verification of these objectifications.

Consequently, legal thinkers have a continuing and prophetic role in the discovering and the symbolizing of the fruits of legal subjectivity.

16. For an analysis of the basis for avoiding radical revision, see Bernard Lonergan, *Method in Theology*, 2nd ed. (New York: Herder and Herder, 1973), pp. 16–20.

The value of their communications is a function of the clarity and the profundity of their differentiated consciousness. The fundamental progression must be from compact consciousness to differentiated consciousness with its various levels. The attainment of differentiation is essential to a jurisprudence of subjectivity, for compact consciousness, although sound in many of its convictions and conclusions, has no adequate awareness of its own mental operations, so it can never be as lucid and as sure as it should be, especially if it is to share its enlightenment with others.

(5) What, finally, is this inner experience of participation in the law? How does the awareness manifest itself? What is its content? To lead into the answer, we say that legal vision is the fruit of authentic decision making; that is, law must become for us a conscious event experienced in a continuum of authentic decisions. Let us consider what that means.

The material for the experience of law is the singular event or legal situation; the focal point is the actual decision; and the context is our habitual attitude, conditioned by past deeds and projected into the future. To phrase it differently, the elements are: first, the here-and-now decision; second, the past decisions rooted in habit and preserved in memory; and, third, the prospective decisions, prompted by habit and characterized by good will.

So the experience of law is the experience of being righteous, specifically in the concrete act being performed but also in the remembered past and foreseeable future. It is an awareness of being in tune through our choices with a transcendent order in the world, of being at peace with ourselves, with others, and with God, by participating in the order that comes from God and is reflected in all his creatures. This experience is a justifiable sense of doing what is right, thereby linking oneself with all that is rightly done everywhere in the world. Law becomes resplendent in the person who fully participates in this cosmic order because in doing so his life has become open, committed, unified, and luminous. Through love he experiences a multi-dimensional oneness—individually, bilaterally, communally, and sacrally.

Through a continual effort at self-appropriation, the legal subject effectively breaks free of the diminished status attributed to him by much of modern juridical thought. Thus it is possible for the subject to achieve integral fulfillment despite his external limitations. Nevertheless, when positive law has isolated itself from the other legal spheres and tries to operate in a logically self-contained and therefore existentially unreal unit, the diminished subject is hard-pressed to participate fully in a legal event. And yet the desperate challenge may well push this legal subject to a more profound grasp of the meaning and value of law.

In other words, the legal subject has within himself the power to transcend the constraints of the political arena. His vision of law is not merely a function of the enlightenment and good will of his rulers, even if his rulers are the dominant majority. Good government certainly facilitates an appreciation of law; bad government, however, does not make a vision of justice impossible. One must face the inevitability of disorder with the confidence that comes from having a principle of reason within us derived from an ultimate source, transcendent Reason. The point of contact is our own responsible decision in the instant case, whatever the set of circumstances characterizing it may be. Authentic decisions are made by the inmates of a concentration camp, by the brutally enslaved, by the victims of torture and of impending death.

The vision of law comes from the depth and the breadth of a commitment to reason and justice and love. This liberating power of free and rational choice enables the legal subject to achieve dignity and to fulfill his destiny, whatever his fate may be. In *Epistle VII*, Plato dramatically described the breakthrough into a philosophical vision: "There is no way of putting it into words. Acquaintance with it must come after a long period of attendance on instruction in the subject itself and of close companionship, when, suddenly, like a blaze kindled by a leaping spark, it is born in the soul and at once becomes self-sustaining."[17] Although for Plato all philosophy had a moral dimension, later in the same Epistle he spoke specifically and similarly of attaining to "the most complete truth in regard to moral concepts":

Hardly after practicing detailed comparison of names and definitions and visual and other sense perceptions, after scrutinizing them in benevolent disputation by the use of question and answer without jealousy, at last in a flash, understanding of each blazes up and the mind, as it were exerts all its powers to the limit of human capacity, is flooded with light.[18]

Without contradicting the master, one might suggest that, in addition to such peak experiences, there are also those which manifest a glow rather than a blaze, a series of flames rather than a conflagration; yet

17. Plato, *Epistle*, VII, 341 C–D.
18. Ibid., 344 B.

such is the drive of the mind for truth and such is the normality of law that perceptive and persistent authenticity will eventually enjoy a "feast of lights."

CONCLUSION

The purpose of this book is to help us find meaning and value in the experience of law. Challenged by absurdity, we seek an ultimate ground for our actions and norms. For all of us, the search has already been long underway. Recalling Goethe's remark—"In the beginning was the deed"—we note that, from our earliest youth, we have responded to our empirical experiences by asking questions. The dual perspective of Eros and Nemesis has given us some insight into the laws operating on us from within and from without, energizing and directing actions as well as sanctioning them. Our questions and our discoveries have pointed us in the direction of both subjectivity and objectivity.

In the past, the jurisprudential tendency has been to overlook the subjectivity and to try to solve all juridical questions on the basis of practical common sense or abstract theory. The answers have not been entirely adequate. A jurisprudence of subjectivity, however, is not an equally limited venture in the other direction. Rather, it is an exercise in reconciliation, an attempt to bring together the two parts of an integral jurisprudence. There is, however, a certain priority, for the subjective side grounds the objective: both facts and norms, whatever their foundation in external reality, are understood through our mental operations. Facts and norms exist in our minds and, if our minds are functioning properly, are consonant with reality.

A jurisprudence of subjectivity keeps us from being limited to a naively compact consciousness. By refined differentiation, we are able to expand our consciousness of mental operations, thus enabling ourselves to assess the precise meaning and value that we can attribute to our objective conclusions. Through the self-appropriation of authentic subjectivity, we find the guarantee of sound objectivity.

A jurisprudence of subjectivity, however, is more than a battery of tests to check the validity of the *corpus juris*. More significantly, it is a means of integrating law into one's whole life. Not that there is any reasonable alternative, for law is clearly part of life. But we can make its presence an instrument of growth or suffer it as an inescapable constraint. A jurisprudence of subjectivity aims at facilitating a vision of law and life through the consciousness that comes from authentic participation in legal events.

Although everyone is challenged by law, those in the legal profession have a special stake in the successful resolution of this human problem. Judges, lawyers, professors, and even law students develop a characteristic mentality. Law transforms them for better or worse. If it remains merely a job, a prestigious way of making a living, a sophisticated, dialectical skill, or a springboard to a position of power and influence, it splits their life into uncoordinated personal and professional compartments. The result is that one may become worldly wise without being truly wise; for true wisdom keeps asking relevant questions and keeps trying to verify and unify insights and to integrate all of life's experiences.

The life of a specialist in law has a beginning, middle, and end. Relevant questions should be entertained at every stage. But, as one grows older, the really important questions, unless they are thoroughly quashed, tend to surface more and more insistently. And yet the answering of these questions is itself a lifetime occupation. We grow in wisdom, but slowly; we do not solve the problem of existence once and for all, as we do a mathematical equation. All of us, not just lawyers, have abundant and multifaceted legal experience, since our lives are structured by law. It would be sad, and the loss would be irremediable, if looking back over a life permeated with law—especially as members of the legal profession—we were forced to admit, in Eliot's phrase, "We had the experience but missed the meaning."[19]

A jurisprudence of subjectivity has a compelling mission—to keep the relevant questions about the life of the law ever alive in our minds. We are all meant to be legal philosophers, in that we are meant to reason, to use our ability to ask and answer fundamental questions about the law and its role in our lives and to try to trace the answers to their source, to the divine ground that alone can give ultimate meaning and value.

The key to legal wisdom is consciousness of our mental operations, operations that we share with all other men and women and that make possible not only dialogue but consensus. For this quest is empirically grounded in the "eros of the human spirit,"[20] as it is manifested in each

19. T. S. Eliot, "The Dry Salvages," from "The Four Quartets," *The Complete Poems and Plays* (New York: Harcourt, Brace, 1952), line 95, p. 133.
20. Bernard Lonergan, *Method*, p. 13.

one's "responsive pursuit of his questioning unrest to the divine source that has aroused it."[21] In short, the inner experience of law is consciousness of the basic thrust of the mind toward reality fulfilling itself in authentic decision making. Through just actions, the legal subject experiences the emergence in himself of his Source and his End. Participating in this divine merger, the subject perfects and transcends himself with a heightened consciousness in an ongoing, realized legal eschatology.

The pattern of this lifelong search, as it is reflected through the spheres of law, is an ascending spiral: we return again and again to the same questions, and they yield richer and richer answers. The answers are but stages in a transforming participation in righteousness. Only thus can the inner experience of law burn brightly in our minds and hearts, dispelling the shadows of absurdity, illuminating the ultimate meaning and value of life, and inaugurating a period of repose, a well-earned juridical sabbath.

21. Eric Voegelin, *Anamnesis*, p. 96.

SELECT BIBLIOGRAPHY

Adler, Mortimer. *Six Major Ideas*. New York: Macmillan, 1981.

Allen, Francis A. *The Decline of the Rehabilitative Ideal*. New Haven: Yale University Press, 1981.

Andenaes, Johannes. *Punishment and Deterrence*. Ann Arbor, Mich.: The University of Michigan Press, 1974.

Aquinas, St. Thomas. *Sententia Libri Ethicorum. Commentary on the Nicomachean Ethics*. Trans. C. I. Litzinger. 2 vols. Chicago: Regnery, 1964.

———. *Summa contra gentiles*. Leonine edition. Rome: Forzanius, 1934.

———. *Summa theologiae*. 60 vols. plus index. Blackfriars edition. New York: McGraw-Hill, 1964–1976.

Arens, Richard, and Lasswell, Harold D. *In Defense of the Public Order: The Emerging Field of Sanction Law*. New York: Knopf, 1971.

Aristotle. *Aristotelis Ethica Nichomachea*. Ed. L. Bywater. Oxford Classical Texts. Oxford: Clarendon Press, 1894.

———. Aristotle. *Aristotelis Politica*. Ed. W. D. Ross. Oxford Classical Texts. Oxford: Clarendon Press, 1957.

———. Aristotle. *Eudemean Ethics*. Trans. H. Rackham. Loeb Classical Library. Cambridge: Harvard University Press, 1935.

———. *Politics*. Ed. W. D. Ross and trans. B. Jowett. Oxford: Clarendon Press, 1921.

Armstrong, R. A. *Primary and Secondary Precepts in Thomistic Natural Law Teaching*. The Hague: Martinus Nijhoff, 1966.

Beccaria, Cesare. *On Crimes and Punishments*. Trans. H. Paolucci. Indianapolis, Ind.: Bobbs-Merrill, 1963.

Bellarmine, Robert. Opera Omnia. 12 vols. Ed. J. Fèvre. Paris: L. Vivès, 1870–1874.

Bender, Ludovicus. *Philosophia Iuris*. 2nd ed. Rome: Officium Libri Catholici, 1955.

Bentham, Jeremy. *A Fragment on Government* and *An Introduction to the Principles of Morals and Legislation*. Ed. W. Harrison. Oxford: Blackwell, 1960.

———. *Works*. Ed. J. Bowring. Edinburgh: W. Tait, 1838–1843.

Berdyaev, Nikoli. *Slavery and Freedom*. New York: Scribner's, 1944.

Beveridge, W.I.B. *The Art of Scientific Investigation*. Rev. edition. New York: Random House, 1957.

Bodenheimer, Edgar. *Jurisprudence*. Cambridge: Harvard University Press, 1962.

Boulding, Kenneth. *The Meaning of the Twentieth Century*. New York: Harper and Row, 1965.

Brod, Max. *Franz Kafka*. 2d ed. New York: Schocken Books, 1960.

Broderick, Albert, ed. *The French Institutionalists: Maurice Hauriou, Georges Renard, Joseph Delos*. Trans. M. Welling. 20th Century Legal Philosophy Series: Vol. VIII. Cambridge: Harvard University Press, 1970.

Buber, Martin. *I and Thou*. Trans. R. G. Smith, 2nd ed. New York: Scribner's, 1958.

Burke, Edmund. *Reflections on the French Revolution*. Ed. T. H. D. Mahoney. Indianapolis: Bobbs Merrill, 1955.

Cahill, Lisa Sowle. "Teleology, Utilitarianism, and Christian Ethics," *Theological Studies* 42 (1977): 601–29.

Cahn, Edmond. "The Consumers of Injustice," *New York University Law Review* 34 (1959): 1166–1181.

Camus, Albert. *The Myth of Sysyphus*. Trans. J. O'Brien. New York: Vantage Book, 1955.

Christie, George. *Jurisprudence*. St. Paul, Minn.: West, 1973.

Code of Canon Law. Latin-English Edition. Translation prepared under the auspices of the Canon Law Society of America. Washington: Canon Law Society of America, 1983.

Comte, Auguste. *The Catechism of Positive Religion*. Trans. R. Congreve. 3rd rev. ed. Clifton, N.J.: A. M. Kelley, 1973.

Copleston, Frederick. *A History of Philosophy*, 9 vols. London: Burns and Oates, 1950–1986.

Creel, Austin. *Dharma in Hindu Ethics*. Columbia, Mo.: South Asian Books, 1977.

Crowe, Frederick E. *The Lonergan Enterprise*. Cambridge: Cowley, 1980.

Crowe, Michael E. *The Changing Profile of the Natural Law*. The Hague: Martinus Nijhoff, 1977.

Curran, Charles E. and McCormick, Richard A. eds. *Readings in Moral Theology*. New York: Paulist Press, 1979, 1989, 1982, 1984.

Davitt, Thomas E. *The Nature of Law*. St. Louis: Herder, 1951.

d'Entrèves, A. P. *Natural Law*. London: Hutchinson, 1951.

Del Vecchio, Giorgio. Justice: *An Historical and Philosophical Essay*. Trans. Lady Guthrie. Edinburgh: Edinburgh University Press, 1956.

———. *Man and Nature: Selected Essays*. Trans. A. H. Campbell. Notre Dame, Ind.: Notre Dame University Press, 1969.

———. *The Philosophy of Law*. Trans. T. O. Martin from 8th edition. Washington: The Catholic University of America Press, 1953.

Deman, T. *La Prudence*. Paris: Desclée, 1949.

Diels, Hermann. *Die Fragmente der Vorsocratiker*. 6th ed. Ed. Walther Kranz. Berlin: Wiedmann, 1968.

Dodd, C. H. *The Epistle to the Romans*. Moffatt New Testament Commentary. London: Hodder and Stroughton, 1932.

Douglas, William O. *The Court Years: 1938–1975*. New York: Vintage Books, 1981.

Dworkin, Ronald. *Taking Rights Seriously*. Cambridge: Harvard University Press, 1978.

Eliade, Mircea. *Images and Symbols*. Trans. P. Mairet. New York: Sheed and Ward, 1952.

———. *The One and the Two*. New York: Harper and Row, 1969.

———. *Yoga: Immortality and Freedom*. Trans. W. R. Trask. Bollingen Series LVI. New York: Pantheon, 1958.

Fejfar, Anthony J. "Insight into Lawyering: Bernard Lonergan's Critical Realism Applied to Jurisprudence," *Boston College Law Review* 27 (1986): 681–719.

Finnis, John. *Fundamentals of Ethics*. Washington: Georgetown University Press, 1893.
———. *Natural Law and Natural Rights*. Oxford: Clarendon Press, 1980.
———. "On 'The Critical Legal Studies Movement,'" *American Journal of Jurisprudence* 30 (1985), 21–42.
Fisher, Roger, and Ury, William. *Getting to Yes*. Boston: Houghton Mifflin, 1981.
Fitzmyer, Joseph A. "The Letter to the Romans," in *The Jerome Biblical Commentary*. Englewood Cliffs, N.J.: Prentice-Hall, 1968.
Frank, Jerome. *Law and the Modern Mind*. New York: Doubleday, 1963.
Fried, Charles. *Right and Wrong*. Cambridge: Harvard University Press, 1978.
Fuchs, Josef. *Natural Law*. New York: Sheed and Ward, 1965.
———. *Personal Responsibility and Christian Morality*. Washington: Georgetown University Press, 1983.
———. *Christian Ethics in a Secular Arena*. Trans. B. Hoose and B. McNeil. Washington: Georgetown University Press, 1984.
Fuller, Lon. *The Morality of the Law*. New Haven: Yale University Press, 1964.
Gadamer, Hans-Georg. *Philosophical Hermeneutics*. Trans. and ed. D. E. Linge. Berkeley: University of California Press, 1976.
———. *Truth and Method*. New York: Seabury Press, 1975.
———. *Reason in the Age of Science*. Trans. Frederick G. Lawrence. Cambridge: MIT Press, 1981.
Gandhi, Mohandas K. *The Collected Works*. Delhi: Government of India, Ministry of Information and Broadcasting, 1958 and following.
Gardner, Howard. *Frames of Mind*. New York: Basic Books, 1983.
———. *The Mind's New Science*. New York: Basic Books, 1985.
Gilmore, Grant. "Legal Realism: Its Cause and Cure," *Yale Law Journal* 70 (1961): 1037–1048.
Gill, Eric. *Beauty Looks After Herself*. New York: Sheed and Ward, 1933.
Gilson, Etienne. *God and Philosophy*. New Haven: Yale University Press, 1941.
Glendon, Mary Ann. *Abortion and Divorce in Western Law*. Cambridge: Harvard University Press, 1987.
Granfield, David. *The Abortion Decision*. Garden City, N.Y.: Doubleday, 1969; rev. ed. Image Book, 1971.
———. *Antinomianism and the Relation of Law and Liberty*. Washington: The Catholic University of America, 1962.
———. "Force, Power, and Law," *The Catholic University of America Law Review* 12 (1963): 79–81.
———. "Rehabilitation: An Ideal in Transition," *Social Thought* 3 (1977): 5–14.
———. "The Scholastic Dispute on Justice: Aquinas versus Ockham." In *Justice*. Ed. Karl Friederich. Nomos VI. New York: Altherton Press, 1963, pp. 229–42.
———. "Towards a Goal-oriented Consensus," *Journal of Legal Education* 19 (1967): 379–402.
Granfield, Patrick. "The Theological Development of the Defendant's Obligation to Reply in a Civil Court," *Theological Studies* 26 (1965): 280–298 and 27 (1966): 401–420.
Gray, John Chipman. *The Nature and the Sources of the Law*. 2d ed. rev. by R. Gray. New York: Columbia University Press, 1921.

Grisez, Germain G. "The First Principle of Practical Reason," *Natural Law Forum* 10 (1965): 168–201.

Grotius, Hugo. *De jure belli ac pacis* (1646). Trans. F. W. Kelsey et al. Classics of International Law. Oxford: Oxford University Press, 1925. Vol. 3.

Guardini, Romano. *Power and Responsibility*. Chicago: Henry Regnery, 1961.

Hall, Jerome. *Studies in Jurisprudence and Criminal Theory*. New York: Oceana Publications, 1958.

Hallowell, John H. *Main Currents in Modern Political Thought*. New York: Henry Holt, 1950.

Hand, Learned. *Lectures on Legal Subjects*. New York: Macmillan, 1926.

Hardie, W.F.R. *Aristotle's Ethnic Theory*. 2nd ed. Oxford: Clarendon Press, 1980.

Hart, H.L.A. "Are There Any Natural Rights?" *The Philosophical Review* 64 (1955): 175–191.

———. *The Concept of Law*. Oxford: The Clarendon Press, 1961.

———. "Positivism and the Separation of Law and Morals," *Harvard Law Review* 71 (1958): 593–629.

———. *Punishment and Responsibility*. Oxford: Oxford University Press, 1968.

Hayek, Friedrich A. *Law, Legislation and Liberty*. 3 vols. Chicago: University of Chicago Press, 1973, 1976, 1979.

Hegel, Georg. *Werke*. Ed. H. G. Glockner. 22 vols. Stuttgart: Frommen, 1927–1939.

Hobbes, Thomas. *The English Works of Thomas Hobbes*. Ed. W. Molesworth. 11 vols. London: J. Bohn, 1839–1845.

———. *Leviathan*. Ed. C. B. Macpherson. Baltimore: Penguin Books, 1968.

Hohfeld, W. N. *Fundamental Legal Conceptions*. Ed. W. W. Cook. New Haven: Yale University Press, 1966.

Holmes, Oliver Wendell, Jr. *Collected Legal Papers*. New York: Harcourt Brace, 1920.

———. *The Common Law*. Boston: Little, Brown, 1938.

———. *The Mind and Faith of Justice Holmes*. Ed. Max Lerner. New York: The Modern Library, 1943.

———. "The Path of the Law," *Harvard Law Review* 10 (1897): 457–478.

Holmes, Oliver Wendell, Jr., and Pollock, Sir Frederick. *Holmes-Pollock* Letters. Ed. Mark DeWolfe Howe. 2nd ed. 2 vols. Cambridge: Harvard University Press, 1961.

Hume, David. *A Treatise of Human Nature*. Ed. L. A. Selby-Bigge. Oxford: Clarendon Press, 1960.

Hutcheson, Joseph C., Jr. "The Judgment Intuitive: The Function of the 'Hunch' in Judicial Decision," *Cornell Law Quarterly* 14 (1929): 274–288.

Jaeger, Werner. *Paideia: The Ideals of Greek Culture*. 3 vols. New York: Oxford University Press, 1943–1945.

James, William. *The Will To Believe and Other Essays in Popular Philosophy*. New York: Longmans, Green, 1917.

Jung, Carl, *Man and His Symbols*. Garden City, N.Y.: Doubleday, 1964.

———. *Memories, Dreams, Reflections*. Ed. A. Jaffé, trans. R. and C. Winston. New York: Random House, 1961.

Kafka, Franz. *Letters*. Ed. Max Brod. New York: Schocken Books, 1958.

————. *The Trial.* New York: Schocken Books, 1968.

Kane, Pandurang Vaman. *History of Dharmasastra* (Ancient and Medieval Religious and Civil Law in India). Poona: Bhandarkar Oriental Research Institute, 1968.

Kant, Immanuel. *Critique of Practical Reason.* Trans. T. K. Abbott. London: Longmans, Green, 1963.

————. *Critique of Pure Reason.* Trans. Norman Kemp Smith. London: Macmillan, 1933.

————. *The Moral Law: Kant's Groundwork of the Metaphysic of Morals.* Trans. and ed., H. J. Paton. New York: Barnes & Noble, 1963.

Kelsen, Hans. *General Theory of the Law and the State.* Trans. A. Wedberg. New York: Russell and Russell, 1971.

————. *The Pure Theory of Law.* Trans. M. Knight. Berkeley: University of California Press, 1967.

Kierkegaard, Søren. *Concluding Unscientific Postscript.* Trans. D. Swenson and W. Lowrie. Princeton: Princeton University Press, 1974.

————. *The Concept of Dread.* Trans. W. Lowrie. Princeton: Princeton University Press, 1944.

Kittle, Gerhard and Friedrich, Gerhard. *Theological Dictionary of the New Testament.* Trans. W. Bromiley. 10 vols. Grand Rapids, Mich.: W. B. Eerdmans, 1964.

Küng, Hans. *Does God Exist?* Trans. E. Quinn. New York: Vintage Books, 1981.

Kuhn, Thomas S. *The Structure of Scientific Revolutions.* Chicago: University of Chicago Press, 1962.

Levi, Edward H. *An Introduction to Legal Reasoning.* Chicago: University of Chicago Press, 1948.

————. "The Nature of Judicial Reasoning," *University of Chicago Law Review* 32 (1965): 395–409.

Llewellyn, Karl. *The Bramble Bush.* New York: Oceana, 1981.

————. "A Realistic Jurisprudence—The Next Step," *Columbia Law Review* 30 (1930): 431–465.

Locke, John. *Essays on the Law of Nature.* Trans. W. von Leyden. Oxford: Oxford University Press, 1954.

————. *Works.* 9 vols. London: Rivington, 1824.

Lonergan, Bernard. *Collection.* Ed. F. E. Crowe. New York: Herder and Herder, 1967.

————. *Insight.* London: Longmans, Green, 1957; New York: Philosophical Library, 1958.

————. *Method.* 2nd ed. New York: Herder and Herder, 1973.

————. *Philosophy of God, and Theology.* Philadelphia: The Westminster Press, 1973.

————. "Questions with regard to Method: History and Economics." In *Dialogues in Celebration.* Ed. Cathleen M. Going. Montreal: Thomas More Institute, 1980.

————. *A Second Collection.* Ed. W. F. J. Ryan and B. J. Tyrrell. Philadelphia: The Westminster Press, 1974.

————. *A Third Collection.* Ed. F. E. Crowe. New York: Paulist Press, 1985.

————. *Understanding and Being.* Ed. E. A. Morelli and M. D. Morelli. Lewiston, New York: Edwin Mellen Press, 1980.

Mahabarata. Trans. P. C. Roy. 18 vols. Calcutta: Baharata Press, 1884–1894.
McCormick, Richard A. *Notes on Moral Theology 1965 through 1980.* Washington: University Press of America, 1981.
———. *Notes on Moral Theology 1981 through 1984.* Washington: University Press of America, 1985.
McCormick, Richard A., and Ramsey, Paul, eds. *Doing Evil to Achieve Good.* Chicago: Loyola University Press, 1978.
McDougal, Myres S., and Associates. *Studies in World Public Order.* New Haven: Yale University Press, 1960.
McDougal, Myres S., and Florentino P. Feliciano. *Law and Minimum World Public Order.* New Haven: Yale University Press, 1961.
McKenzie, John L. *Light on the Epistles.* Chicago: Thomas More Press, 1975.
Menninger, Karl. *The Crime of Punishment.* New York: Viking Press, 1966.
Moore, Thomas Verner. *Cognitive Psychology.* Chicago: Lippincott, 1939.
Morris, Norval. *The Future of Imprisonment.* Chicago: University of Chicago Press, 1974.
Muck, Otto. *The Transcendental Method.* New York: Herder and Herder, 1968.
Murphy, Cornelius, F., Jr. *Modern Legal Philosophy.* Pittsburg: Duquesne University Press, 1978.
Newman, John Henry. *A Grammar of Assent.* New York: Longmans, Green, 1947.
Noonan, John T., Jr. *Persons and Masks of the Law.* New York: Farrar, Straus, and Giroux, 1976.
Nozick, Robert. *Anarchy, State, and Utopia.* New York: Basic Books, 1974.
O'Connor, William R. *The Eternal Quest: The Teaching of St. Thomas Aquinas on the Natural Desire for God.* New York: Longmans, Green, 1947.
Organ, T. R. *The Hindu Quest for the Perfection of Man.* Athens, Ohio: Ohio University Press, 1970.
Ortega y Gasset, José. *Meditations on Quixote.* San Juan, Puerto Rico: University of Puerto Rico Press, 1957.
———. *Obras Completas.* 6 vols. Madrid: Revista de Occidente, 1957–1958.
———. *The Revolt of the Masses.* New York: Norton, 1932.
———. *What is Philosophy?* Trans. M. Adams. New York: Norton, 1960.
Packer, Herbert L. *The Limits of the Criminal Sanction.* Stanford: Stanford University Press, 1968.
Penfield, Wilder, M.D. *The Mystery of the Mind.* Princeton: Princeton University Press, 1975.
Piaget, Jean. *The Child's Conception of the World.* Trans. A. and J. Tomlinson. New York: Harcourt, 1929.
Plato. *Collected Dialogues.* Ed. E. Hamilton and H. Cairns. New York: Pantheon Books, 1961.
Poincaré, Jules Henri. *Science and Method.* Trans. F. Maitland. London: Nelson, 1914.
Polanyi, Michael. *Personal Knowledge.* Chicago: University of Chicago Press, 1962.
Pound, Roscoe. *Outlines of Jurisprudence.* 5th ed. Cambridge: Harvard University Press, 1943.
———. *The Philosophy of Law.* New Haven: Yale University Press, 1943.
———. "Philosophy of Law and Comparative Law," *University of Pennsylvania Law Review* 100 (1951): 1–19.

Rahner, Karl. *Foundations of Christian Faith: An Introduction to the Idea of Christianity.* Trans. W. V. Dych. New York: Seabury, 1978.

Rahner, Karl, Ernst, Cornelius, and Smyth, Kevin, eds. *Sacramentum Mundi: An Encyclopedia of Theology.* New York: Herder and Herder, 1968.

Rawls, John. "Justice as Fairness," *The Philosophical Review* 67 (1958): 164–94.

———. *A Theory of Justice.* Cambridge: Harvard University Press, 1971.

Renard, Georges. *La théorie de l'institution.* Paris: Sirey, 1930.

Riley, Lawrence J. *The History, Nature and Use of Epikeia in Moral Theology.* Washington: The Catholic University of America Press, 1948.

Risk, J. M., ed. *The Stoics.* Berkeley: University of California Press, 1978.

———. *Stoic Philosophy.* Cambridge: Cambridge University Press, 1969; paperback edition, 1977.

Robinson, John Mansley, *An Introduction to Early Greek Philosophy.* Boston: Houghton Mifflin, 1968.

Rodes, Robert E., Jr. *The Legal Enterprise.* Port Washington, N.Y.: National University Publications, 1976.

Rommen, Heinrich A. *The Natural Law.* Trans. T. R. Hanley. St. Louis: Herder, 1949.

Rooney, Miriam Theresa. *Lawlessness, Law, and Sanction.* Washington: The Catholic University of America, 1937.

Russell, Bertrand. *Power.* London: Unwin Books, 1938.

Santayana, George. *The Sense of Beauty.* New York: Scribner's Sons, 1936.

Sartre, Jean-Paul. *Being and Nothingness.* Trans. H. E. Barnes. New York: Philosophical Library, 1956.

———. *L'Existentialisme est un humanisme.* Paris: Les Editions Nagel, 1947.

———. *Huis Clos.* Paris: Gallimard, 1947.

Schubert, A. *Augustins Lex-Aeterna-Lehr nach Inhalt und Quellen.* Münster: W. Aschendorff, 1924.

Seneca, *Epistulae Morales.* Trans. R. M. Grummere, Loeb Classical Library. 2 vols. Cambridge: Harvard University Press, 1953.

Simon, Yves. *Authority.* Notre Dame, Ind.: Notre Dame University Press, 1962.

———. *Philosophy of Democratic Government.* Chicago: University of Chicago Press, 1951.

Skinner, B. F. *Beyond Freedom and Dignity.* New York: Knopf, 1971.

Smith, Adam. *The Wealth of Nations.* Ed. E. Cannon. New York: Putnam's Sons, 1904.

Sohm, Rudolph. *Institutes.* Trans. J. Ledlie. 3rd ed. Oxford: Clarendon Press, 1907.

Stammler, Rudolf. *The Theory of Justice.* Trans. I. Husik. New York: Macmillan, 1925.

———. *Wirtschaft und Recht nach der Materialisticschen Geschiechtsaffassung.* 2nd ed. Leipzig, 1906.

Suarez, Franciscus. *Omnia Opera,* 28 vols. Paris: L. Vivès, 1856–1858.

Sykes, G. M. *The Society of Captives.* New York: Atheneum, 1965.

Teilhard de Chardin, Pierre. *The Divine Milieu.* New York: Harper and Row, 1960.

Tillich, Paul. *The Courage to Be.* New Haven: Yale University Press, 1952; Yale Paperbound, 1959.

———. *Love, Power, and Justice.* New York: Oxford University Press, 1954; Galaxy Books, 1960.

Toynbee, *A Study of History*. London: Oxford University Press, 1939.

Tracy, David. *Blessed Rage for Order*. New York: Seabury Press, 1975.

Unger, Roberto Mangabeira. "The Critical Legal Studies Movement," *Harvard Law Review* 96 (1983): 461–675.

———. *Politics and Knowledge*. New York: the Free Press, 1975.

van Buitenen. "*Dharma* and *Moksa*," *Philosophy of East and West* 7 (1957): 37.

Voegelin, Eric. *Anamnesis*. Trans. G. Niemeyer. Notre Dame, Ind.: Notre Dame University Press, 1978.

———. *Conservations with Eric Voegelin*. Ed. Eric O'Connor. Montreal: Thomas More Institute, 1980.

———. *Order and History*. 5 vols. Baton Rouge: Louisiana State University Press, 1956–1987.

———. *The New Science of Politics*. Chicago: The University of Chicago Press, 1952.

———. *Science, Politics and Gnosticism*. South Bend, Ind.: Gateway, 1968.

———. "Wisdom and the Magic of the Extreme," *The Southern Review* 17 (1981): 235–286.

Von Hirsch, Andrew. *Doing Justice: The Choice of Punishments*. New York: Hill and Wang, 1976.

Von Jhering, Rudolf. *Law as a Means to an End*. Trans. I. Husik. Boston: The Boston Book Co., 1914.

Weil, Simone. *Gravity and Grace*. Trans. A. Willis. New York: Putnam's Sons, 1952.

Wheelwright, Philip. *The Presocratics*. New York: The Odyssey Press, 1966.

Zaehner, R. C. *Hinduism*. Oxford: Oxford University Press, 1962.

Zimmer, Heinrich. *Philosophies of India*. Bollingen Series XXVI. Princeton: Princeton University Press, 1971.

NAME INDEX

SUBJECT INDEX

Absolute ownership, 135
Absolute spirit, 22–23
Absolutes, rejection of, 210–11
Absolutism, 18–19
Abstraction: abstract principles of natural
  law, 180–92; distributist state, 135,
  140; masks and abstractions, 36; minimal state, 135; natural law, 178–79;
  practical decision making, 192–93;
  premoral evil, 212; revisionist rules,
  211; subjectivity, 37; Stoic ethics, 231
Absurd, the, 5, 9–14, 224, 240–41, 243,
  248, 252
Action(s): ability to act, 151; action and
  intention, 183; action and norms, 130;
  consciousness and action, 53; crimes
  against nature, 188–89; disproportionate action, 68, 184; *Im Anfang
  war die Tat*, 255, 273; intrinsically
  evil actions, 214; juridic daimon, 45;
  justice and doing, 104; justification of
  actions, 246; knower and doer, 56, 79,
  194, 202, 238–39, 247, 264, 266;
  minimalist state, 135; moral actions,
  231; moral precepts, 188; revisionist
  rules, 210–15; rules and principles,
  232; subjective focus, 38; values and
  actions, 178, 256; vision of law, 262
Actualization of powers, 152
Actus reus (guilty act), 162
Adiaphora (indifferent things), 93
Adjudication, rules of, 141
Adversarial legal structure, 61, 107,
  115–16, 118, 147
Aesthetic balance, 101–5
Affirmation of God, 240–51
Agnoia (ignorance), 69
Agnosticism, 246
Alienation and ideology, 80–81
All or nothing rules, 232
Allegoresis (allegory), 230
Altruism, 134–35, 137
Ambiguity, natural law, 183–84
American colonies, 20
Amoral universe, 250
Analytical school, 24–26, 28, 30
Anamnesis (recollection), 180

Anarchy, 98–99, 167
"Angelism," 16
Anger, wrath of God, 76
Anglo-American law, 124
Angst, 37
Animals, 181
"Animate justice," 122, 261
Answering questions. *See* Question and
  answer.
Appetite(s): good of appetite, 120; natu-
  ral appetite, 17; right appetite, 199,
  200. *See also* Inclinations.
Appropriation and subjectivity, 38
Arbitration, 125
Arete (excellence), 222
Arrest, 149–50
Arrogance and complacency, 78
Arts, fine arts, 198
Assent, real and notional, 39–40
Ate (spirit of infatuation), 70
Atheism, 243, 245–46
Athens, 222, 233
Attention: attending to data, 54, 81;
  attention and observation, 62
Attica uprising (1971), 164, 166
Attributive evaluation, 98
Austin's imperative theory, 149, 170
Authentic decisions, 266–67
Authority: dynamics of governance,
  149–73; functions of authority, 167;
  liberty and authority, 255; limits on
  authority, 169–70; notion of authority,
  166–67
Autonomy, 15, 16, 25

"Basic norm," 244
"Basic sin," 78–79
Beauty, 49, 101, 262
Being and becoming, 179
Being and non-being, 153
Benefits and obligations, 138
Benevolence and equality, 146–47
Bhagavad-Gita, 71, 116
Bias, 137, 257, 258
Bible, 238
Bible, OT, Exod., 89
Bible, OT, Gen., 97

288

INDEX OF GREEK WORDS
TRANSLITERATED IN THE TEXT